AF712506

Global Pharmaceutical Marketing

A practical guide to codes and compliance

Global Pharmaceutical Marketing

A practical guide to codes and compliance

Judith Grice

Managing Director, PharmaCodes Medical Communications Ltd, UK

London • Chicago

Pharmaceutical Press

Published by the Pharmaceutical Press
An imprint of RPS Publishing

1 Lambeth High Street, London SE1 7JN, UK
100 South Atkinson Road, Suite 200, Grayslake, IL 60030–7820, USA

(PhP) is a trade mark of RPS Publishing
RPS Publishing is the publishing organisation of the Royal Pharmaceutical Society of Great Britain

First published 2008

Index provided by Indexing Specialists, Hove, East Sussex
Typeset by J&L Composition, Filey, North Yorkshire
Printed in Great Britain by TJ International, Padstow, Cornwall

ISBN 978 0 85369 717 6

A catalogue record for this book is available from the British Library

Contents Overview

Contents

CHAPTER 1

Introduction

The pharmaceutical industry is in the global media spotlight and has received heavy criticism from politicians, and the lay and medical press for the way that it commercialises its products.[1–3] It is mainly as a result of this criticism that regulatory and self-regulatory controls for the promotion of prescription medicines have been or are being revised in many countries around the world. In most countries both legal regulation and self-regulation (i.e. codes of practice of trade associations) operate but the balance between the two can differ; in the best national models they work synergistically.[4] In some countries the national regulatory authorities vet promotional materials as well as dealing with complaints; in others the primary route is self-regulatory codes of practice. This information is summarised in Table 5.1 in Section 5.5 (p. 33).

Many pharmaceutical companies have realised that they must improve their public image, and business reports, such as the one from Price Waterhouse Coopers,[5] have reinforced this making sound business sense, with the result that companies are producing internal guidance on promotional activities, additional compliance officers are being appointed, there are more internal audits and there is generally a tightening of company procedures for approval of promotion. This, in turn, has placed increasing pressure on those involved in the promotion of pharmaceuticals in terms of both the sales and marketing departments and the medical and regulatory departments, which have to approve promotion to ensure compliance. There has been further intensification within the market place for pharmaceuticals becoming more and more global; this has resulted in sales and marketing campaigns often being prepared at a global or at least a pan-European level. Therefore sales, marketing, medical and regulatory departments within regional or international pharmaceutical company offices need to be aware of the plethora of regulations and self-regulatory codes that exist.

This does not mean that those working at a national level need be aware only of their national code; there are many examples where referral to the codes of other countries is important. An example of this would be international or company meetings held overseas.

Whilst working within the pharmaceutical industry as European and later as International medical information manager, with responsibility for compliance of promotional materials across the region, I was regularly required to approve the use of promotional materials such as stand panels and giveaways for use at international meetings, or to approve marketing campaigns for pan-European or international use. This involved finding the relevant code of conduct or, if it was for an international campaign, numerous codes of conduct.

In some instances finding the self-regulatory code of practice in the English language was difficult and time-consuming. Even when they were found, comparison of one code with another would often be time-consuming because they were structured differently. Therefore this book was started to make my life easier by providing me with a quick reference guide to the self-regulatory codes of practice and so facilitate production or review of promotional practices.

1.1 Remit of this book

This book is focused mainly on the self-regulatory codes of conduct for the promotion of pharmaceutical products covering many of the major pharmaceutical markets located in the following geographical areas: Australia, Brazil, Canada, the Czech Republic, France, Germany, Greece, India, Ireland, Italy, Japan, the Netherlands, Norway, Spain, Sweden, Switzerland, Turkey, the United Kingdom and the United States of America.

It also contains some information on the regulatory framework in these countries. There is some information about Mexico, but the self-regulatory code could not be found. In addition there are some overarching international codes of conduct, such as the International Federation of Pharmaceutical Manufacturers and Associations (IFPMA) code, the World Health Organization (WHO) guidelines and the European Federation of Pharmaceutical Industries and Associations (EFPIA).

1.2 How this book is structured

The three chapters at the start of the book deal with planning core campaigns, planning promotion at international congresses and planning advisory boards.

They give an overview and some guidance on the processes that staff involved in marketing products at the European, global or international level need to consider when planning the above. They contain checklists and also reference where the information can be found in other chapters of this book.

Chapter 4 contains the legal regulatory/self-regulatory framework for each country and an overview on the balance between the two.

The next six chapters contain the subjects that I selected from the codes for inclusion in the book; in my experience, they are the topics most often required by staff preparing global, international or pan-European campaigns. Subjects normally managed at national levels have been omitted.

The self-regulatory codes for the countries mentioned earlier and the overarching codes were fitted into a uniform structure under these selected topics, with a summary at the start of each chapter or, when relevant, at the start of a section. The selected topics are:

- basic principles of the self-regulatory codes
- gifts, sponsorship and payments
- events and hospitality
- printed promotional materials
- internet and electronic communication media
- research.

In many cases the information has been quoted directly from the national code but in other instances, for the sake of brevity, the information from the relevant code has been summarised or two or more clauses merged. This book is therefore my interpretation and summary of the national codes and is not intended as a verbatim copy of all the codes. With this in mind, the clause where the information has been sourced is provided as a heading below the country heading.

Paragraphs and sentences starting and ending with * contain information that I have found during the course of my work and I have included it because I found it useful. However, it has not been source verified and is therefore unreferenced.

1.3 Who might use this book and why

I have written this book for those involved in pharmaceutical marketing, whether in the creation, production or review and approval of campaigns. They might be involved in the commercial departments of a pharmaceutical company or an advertising agency, or engaged in compliance in departments such as those for regulatory, legal or medical information.

I do not anticipate that the book would be read from cover to cover, but rather used as a quick reference guide when starting to plan core promotional campaigns, advisory boards or international congresses, or even just dipped into when thinking about planning internet sites or market research. In addition, for those starting out in pharmaceutical marketing, Chapter 6 may give an indication of where the pharmaceutical industry differs from marketing in other sectors.

1.4 Limitations of this book

It is important to understand the limitations of this book:

- This book is **NOT** intended to replace reading the codes themselves and, although every attempt has been made to ensure accuracy, the interpretations and summaries are my own. However, where there are any discrepancies, the actual codes of conduct should be followed. To facilitate the use of the codes a list of the websites where they can be found is located in Appendix 1.
- This book is **NOT** intended to centralise certification and approval of promotion and advertising in a global or international headquarters, thereby replacing country-specific approval and certification of promotional materials.
- This book is **NOT** a comprehensive guide to the laws regulating advertising and promotion in the individual countries and is intended only as an overview.

CHAPTER 2

Planning Core Promotional Campaigns

The headquarters of many companies are producing core promotional campaign materials because of the advantages in cost savings, the consistency of messages and the branding. This means that those compliance or promotional affairs staff who work in medical information, regulatory and legal departments often have to approve materials that are intended for global, international or pan-European use.

These materials are not normally printed centrally but are sent to the various affiliate countries around the world for adaptation in order to comply with both local regulations and self-regulatory codes of conduct. The core campaigns will often be prepared in accordance with overarching codes of conduct, such as the International Federation of Pharmaceutical Manufacturers and Associations (IFPMA) or European Federation of Pharmaceutical Industries and Associations (EFPIA) code. However, these codes are intended to convey the minimum standards for the industry and are therefore more skeletal than national codes of conduct such as those of the Association of the British Pharmaceutical Industry (ABPI). Although the core materials will be certified locally before use, there is no point in producing materials intended for global use that can, in reality, be used only by one or two countries without undergoing radical change. The aim is therefore to produce campaigns that are acceptable in most markets after just minor modifications. An example of this is shown by many countries that do not allow data on file to be used as a standard of proof for claims in promotional materials. If this were to be overlooked and used as part of a global campaign, significant changes would be required at the national affiliate level before the materials could be used.

It is important that those involved in producing or approving core campaign materials be at least aware of the self-regulatory framework in those countries where the campaign will be used. Table 2.1 is a checklist of action items that could serve as a reminder of the issues to consider when producing materials that are intended for use in more than one country.

Even when all of the above points have been considered it will not be possible to ensure that a campaign will be acceptable in all countries where it is intended for use. Therefore it is extremely important and mandated in most countries that it should be reviewed, approved and certified for use locally.

TABLE 2.1 Key issues when planning core promotional campaigns

Action/Checklist	Reference in book
At the concept stage, confirm that proposed visuals/images would be acceptable in the countries where it is intended to use the material	Where this is mentioned in the codes it is found in Section 9.4 (p. 158), but it is often not mentioned and so it is recommended that local affiliate country staff are asked for advice
If licensed, are any claims consistent with the licence in the countries where it is intended to use the promotional material?	Check with a company's local national regulatory departments or the summary of product characteristics for the countries where it is intended to use the promotional item
Do the materials have to be pre-approved or submitted to the Ministry of Health in any of the countries where they are to be used?	See Section 5.5, p. 33
Are the claims accurate, balanced, based on up-to-date information, capable of substantiation?	See Chapter 6, p. 35 and Section 9.3, p. 150
Check if the words used in the promotional claims are acceptable when translated	It is possible that words do not translate well into other languages, so it is advisable to check at this stage with staff in the affiliate country
It is often advisable to put campaign concepts and images into market research The extent of this with respect to the number of countries depends upon available budget The rules for conducting market research vary	See Section 11.2, p. 201
Check what types of references are allowed as standard of proof for substantiation of claim, e.g. are data on file allowed? Many countries only allow peer-reviewed published data to be used to substantiate claims	See Section 6.1, p. 35 and Table 6.1, p. 36
If planning to use the word 'new' check when it can be used	See Section 6.4, p. 52
Check what the relevant code(s) say about hanging comparatives, superlatives and quotes	See Section 6.2, p. 43
Check that artwork, such as graphs and statistics, are not misleading	See Section 6.6, p. 58
Is information on how to report adverse events required?	See Section 9.4, p. 158
Is there a requirement for prescribing information to be an integral part of the promotional item? If so, what must this contain?	See Section 9.4, p. 158, Table 9.1, p. 148 and Table 9.2, p. 151

CHAPTER 3

Promotion at International Congresses

International congresses are meetings that are organised independently rather than by pharmaceutical companies, although companies will often sponsor congresses. They are usually held in a different country each year and are intended for an international audience. Examples would be the European Association for Study of the Liver (EASL), the American Academy of Dermatology (AAD) or the World Congress of AIDS (WAIDS). However, national meetings of organisations are intended mainly for an audience from a particular country, for example, the British HIV Association (BHIVA) is intended primarily for a British audience and the German Aids Society (DAH) is intended primarily for a German audience. This difference, between international congresses and national meetings, is important because the codes of some countries allow medicines that are either not licensed or not licensed for a particular indication in the host country to be promoted at international congresses, provided that the product is appropriately licensed elsewhere.

The organisation for pharmaceutical companies attending these events is often handled centrally via European, international or global headquarters. Before considering these categories there are several important points that must be taken into account:

- the congress organisers' rules
- the location of the congress (inside or outside Europe?)
- the applicable national code.

Location of the congress

Promotion, which takes place within Europe, must comply with applicable laws and regulations. In addition, promotion that takes place within Europe must also comply with each of the following 'applicable codes':

- In the case of promotion that is undertaken, sponsored or organised by a company located within Europe, the member association national code of the country in which such company is located
- In the case of promotion that is undertaken, sponsored or organised by a company located outside Europe, the EFPIA (European Federation Pharmaceutical Industry Association) code
- The member association national code of the country in which the promotion takes place.

In the event of a conflict between the provisions of the applicable codes, the more restrictive of the conflicting provisions will apply.

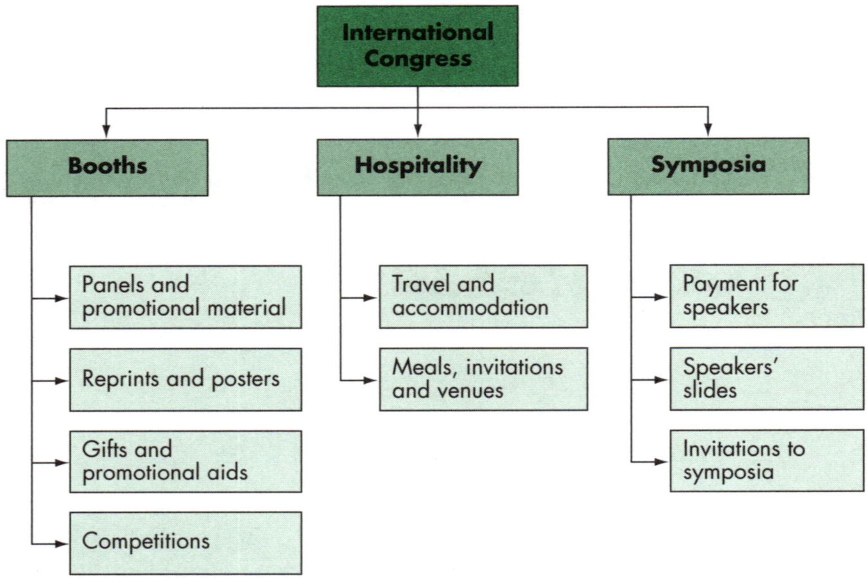

FIGURE 3.1: Planning international congresses.

3.1 Booths

3.1.1 BOOTH PANELS AND PROMOTIONAL MATERIALS

The promotional materials that are used by pharmaceutical company staff at their company booth for advertising products to conference delegates at international congresses must be produced and certified for use, in accordance with the legal and self-regulatory frameworks in the applicable countries. These promotional materials include: printed detail aids, electronic detail aids, leave pieces and product monographs.

In addition to promotional materials the booth panels also need to be certified (approved). (See Section 8.5, p. 139 for the relevant code(s).)

Table 3.1 is intended as a prompt for what needs to be considered when producing both promotional materials and booth panels; the right-hand column is a quick reference guide to where this information can be found in this book.

3.1.2 REPRINTS AND POSTERS

The distribution of reprints of clinical papers or posters by sales representatives on a booth is regarded as promotional. Therefore only reprints and posters that are within the terms of the licence may be used. In many countries they must be certified as a promotional item.

If there is a separate medical information portion of the booth, reprints and posters can usually be provided in response to unsolicited questions.

It is recommended that Table 3.2 be checked for the applicable country before ordering any reprints for an international congress booth.

TABLE 3.1 Key issues when planning for booths at international congresses

Action/Checklist	Reference in book
Is the product or indication licensed in the country where the conference is being held?	Check with company national regulatory department or summary of product characteristics for the country where conference being held
If not, what are the rules about unlicensed or off-label promotion, e.g. is a statement required about where the product or indication is licensed or is it forbidden to promote the products?	See Section 8.5, p. 139
Do the materials have to be pre-approved or submitted to the Ministry of Health in any of the countries where they are to be used?	See Section 5.5, p. 33
Does the information have to be in the language of where the product is licensed?	See Section 8.5, p. 139
If licensed, are any claims consistent with the licence?	Check with company national regulatory department or summary of product characteristics for the country where conference being held
Are the claims accurate, balanced, based on up-to-date information, capable of substantiation?	See Chapter 6, p. 35 and Section 9.3, p. 150
Check what types of references are allowed as standard of proof for substantiation of claim, e.g. are data on file allowed? Many countries allow only peer-reviewed published data to be used to substantiate claims	See Section 6.1, p. 35 and Table 6.1, p. 36
If planning to use the word 'new' check that it can be used	See Section 6.4, p. 52
Check what the relevant code(s) say about hanging comparatives, superlatives and quotes	See Section 6.2, p. 43
Check that artwork, such as graphs, statistics, are not misleading	See Section 6.6, p. 58
Does the code specify that a unique identification number is required to be printed on the promotional piece?	The ABPI code in the UK recommends that, when items are certified, they be given a unique number; this number should appear on promotional items
Is a warning symbol required, e.g. black triangle for adverse events?	
Is information on how to report adverse events required?	See Section 9.4, p. 158
Is there a requirement for prescribing information to be an integral part of the promotional item/booth panel? If so, what must this contain?	See Section 9.4, p. 158, Table 9.1, p. 148 and Table 9.2, p. 151

TABLE 3.2 Key issues for reprints and posters at international congresses

Action/Checklist	Reference in book
Is the reprint or poster within the terms of the product licence in the applicable country?	Check with company national regulatory department or summary of product characteristics for the country where the conference is being held
If not, is it within the licence in any country and what are the rules about promotion of unlicensed/off-label information in the country where the congress is being held?	See Section 8.5, p. 136
Does the reprint/poster give a balanced/accurate view of the available information?	See Chapter 6, p. 35
Could the reprint or poster be considered to be misleading?	Check the graphs and statistics: see Section 6.6, p. 58
Do the applicable codes require reprints to be certified as other promotional items?	Refer to Section 9.5, p. 174
Has the paper been published in a peer-reviewed journal/independently refereed?	If not peer reviewed, it may need to be approved as any other item of promotion, so may require prescribing information
Do the applicable codes require prescribing information to be supplied with the reprint and does this need to be an integral part of the paper or poster or can/must it be given separately?	Refer to Section 9.5, p. 174

TABLE 3.3 Key issues for gifts and promotional aids at international congresses

Action/Checklist	Reference in book
What is the cost and perceived value?	See Chapter 7, p. 83
Does the relevant code require that it be relevant to professional practice? Is it on a list of items allowed/not allowed in the appropriate country's code(s)?	See Chapter 7, p. 83
What is allowed to appear on the item?	See Chapter 7, p. 83 and Section 9.4, p. 158
What must appear on the item?	See Chapter 7, p. 83

3.1.3 GIFTS AND PROMOTIONAL AIDS

Gifts and promotional aids are usually inexpensive items that are branded with a product name; as the name suggests, they are given to health professionals who visit the booth as part of the product promotion. In many countries they are referred to as 'reminder items' and are intended for use by healthcare professionals in their daily practice and so act as a reminder of the product name.

3.1.4 COMPETITIONS

Competitions are not allowed in some countries, because they are not considered acceptable methods of promotion. Therefore, if a competition is planned for a booth at an international congress, the first step should be to find out whether this is allowed in the relevant country or countries (see Section 7.2, p. 93).

3.2 Hospitality

One of the first considerations in respect of sponsorship of healthcare professionals attending international congresses, in terms of travel, accommodation or congress registration fees, is whether the authorities in the health professional's country require notification of this sponsorship. This is true in France, for example, where the national medical board, Consiel national de l'Ordre des Médecins (CNOM), and the national board of pharmacists, Consiel national de l'Ordre des Pharmacists (CNOP), require 30 days' advance notification of hospitality or sponsorship. Details of this can be found in Section 8.3, p. 131.

3.2.1 TRAVEL AND ACCOMMODATION

See Table 3.4 for details of travel and accommodation.

TABLE 3.4 Key issues for travel and accommodation at international congresses

Action/Checklist	Reference in book
Is reimbursement for travel costs allowed? Is class of travel, e.g. coach or business class, specified in the code of the country where the healthcare professional is employed?	See Section 8.3, p. 131
Is accommodation necessary? If so can the healthcare professional be reimbursed for the cost?	See Section 8.3, p. 131
Are there any restrictions on who can be reimbursed for travel and/or accommodation, e.g. accompanying persons such as spouses who do not qualify as delegates in their own right?	See Section 8.2, p. 129

3.2.2 MEALS, INVITATIONS AND VENUES

The guidance with respect to food and drink provided by pharmaceutical companies for healthcare professionals in many countries is that it should not be lavish and should be of a standard that health professionals would pay for themselves. This is obviously vague so it is suggested that individual pharmaceutical companies should provide guidance for their employees on what is considered acceptable in terms of cost, etc.

Information that is available in the codes for the countries can be found in Chapter 8.

3.3 Symposia

3.3.1 PAYMENT OF SPEAKERS

In general terms, speakers in company-organised symposia can be paid for the time that they have spent preparing and delivering their presentations or chairing debates. However, this payment should normally be in line with commercial rates of pay for the amount of time spent. For country-specific requirements, refer to Section 7.5, p. 105.

3.3.2 SPEAKERS' SLIDES

New clinical data relating to unapproved uses or indications are often presented as part of a legitimate scientific exchange, but this must not be carried out in a promotional manner.

If the slides are promotional, e.g. containing product logos or branding, they will be considered promotional and must be certified as for any other promotional item used at the conference (see Section 3.1.1 above).

3.3.3 INVITATIONS TO SYMPOSIA

Invitations to symposia at international congresses may be promotional; therefore, if there is mention of a product and claim, they must meet the requirements of a promotional item.

CHAPTER 4

Planning Advisory Boards

Pharmaceutical companies set up advisory boards for the purpose, as the name suggests, of getting advice on a particular aspect of the commercialisation of their products. Advisers/consultants generally advise the pharmaceutical company on marketing and clinical issues and help to answer questions, so that the company can better direct medical/clinical and marketing efforts. Advisory boards are therefore for the benefit of the company and the participants are usually paid for their services, which are normally delivered under the terms of a contract.

Advisory boards are not considered promotional and differ from other types of company-organised meeting that have an educational content but are considered promotional.

Advisory boards must be organised appropriately and their objectives clearly defined or they may be considered as promotion or disguised promotion. The organisation of the advisory board and the rationale for it must be able to withstand independent scrutiny. Figure 4.1 represents the organisation of advisory boards and each area is considered in this chapter.

Any company personnel attending the advisory board should attend in a non-promotional role; for this reason, members of the sales force should not normally even attend an advisory board.

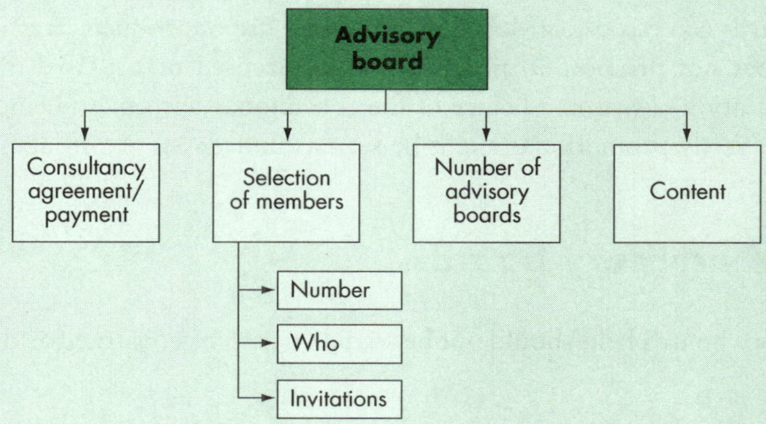

FIGURE 4.1 Organising an advisory board.

4.1 Consultancy agreements and payments

As mentioned above, it is usual for members of advisory boards to be paid a consultancy fee as laid down in a formal contract. The guidance given with respect to the amount in most codes of conduct is that this should be in line with professional rates of remuneration and should reflect the amount of time spent in the advisory capacity. For individual country guidance, consult Section 7.5, p. 105.

4.2 Selection and invitation of members

4.2.1 NUMBER AND WHOM TO INVITE

Advisers must be selected based on their knowledge, experience or other skill-based qualification that will allow the objectives of the advisory board to be met. They must not be selected on the basis of their history of, or potential for, prescribing the pharmaceutical company's products.

The number of advisers/consultants selected for any one advisory board meeting should not be too numerous, both for the sake of efficiency and from an ethical perspective. A large number of invitees may give the impression that the company is pursuing commercial objectives. The number invited should therefore be limited to a number that could reasonably contribute in an interactive forum. This number is not specified in most countries; Canada is an exception, however, and specifies a maximum of 20 advisers/consultants.

If the disease area involves different specialities or professions, representation from the various groups should be considered.

4.2.2 INVITATIONS

Invitations must make it clear that they are invitations to participate in an advisory board. The objectives of the meeting and what the adviser is expected to do at the meeting should be made clear. It is good practice to include an agenda.

Although the advisory board is not promotional (if it is organised correctly), the initial invitation is considered promotional, in the same way as any mailing to a healthcare professional is, because the invitee may ultimately not want to be on the advisory board.

This can present a dilemma: the objectives of the advisory board must be made clear in the invitation and advisory boards can discuss off-label or unlicensed use of products. It is important, however, that the invitation does not promote a product in an unlicensed or off-label manner, which could result because the invitation is sent in advance of the consultancy agreement being established and an invitation that is too overtly promotional might be seen as unlicensed or off-label promotion.

4.3 Number of advisory boards

The number of advisory boards held should not be so many as to be construed as disguised promotion.

4.4 Content of the advisory board meeting

If the advisory board is correctly organised, the content is not normally considered promotional. It is quite legitimate for unlicensed and off-label information to be discussed at the advisory board, but care must be taken in the meeting's organisation to ensure that the content is not allowed to slip into the promotional arena. Therefore it is important to avoid the following:

- Frequent use and prominently displayed brand names on communication material, such as presentation slides.
- Brand reminder items and promotional aids being used in the meeting, e.g. Post-It pads, writing pads and pens.
- An accent on a presentational style, with prominence given to the presentation of data rather than an interactive discussion.

4.5 Hospitality during advisory board meetings

In general this is the same as for hospitality at other types of meetings. There are exceptions to this, for example in the UK the ABPI does not restrict advisory board members to economy class travel.

A rule of thumb is that hospitality should not be lavish and should be of a level that the health-care professional could afford if paying for it personally. Refer to Chapter 8 for more specific country guidance on hospitality.

CHAPTER 5

Regulatory and Self-Regulatory Overview

Promotion is often defined as any activity undertaken, by a pharmaceutical company or with its authority, that promotes the prescription, supply, sale or administration of its medicines. This includes the following:

- Advertisements in medical and pharmaceutical journals and other print media, as well as on objects
- Mailings to healthcare professionals or their auxiliary personnel
- Activities of pharmaceutical representatives
- The use of audiovisual aids and other information media
- Free samples and gifts
- Granting of hospitality, and organising and sponsoring of symposia, congresses and similar events.

The governance of this promotion varies from country to country and is by either legal regulation or self-regulation but is often a mixture of the two.

5.1 Certification of promotional material

In most countries, before promotional material can be used, it must be approved or certified for use. This certification is often by a scientific service that must ensure the existence of the proper internal procedures for certification of promotional material. This, in turn, ensures implementation of the legislation and compliance with the self-regulatory code.

5.2 Global and regional self-regulatory codes

5.2.1 IFPMA CODE[6]

The International Federation of Pharmaceutical Manufacturers and Associations (IFPMA) code is intended to provide minimum standards and universal principles for ethical marketing conduct on which national codes can be based. It is used as an operational code only in those countries (e.g. less developed countries) where no other code exists. In practice the self-regulatory national codes in developed countries are usually stricter and more detailed than the IFPMA code.

An important feature of the code is its universal applicability. All companies that are members of an affiliated trade association (e.g. ABPI [Association of British Pharmaceutical Industries], LEEM [Les enterprises du médicament or French Pharmaceutical Companies Association], LIF [Swedish Association of the Pharmaceutical Industry], Interpharma) are required to apply the minimum standards of the code wherever they do business. Companies entering into licensing and agency agreements are expected to require their licensees and agents to respect the provisions of the IFPMA code.

5.2.2 EFPIA CODE[7]

The European Federation of Pharmaceutical Industries and Associations (EFPIA) is the representative body of the pharmaceutical industry in Europe. Its members are the national industry associations of over 20 countries producing pharmaceuticals in Europe.

The EFPIA code outlines the minimum standards that must be incorporated into the national codes of its member associations, e.g. ABPI, LEEM, LIF, Interpharma. This code has been revised to make it consistent with European Council Directive 2001/83/EC, as amended in 2004. National member associations were required to revise their codes to meet the minimum standards of the EFPIA by the end of 2005.

5.2.3 WORLD HEALTH ORGANIZATION ETHICAL CRITERIA[8]

The World Health Organization (WHO) issued the *Ethical Criteria for Medicinal Drug Promotion* in the late 1980s, which set out suggested standards to be implemented via regulation, international and national codes of practice.

5.3 Regulations and self-regulatory codes by country

5.3.1 AUSTRALIA[9]

Regulation

The advertising of medicines or therapeutic goods (as they are often referred to in Australia) is regulated by the Therapeutic Goods Administration (TGA). The TGA administer the main legislative acts, the Therapeutic Goods Act 1989 (TG Act) and the Therapeutic Goods Regulations 1990 (TG Regulations). The advertising of medicines is also subject to the same laws that regulate advertising generally – the Trade Practices Act 1974 (TP Act). The Australian Competition and Consumer Commission (ACCC) administer the TP Act.

Self-regulation

There is also a self-regulatory code of practice with supporting guidelines covering the promotion and advertising of prescription-only medicines, namely the Medicines Australia code of conduct.

5.3.2 BRAZIL[10]

Regulation

The advertising of medicines is regulated legally by the Brazilian Congress and via Resolutions and Ordinances issued by the Brazilian Sanitation Agency (Anvisa). Anvisa is an agency reporting to the Ministry of Health; their function is to promote public health and they also control the advertising of medicinal products.

The main federal laws are: 6360/76, 6437/77, 9294/96 and 8.078/90. The main Anvisa Resolutions and Ordinances on medicine advertising are: Anvisa Ordinance 344/98 and Anvisa Resolution 102/00.

Self-regulation

In addition to the regulation mentioned above, advertising of medicinal products is also subject to the ethical rules of the Brazilian Advertising Self-regulation Council (Conar). Conar is a non-governmental agency made up of advertising agencies, media vehicles, advertisers, consumers and representative associations. Their main objective is the enforcement of the Brazilian Advertising Self-regulation Code, which also establishes ethical rules on the advertising of medicines.

5.3.3 CANADA[11]

Regulation

In Canada the federal Food and Drugs Act regulates the advertising of medicines. This Act establishes the basic principles that drugs should not be advertised in a manner that is false, misleading, deceptive or likely to create an erroneous impression about its character, value, quantity, composition, merit or safety. The Act is administered by Health Canada.

Self-regulation

The Pharmaceutical Advertising Advisory Board (PAAB) administers the PAAB Code of Advertising acceptance, which applies to both prescription-only and non-prescription medicines. Compliance with the PAAB is in theory voluntary; however, it is strongly advocated by Health Canada.

Additional self-regulatory industry associations include: Canada's research-based pharmaceutical companies which have a code of marketing practice based on the principles of the IFPMA, called the Advertising Standards Canada (ASC); this administers the Canada Code of Advertising Standards (ASC). It is not specific to the pharmaceutical industry but relates to advertising in general.

Health Canada encourages compliance with these standards.

5.3.4 THE CZECH REPUBLIC[12]

Regulation

The advertising of medicines in the Czech Republic is regulated by legislation in the Advertising Act (Act no. 40/1995 Coll.). This was amended to comply with Directive 2001/83/EC when the Czech Republic became part of the European Union in 2004.

Other relevant legislation is the Act on Medicaments, Commercial Code and Civil Code. The State Institute for Drug Control (SÚKL) issues instructions, clarification and interpretation of the legislation.

Self-regulation

The self-regulatory body, the International Association of Pharmaceutical Companies (MAFS), has issued a code of conduct.

5.3.5 FRANCE[13]

Regulation

The advertising of prescription-only medicines in France is regulated by Directive 2001/83/EC as amended, which has been incorporated into French law specifically by:

- The French Public Health Code concerning promotion of pharmaceutical products
- The French Consumer Code, which refers particularly to comparative advertising
- The French Drug Agency (Agence Française de Sécurité Sanitaire des Produits de Santé – AFSSAPS) guidelines.

Although the AFSSAPS guidelines have no binding force from a legal standpoint, French courts consider that pharmaceutical companies must take them into account.

Self-regulation

The French pharmaceutical industry association, LEEM, has issued guidelines regarding promotion of medicines. In December 2004 LEEM signed an agreement with the Economic Committee of Health Products (CEPS) regarding the promotional practices of sales representatives.

5.3.6 GERMANY[14]

Regulation

The main legal provisions governing the advertising and promotion of medicinal products in Germany are:

- the law on Advertising in the Field of Healthcare (Heilmittelwerbegesetz – HWG)
- the Unfair Competition Act (UWG).

In addition, as Germany is part of the European Union, Directive 2001/83/EC (as amended) has been incorporated into national law.

Self-regulation

The voluntary self-regulation of the Pharmaceutical Industry or FSA code is based on the recommendations of the collaboration of physicians issued by the German Association of Research-based Pharmaceutical Companies (VFA), the German Federal Association of Pharmaceutical Manufacturers (BAH) and the German Association of the Pharmaceutical Industry (BPI). Although these recommendations have no legal authority, member companies agree to abide by this code.

5.3.7 GREECE[15]

Regulation

Greece has implemented Directive 2001/83/EC (as amended) into their national legislative framework of ministerial decrees. Some of the main provisions about prescription-only medicines include:

- the ministerial decree regarding the provision of medical information about medicines by pharmaceutical companies
- the ministerial decree regarding promotional expenses incurred by pharmaceutical companies.

Self-regulation

The Greek pharmaceutical industry association, the Hellenic Association of Pharmaceutical Companies (SFEE), has issued a code of practice on the promotion of prescription-only medicines.

5.3.8 INDIA

Regulation

No information found.

Self-regulation[16]

The Organisation of Pharmaceutical Producers of India (OPPI) has developed a code of practice for its members, based on the IFPMA.

5.3.9 IRELAND[17]

Regulation

The primary Irish legislation relating to the advertising of medicinal products in Ireland is the Medical Preparations Advertising Regulations, 1993 and 1996, as amended. Ireland, as part of the EU, implemented Directive 2001/83/EC (as amended with regard to the advertising of medicinal products for human use) and covers advertising to both health professionals and the general public.

Self-regulation

The Irish Pharmaceutical Health Authority (IPHA) code provides guidance on the advertising and promotion of prescription-only and non-prescription medicines to doctors, dentists and pharmacists, but does not deal with the promotion of such products to the general public.

The Pharmaceutical Code is voluntary but, as they have been prepared in consultation with the Department of Health and Children, incorporating guidelines published by the Irish Medicines Board (IMB), pharmaceutical companies are usually compliant.

The Code of Advertising Standards for Ireland and the Code of Sales Promotion Practice are implemented by the Advertising Standards Authority for Ireland (ASAI) and are referred to as the ASAI codes. They contain general rules relating to all advertisements, together with rules specific to the advertising of medicinal products to the general public. The ASAI codes are self-regulatory and do not have any legislative standing, so only members of the ASAI are obliged to adhere to them and only the ASAI may enforce them.

5.3.10 ITALY[18]

Regulation

Advertising of medicinal products is governed by Legislative Decree n. 541 1992, and Italy, as part of the EU, has implemented Directive 2001/83/EC (as amended).

Self-regulation

The Association of the Pharmaceutical Industry, Farmindustria, has issued a code of practice containing provisions for the advertisement of prescription-only medicines. This code of practice is not legally binding and applies only to members of the association.

5.3.11 JAPAN[19]

Regulation

In Japan, the Pharmaceutical Affairs Law 1960, as amended, and the Standards for Fair Advertising Practices concerning Medicinal Products define the standards for marketing practices with respect to medicinal products. The Fair Competition Rules were established by the Japan Fair Trade Commission, in accordance with the Law for Preventing Unjustifiable Extra or Unexpected Benefit and Misleading Representation.

Self-regulation

Japan Pharmaceutical Manufacturers Association (JPMA) established the self-regulatory code 'Code of Practices for Promotion of Ethical Drugs' in 1993.

5.3.12 MEXICO[20]

Regulation

The General Health Law mainly governs advertising of medicinal products in Mexico. The authority in charge of enforcing the advertising provisions is the Federal Commission for Protection against Sanitary Risks (COFEPRIS), part of the Ministry of Health.

In addition to the Law and Regulations, there are also opinions issued by the Advertising Council, which includes representatives from the Ministry of Health, the academic and scientific communities, the business sector, the media and consumer groups.

Self-regulation

The National Chamber of the Pharmaceutical Industry has a code of ethics that includes provisions about advertising. Although this code of ethics is not mandatory, failure to comply can result in suspension or expulsion from membership.

5.3.13 THE NETHERLANDS[21]

Regulation

In the Netherlands the Medicines Act 1958 provides the legal basis for the advertising of medicines. However, more detail is included in the Medicines Advertising Decree 1994, which implements the EU Directive on the Advertising of Medicinal Products (92/28/EEC), now included in the human use Directive 2001/83/EC (as amended) relating to medicinal products for humans.

Self-regulation

The Code of Conduct for Pharmaceutical Advertising (CPA) lays down rules similar to those included in the Medicines Advertising Decree. Most pharmaceutical companies have agreed to comply with this code via the industry association Nefarma. Nefarma and other industry associations have established a self-regulating body (the Code geneemiddelenreclame or CGR). The Minister of Health, Welfare and Sport has stipulated that the rules on advertising should be enforced by the CGR as well as by the Public Health Inspectorate.

5.3.14 NORWAY[22]

Regulation

The Norwegian Act of 1992 on Medicinal Products is the principal law concerning medicinal products. Chapter VII provides the legal framework for the Advertising of Medicines. In addition, the Norwegian Marketing Control Act 1972, the Norwegian Act 1999 relating to Health Personnel and the Norwegian Regulation 1999 on Medicinal Products contain relevant provisions with regard to marketing of medicines.

Self-regulation

The Norwegian Association of Pharmaceutical Manufacturers (LMI) has a voluntary code of conduct that promotes the practice of fair and ethical marketing.

In December 2004, the Norwegian Medical Association and LMI jointly laid down an ethical code and guidelines on cooperation and interactions between physicians and the pharmaceutical industry.

5.3.15 SPAIN[23]

Regulation

The advertising and promotion of medicines in Spain are governed both by the laws that apply to advertising in general, i.e. the Advertising Act, and by the Act that specifically addresses the advertising and promotion of medicines, i.e. the General Health Act. In addition, as Spain is part of the EU, Directive 2001/83/EC, as amended, has been implemented.

Self-regulation

Farmaindustria is the trade association of pharmaceutical industries and represents most of the pharmaceutical industry in Spain. The association has issued a self-regulatory code, 'The Code on Good Practices for the Promotion of Medicines', which provides clear guidance on industry practice. This code is binding on the association members and therefore important, although not legally binding.

5.3.16 SWEDEN[24]

Regulation

The advertising and promotion of medicines are basically covered by two acts: the Medicinal Products Act and the Market Practices Act. The former includes a basic provision that all advertising of medicinal products shall be kept up to date, factual and balanced, and must not be misleading. The latter is applicable to advertising for products and services, including medicinal products, and contains a general requirement that all marketing must be compatible with good marketing practice and fair towards consumers and the industry. This Act also sets out specific rules on, among other things, misleading advertising, comparative advertising and special offers. Directive 92/28/EEC, regarding advertising of medicinal products (now Directive 2001/83/EC, as amended), has now been implemented and changes have been made to the Medicinal Products Act in 2006.

Self-regulation

The LIF have issued an ethical code containing much more detailed rules relating to pharmaceutical advertising. Although these have not been laid down in statute law, and therefore are not legally binding, the LIF rules are widely recognised by the pharmaceutical industry and applied by courts as an expression of fair and ethical marketing. The LIF rules include prohibitions on, among other things, promotion of prescription drugs to the general public, off-label promotion and pre-launch marketing. They also list rules with respect to comparative advertising, misleading, incomplete or unsubstantiated information, and disguised promotion.

5.3.17 SWITZERLAND[25]

Regulation

The Federal Law on Medicinal Products and Medical Devices 2000 (otherwise known as the Law on Therapeutic Products) and the Ordinance on Advertising for Medicinal Products 2001 regulate the advertising of medicines.

Self-regulation

The Swiss Pharmaceutical Industry has a self-regulatory code of conduct: the 'Pharma' code. This code takes into account, in particular, the codes issued by the IFPMA and the EFPIA, as well as the recommendations of the Swiss Academy of Medical Sciences relating to collaboration between the medical profession and the industry. In addition, the provisions of the Federal Law against Unfair Competition of 1986 must be observed.

5.3.18 TURKEY[26]

Regulation

The advertising of medicines is governed by the Regulation on the Promotion of Medicinal Products for Human Use. The General Directorate of Pharmaceuticals and Pharmacy under the Ministry of Health (MoH) is in charge of all matters related to pharmaceuticals and has issued a code of conduct.

Self-regulation

This is not applicable in Turkey.

5.3.19 THE UNITED KINGDOM[27]

Regulation

The advertising of medicinal products in the UK is controlled by a combination of legislation and codes of practice.

The principal sets of regulations implementing Directive 2001/83/EC (as amended) are the Medicines Advertising Regulations 1994 and the Medicines Monitoring of Advertising Regulations 1994. Further provisions are set out in Part VI of the Medicines Act 1968. The Medicines and Healthcare Products Regulatory Agency (MHRA) supervises the advertising of medicinal products on behalf of the Licensing Authority. The Regulations are supplemented by guidelines published by the MHRA. The latest version is called *The Blue Guide — Advertising and Promotion of Medicines in the UK* and was published in February 2005.

Self-regulation

Day-to-day control over the advertising of prescription-only medicines is provided by the Prescription Medicines Code of Practice Authority (PMCPA), part of the Association of the British Pharmaceutical Industry (ABPI). The PMCPA administers the code of conduct for pharmaceutical companies – often referred to as the 'ABPI code'.

5.3.20 THE UNITED STATES OF AMERICA[28]

Regulation

Both the Federal Food, Drug and Cosmetic Act (FDCA) and the US Food and Drug Administration (FDA) regulations govern prescription-only drug advertising. The FDCA sets out broad requirements for prescription-only drug advertisements and authorises the FDA to circulate related regulations.

The dissemination of false advertisements likely to induce the purchase of food, drugs, devices, services or cosmetics is unlawful and subject to enforcement by the Federal Trade Commission (FTC).

Self-regulation

The Pharmaceutical Research Manufacturers of America (PhRMA) code of conduct addresses how pharmaceutical companies should interact with healthcare professionals. The interactions should be focused on informing these professionals about products, providing scientific and educational information, and supporting medical research and education to benefit patients.

5.4 Regulatory and self-regulatory enforcement, sanctions and penalties

5.4.1 IFPMA CODE[6]

The IFPMA can deal with complaints of alleged breaches of the code but it is not often used because the national codes take precedence. However, in some less developed countries where there is no national code it will adjudicate in cases of complaint.

5.4.2 EFPIA CODE[7]

Complaints about promotional activities may be lodged with the EFPIA as well as with member associations; however, any complaints would be referred to the national trade association for adjudication. It would then be up to the individual national trade association to impose sanctions, which may include administrative fines and suspension or expulsion from the trade association.

5.4.3 WHO ETHICAL CRITERIA[8]

The WHO does not deal with complaints about unethical promotion or advertising.

5.4.4 AUSTRALIA[9]

It may be a criminal offence to breach the Therapeutic Goods Act or Therapeutic Goods Regulations relating to advertising. The penalties that can be imposed by the Therapeutic Goods Administration (TGA) for a breach of these provisions are fines of up to $AU7000.

In addition, the Trade Practices Act contains provisions with regard to the advertising of medicinal products. This Act prohibits a company from engaging in 'misleading and deceptive conduct' in the course of 'trade or commerce' and has been widely used to challenge advertisements.

On a day-to-day basis, it is the more informal measures that ensure compliance with the rules, in relation to the promotion and advertising of medicines. These measures are via either the Complaints Resolution Panel (CRP), established by the TG Regulations, or the Medicines Australia Code of

Conduct, established by the pharmaceutical industry. Prosecutions for breaches of the TG Act are extremely rare. Complaints about advertising through the CRP or through the industry body Medicines Australia are common and often initiated by competitors. Although the sanctions available to these bodies are not, strictly speaking, enforceable in law, the risk of TGA scrutiny is usually enough to ensure that advertisers comply with their rulings.

The CRP considers whether advertisements in newspapers, magazines, radio, television or film breach the provisions of the TG Act or the TG Regulations. The CRP acts only on receipt of a complaint and has no power to impose sanctions, although it can refer a matter to the TGA and recommend further action.

The Medicines Australia Code of Conduct is the self-regulatory body for the pharmaceutical companies in Australia. It has a Committee, which hears complaints relating to prescription-only medicines, and can impose sanctions on Medicines Australia members. This includes fines of up to $AU200 000, corrective advertising, and suspension or expulsion of members.

The chief recourse for Australian companies that believe that their competitors are using advertising to gain an unfair competitive advantage is the Trade Practices Act.

5.4.5 BRAZIL[10]

Advertising of medicines that do not comply with regulations may be subject to one or more of the following penalties:

- A warning
- Definitive or temporary suspension of the sale of the medicine
- Suspension of any other advertising of the product in the same media for a period of up to 30 days
- Imposition of a rectifying message
- A fine (article 10, Law 6437/77).

The fines range from $US700 to $US1million, depending on the seriousness of the sanitary violation, receptiveness of the offender and their financial position.

Anvisa is in charge of enforcing the law on advertising of medicines and reviews advertising samples from pharmaceutical companies. It issues an infraction notice and initiates an administrative proceeding when it considers that advertising fails to comply with the regulations.

Lawsuits about advertising between competing pharmaceutical companies are commonplace in Brazil. The major issues covered by such lawsuits are comparative advertising, unfair competition, and infringement of trademark, patent and trade dress.

Unfair competition is generally understood to mean any commercial act that is contrary to honest practice in industrial, commercial and trade matters. Complaints are also filed at Conar by competing pharmaceutical companies. The penalties imposed by Conar range from a mere warning to advertising suspension or change of advertisement.

5.4.6 CANADA[11]

In Canada it is a criminal offence to fail to comply with the legislation for drug advertising, and this falls under the jurisdiction of the Minister of Health. It is punishable by 6 months' imprisonment and/or a fine of up to $CDN5000. However, because of the Minister's power to refuse drug licences or create regulatory difficulties for non-compliant drug manufacturers, criminal enforcement of the rules is infrequent.

In practice self-regulatory industry codes provide mechanisms for the resolution of complaints between competing manufacturers. Sanctions for violations of the PAAB code may include a direction to publish corrective notices in annual reports or newsletters, or to issue public letters of apology. Violations of the research and development (Rx&D) Code will be published in the Rx&D Update newsletter and subject to a fine of $CDN10 000/$CDN15 000/$CDN25 000 for the first/second/third violation, respectively, within a 12-month period. Upon the third violation, the Chief Executive Officer of an offending company will also be required to appear before Rx&D's board of directors. Each additional violation after the third one results in publication of the violation in the Rx&D Update and a fine of $CDN50 000. Compliance with sanctions is a condition of continued membership.

An action for unfair competition may be brought under the common law action of passing off, or under the Trade-marks Act. Individuals, trade associations and pharmaceutical companies may be able to initiate legal proceedings for unfair competition.

5.4.7 THE CZECH REPUBLIC[12]

The SÚKL supervises pharmaceutical advertising (except for TV and radio advertising). The supervisory authorities can impose a penalty of up to CZK10 000 000 (€1 = approximately CZK30), depending on the type of breach, its seriousness, manner of commission, duration and consequences. The Council for Radio and Television Broadcasting supervises advertising in these media.

Competitors can take direct actions through the courts in cases that are a breach of the rules on advertising of pharmaceuticals and, at the same time, a breach of civil or commercial law. In most cases, this would be classified and actionable as unfair competition. The following are examples mentioned in the Commercial Code of unfair competition: misleading marking of goods and services, bribery, disparagement and violation of trade secrets.

5.4.8 FRANCE[13]

Pharmaceutical companies, which conduct unlawful communication campaigns, may incur both administrative sanctions and criminal penalties.

Administrative sanctions

Advertising directed at the general public:

- Withdrawal of the AFSSAPS authorisation
- Product is removed from the list of medicines reimbursed by French social security schemes.

Advertising directed at healthcare professionals:

- AFSSAPS decision to suspend or prohibit any use of the advertising material
- Product being removed from the list of reimbursed medicines or decision from the Economic Committee of Health Products (CEPS) to pronounce a fine with a maximum amount equal to up to 10 per cent of the turnover made by the pharmaceutical company in connection with the product.

Criminal sanctions

- Breach of the requirements contained in the French Public Health Code: fine of up to €37 500.
- Misleading promotion for infringements of the French Consumer Code: a fine of up to €37 500 may be imposed. In addition, fines of up to €187 500 can be imposed for misleading advertising.
- Courts may also prohibit or suspend the use of a given promotional material, pronounce criminal penalties or grant financial compensation to competitors.
- Competitors may take direct action before the courts (on the grounds of unfair competition/unlawful comparative advertising), provided that they are able to prove that they have suffered injury as a result of the unlawful advertising.

5.4.9 GERMANY[14]

The supervisory authority for medicinal products in the relevant German Federal State is responsible for controlling the promotion of medicinal products. Where the competent authority considers an advertisement to be in breach of the regulations, it may stop further publication of the advertisement in question.

The intentional breach of the HWG Regulations on misleading advertisements constitutes a criminal offence with penalties of up to 1 year's imprisonment. An administrative fine of up to €20 000 may be incurred for the negligent breach of such provisions. All other intentional or negligent breaches of the HWG may result in fines of up to €50 000. However, infringements of the provisions of the HWG are prosecuted only in exceptional cases.

Competitors may take action directly through the civil courts and they often seek injunctive relief to stop advertisements that are considered to be violating their rights on the basis of the German Law against Unfair Competition.

In addition to the fines imposed via the legal system in Germany, a sanction may also be imposed by the self-regulatory body, the FSA, which can impose fines of €5000–250 000.

5.4.10 GREECE[15]

The national regulatory authority for the control of advertising of medicinal products is the National Organisation for Medicines (EOF). It can apply fines for advertisements and promotion that do not comply with the relevant legislation. The fines increase significantly for repetitive breaches and can be up to €44 000; the company responsible can also be sanctioned to make an announcement in the press. More serious cases can result in a prison sentence of up to 6 months.

Day-to-day breaches are handled by the Hellenic Association of Pharmaceutical Companies (SFEE) under their self-regulatory code.

Sanctions that may be imposed on a member of the SFFE include:

- Immediate publication of the text of the decisions in the SFEE newsletter
- Correction of promotional material and an obligation to send the corrected material to the recipients of the offending material, accompanied by a letter referring to the modifications
- Publication of the text of the decision in scientific journals addressed to relevant health professionals.

In addition, the SFEE Committees may impose monetary sanctions.

5.4.11 INDIA[16]

The Organisation of Pharmaceutical Producers of India (OPPI) adheres to the principles of the IFPMA code.

5.4.12 IRELAND[17]

According to the Irish Medicines Board Act 1995, any person (or body corporate) contravening the regulations is guilty of an offence and shall be liable:

- on conviction to a fine of up to €2000 and/or imprisonment for a term of up to a year
- on conviction on indictment to a fine of up to €120 000 (in respect of a first offence) or up to €300 000 (in the case of a second or subsequent offence)
- to imprisonment for a term of up to 10 years. Where an offence is committed by a corporate body with the consent, connivance or by reason of neglect of any person who is, or who holds him-/herself out as, an officer of that corporate body, such person shall also be personally liable under the 1995 Act.

The Minister, the IMB, the Pharmaceutical Society of Ireland or the health board in the functional area of which the offence has been committed may prosecute an offence.

There is no concept of 'unfair competition' under Irish law. It would be possible to take action under the law for passing off, trademark law or injurious falsehood. A party whose goods are being misrepresented as the goods of another party may bring a passing-off action. The proprietor of the trademark that has been infringed would bring a trademark action.

The aim of the IPHA code is to secure acceptance of high standards of conduct in the marketing of medicines. It emphasises the importance of providing healthcare professionals with accurate, fair and objective information about medicinal products, so that rational decisions can be made as to their use.

The code council has the right to:

- reprimand the party for transgression of the code
- publish details of the reprimand
- order whatever corrective action the code council may consider appropriate in light of the gravity of the complaint.

5.4.13 ITALY[18]

The regulatory body responsible for the control of promotion of medicinal products in Italy is the Italian Medicines Agency, i.e. Agenzia Italiana per il Farmaco (AIFA). In the event that the AIFA considers that advertising material is issued in breach of the rules on advertising of medicinal products, it may order an immediate halt of the infringing activity and require rectification. Penalties imposed in Italy for infringement of the requirement to obtain prior authorisation of promotional materials by the competent authorities have recently been converted from criminal sanctions into administrative fines from €2600 to up to €15 600. In addition, when the infringement involves a product included in the list of reimbursable products, AIFA may also impose a suspension from reimbursement for a period of from 10 days to 2 years, depending on the seriousness of the infringement. The bodies set up to control and implement procedures with regard to the code of self-regulation are the Farmindustria Monitoring Committee, the Jury and the Solo Judge. The following sanctions may be applied in the event of an infringement of the code:

- Warning with the request for the immediate cessation of the infringing behaviour
- Written reprimand
- Temporary suspension
- Expulsion.

In addition, a pecuniary sanction can be applied, varying in accordance with the seriousness of the infringement. The council of Farmindustria must formally approve written reprimands. The company sanctioned should inform the persons responsible for certifying the advertising about the final sanction. If the Solo Judge or the Jury is required to impose a specific sanction twice against the same company in a period of 12 months, Farmindustria will publicise the decision in a national publication, disclosing the name of the company in question.

5.4.14 JAPAN[19]

Cases of a serious offence against the Pharmaceutical Affairs Law and the Fair Competition Rules are subject to criminal sanction (i.e. up to 2 years in jail and/or a fine of up to 1 million yen). Such serious sanctions against a company, together with a public announcement, would place the company at a considerable disadvantage with respect to its business in Japan.

In respect of procedures for pursuing violations of these rules, the scope for direct action taken by competitors through the courts is limited. Any act that falls under the definition of unfair competition is prohibited by the Antitrust Law and guidelines prescribed by the Japan Fair Trade Commission as well as the Unfair Competition Prevention Law. If a pharmaceutical company is in breach of the Antitrust Law or the Unfair Competition Prevention Law, it is subject to criminal, administrative or civil sanctions in accordance with the type, nature and material nature of such breach. The Japan Fair Trade Commission may bring criminal or administrative proceedings.

5.4.15 MEXICO[20]

The Ministry of Health is responsible for the regulation of advertising via COFEPRIS. The penalties for failing to comply with rules related to advertising are the suspension of advertising activities and the imposition of a fine, which can range from 1000 to 10 000 times the official daily minimum wages (around $US4.00/day). The imposition of these fines has been steadily increasing and the Ministry of Health constantly monitors advertising activities.

There has also been a strong coordination effort between COFEPRIS and pharmaceutical companies for the self-regulation of advertising. Competitors can complain directly to COFEPRIS about advertising activities under the provisions of the General Health Law and the Regulations of the Health Law. In addition, companies who belong to the Self-regulation and Publicity Ethics Council can also file a complaint about another member's advertising. The Council can issue recommendations and sanctions after hearing both parties, but these are not binding.

There is also the possibility for an action for unfair competition under Mexican law as a result of a company's advertising activities; this is based on the provisions of the industrial property law. The affected party can also claim damages and lost profits in a civil court, as a result of unfair competition activities.

The federal law for consumer protection has provision for filing a complaint before the Bureau of Consumer Protection with regard to false or tendentious advertising, which can lead to the imposition of a fine and an order to stop the specific advertising activities.

5.4.16 THE NETHERLANDS[21]

In the event of non-compliance with advertising rules, competitors, the Public Health Inspectorate and more particularly the special advertising enforcement department of the Ministry of Health, Welfare and Sports may initiate civil proceedings, possibly after a decision has been obtained from the self-regulatory body (CGR). In urgent matters, preliminary relief may be sought. An injunction against the use of the advertisement, the imposition of penalty payments, as well as compensation, may be claimed in those proceedings.

Both competitors and practitioners can file complaints with the CGR in the event of non-compliance with the Code of Conduct for Pharmaceutical Advertising (CPA). The CGR can issue a preliminary or final recommendation. It is possible to appeal against such a recommendation; the appellate decision will be considered to be a 'binding advice'. Non-compliance with the latter will be deemed to constitute a breach of contract. It is not clear whether decisions of the CGR are binding upon companies that are not members of any of the industry associations that founded this self-regulatory body.

Finally, the Inspectorate can also request that the Public Prosecutor initiate a criminal prosecution and the Inspectorate became much more active in this respect in recent years. Failure to comply with the relevant rules may result in the imposition of fines or even (theoretically) a prison term of up to 6 months.

There is no specific legislation on unfair competition.

5.4.17 NORWAY[22]

The Norwegian Medicines Agency (NMA) monitors advertising and other marketing activities of the pharmaceutical industry and may impose bans on specific marketing activities or, in the event of repeated violation of the law, ban all advertising for a specific pharmaceutical product.

Breaches of the advertising provisions may carry a criminal sanction and therefore the NMA may also notify the prosecution authorities of possible breach of law. In practice, this will be relevant only to serious or repeated breaches of the law.

In the case of intentional breach or gross negligence of the relevant legislation, a court may impose a fine or, in the case of serious offences, pass a custodial sentence. However, this procedure requires that the prosecution authorities decide to bring a criminal charge against the offender, which very rarely occurs.

It is usually the Committee for Drug Information of the LMI (Norwegian Association of Pharmaceutical Manufacturers) that supervises promotional activities and may impose fines on pharmaceutical companies in cases of breach of ethical rules and guidelines. *The fines may be in the order of NOK5000–300 000*. The Committee is authorised to make decisions only in cases where the defendant is a member of the LMI or has approved the industry's ethical guidelines. This is the case for the vast majority of companies responsible for the sale of pharmaceutical products in Norway, and in practice the Committee is an important authority.

Competitors may lodge a complaint against a pharmaceutical company either to the Agency or to the Committee for Drug Information. In principle, competitors may also approach the ordinary courts, but the other two procedures are most commonly used.

The Norwegian Marketing Control Act contains stipulations in respect of fair competition and good marketing practice among businesses. Both private individuals and companies may bring an action based on breach of the Act. A court may impose a fine or, in the case of serious offences, pass a custodial sentence.

Enterprises such as pharmaceutical companies, including competitors, are entitled to bring an action before the Norwegian Council dealing with unfair marketing practices. This is a dispute resolution agency that gives statements in conflicts between businesses. The statements are mainly based on the Norwegian Marketing Control Act. The agency cannot award compensation or impose fines. However, statements of the agency would in most cases give a clear indication of whether or not the matter should be taken to court. In addition, companies may lodge a complaint with the Norwegian competition authority or Norwegian courts for breach of the prohibitions against anti-competitive cooperation or abuse of dominant position in the Norwegian Competition Act.

5.4.18 SPAIN[24]

In Spain the affected parties can take legal action under the laws generally applicable to advertising (e.g. the ceasing and rectification actions set forth in the Advertising Act).

In addition, in the case of medicines, the violation of the provisions governing advertisement can also trigger the application of penalties under the Medicine Act. The penalty incurred depends on the type of violation and its surrounding circumstances. In the most serious cases, the penalty may be €1 000 000.

However, it is more usual for breaches of the ethical code and disputes between competitors with regard to advertising to be handled by the self-regulatory body Farmaindustria. Infringement of the code will be classified as minor, serious or very serious based on the following criteria:

- Damage to the image of the pharmaceutical company
- Magnitude of the infringement
- Potential harm to public health
- Degree of intent
- Impact on the scientific/medical community
- Failure to comply with previous warning
- Unfair competition

- Generalisation of the infringement
- Tendency to re-offend.

The cost of infringement is as follows:

- Minor = €6000–120 000
- Serious = €120 001–240 000
- Very serious = €240 001–360 000.

5.4.19 SWEDEN[23]

The Market Practices Act provides for several remedies or sanctions depending on the nature of the violation. Misleading advertisements and special offers carry a sanction of both prohibitive injunction (subject to fines upon non-compliance), market disruption fees between SEK5000 and SEK5000 000 and third party damages, whereas in cases of violation of the general clause on unfair marketing only prohibitive injunction is available. The Consumer Ombudsman, a competitor or a trade or consumer association can initiate actions.

In day-to-day practice the two self-regulatory bodies, the IGM and the NBL, handle most cases with regard to advertising of medicinal products. The IGM monitors the market and may open a case without a formal complaint, or refer a case to the NBL. Private individuals and pharmaceutical companies, including competitors, are also entitled to bring an action before the IGM. The IGM and the NBL have contractual authority to fine member companies who violate the LIF rules with the maximum fine being SEK250 000.

The Market Practices Act, the LIF rules and the Medicinal Products Act govern unfair competition based on unlawful marketing measures.

5.4.20 SWITZERLAND[26]

Swissmedic exercises control over advertising activities and is responsible for enforcement of the law. It supports the Swiss Society of Chemical Industries with respect to advertising activities addressed to health professionals. As anyone is entitled to notify the Secretariat of any incident suspected of constituting an infringement of this code and the Secretariat is entitled to follow up suspected infringements on its own initiative, the rules are very strictly enforced. As a rule, however, the details of any action taken are not published.

The Swiss Society of Chemical Industries (SSCI) employs an independent healthcare professional to verify the observance of the code. The individual reports to the management of the SSCI and has the following duties:

- Objective and unprejudiced supervision of the observance of the obligations assumed by signing the code
- Random checks of promotional measures and materials of firms
- Examination and assessment of complaints received concerning promotional measures and materials, contacting the firm(s) concerned to clarify the situation and making an effort to reach mutual agreement on the settlement of complaints as far as possible
- Application to the supervisory board in cases where efforts to reach a settlement were unsuccessful
- Taking care of administrative matters and enforcing the decisions of the supervisory board
- Presentation of an annual report on his or her activities to the signatories of the Certificate of Obligation and to any other interested bodies, according to the decisions of the supervisory board.

The criminal sanctions for violating the rules on the advertising of medicinal products are imprisonment for up to 3 months or a fine of up to CHF50 000 if the perpetrator acted intentionally. If the person in question was acting in his or her professional capacity, the penalty is imprisonment for up to 6 months and a fine of up to CHF100 000. If the perpetrator acted negligently, the penalty is a fine of up to CHF10 000.

Competitors may take action directly through the courts and/or file a penal complaint, and seek to obtain injunctive relief and the seizure of illegal advertising media in cases where the violation of the rules on the advertising of medicinal products also qualifies as an act of unfair competition.

Such actions through the courts may be taken by anyone whose clientèle, credit, professional standing, business or other economic interests are threatened or injured by unfair competition. The criminal sanctions for committing acts of unfair competition are imprisonment for up to 3 years or a fine of up to CHF100 000.

5.4.21 TURKEY[26]

The Ministry of Health is the enforcement authority but it is rare for it to take action of its own accord against unethical promotion unless it is a serious breach. If a complaint is received from a competitor or third party, it will consider the facts and decide whether to take action. However, before submitting official applications to the MoH companies usually try to resolve them between themselves.

According to Turkish Commercial Law all acts contrary to good faith may constitute legal grounds for unfair competition action.

5.4.22 THE UNITED KINGDOM[27]

The UK Regulations provide a number of offences for failing to comply with the relevant laws. Enforcement is by the MHRA, which prefers to resolve complaints quickly and informally, with companies agreeing to take voluntary action to amend their advertising, so prosecutions for advertising offences are extremely rare. A person or company contravening the legislation faces a fine of up to £5000 per offence if the Magistrates' Court deals with the matter. Examples of this type would be cases of failure to comply with the rules on samples or the solicitation or acceptance of inducements by health professionals. If the matter is dealt with by the Crown Court, there is no statutory maximum fine legislated and the Court will impose a higher figure in the case of a serious breach. In addition to the fines, a period of up to 2 years' imprisonment may be imposed. The MHRA also has the power to issue notices prohibiting the publication of specified advertisements. The MHRA posts details of cases resolved informally on its website.

On a day-to-day basis most complaints are handled by the self-regulatory authority the Prescription Medicines Code of Authority (PMCPA), part of the Association of the British Pharmaceutical Industry (ABPI) and they work very closely with the MHRA.

Under the ABPI code, the PMCPA's internal panel first makes a decision but there is a right to appeal to a board consisting of representatives of industry and the medical profession chaired by an independent lawyer. It is possible for the PMCPA to impose an administrative fine on members of £2500 per breach of the code or £10 000 per breach, if the matter is unsuccessfully appealed. The Authority also has the power in serious cases to require an audit of a company's promotional procedures, or to suspend or expel the company from the ABPI.

Generally it is not usual for competitors to take direct action through the courts, although they can make complaints to the MHRA or PMCPA. There is no unfair competition statute, which provides a ready basis for a complaint in the UK.

5.4.23 THE UNITED STATES OF AMERICA[28]

In the USA a prescription drug is considered 'misbranded' if an advertisement fails to satisfy the requirements of the FDCA and FDA regulations. The FDCA prohibits the introduction of a misbranded drug into interstate commerce or the misbranding of a drug already in interstate commerce.

Potential penalties for misbranding violations include injunction proceedings, civil penalties, seizure proceedings and even criminal prosecution. The US government is responsible for the enforcement of the FDCA and FDA regulations.

The FDA's division of Drug Marketing, Advertising and Communications (DDMAC) polices prescription-only drug advertising. Before pursuing the remedies listed above, DDMAC will often issue a warning letter to the manufacturer outlining any violations and requesting that certain actions be taken, including, in some circumstances, discontinuation of an advertisement.

Although the FDCA does not provide for competitors to take action in court, the Lanham Act permits false advertising claims. A competitor has standing under the Lanham Act to challenge false or misleading advertising if such a competitor believes that it is likely to be damaged.

The Pharmaceutical Research Manufacturers of America (PhRMA) code of conduct addresses how pharmaceutical companies should interact with healthcare professionals, but there is no formal complaints mechanism for the code.

In July 2005, California enacted legislation that was the first of its kind to require pharmaceutical companies doing business in the state to put into place a compliance programme. This programme must be in accordance with the Office of the Inspector General (OIG) guidelines and the PhRMA code. It requires that the company make a public written declaration of compliance on an annual basis. However, the law does not specify which state agency is responsible for enforcement of the law nor does it specify any penalties for non-compliance.

5.5 Overview of control: regulation or self-regulation

TABLE 5.1 Summary of control mechanisms by country

Country	Regulatory authority (RA)	Pre-approval mandatory by RA?	Active monitoring by RA?	Control by RA / self-regulation?	National self-regulatory agency	Complaints handled by
Australia	TGA	No	No	Self-regulation	IAMA	IAMA
Brazil	Anvisa	Yes in theory, no in practice	Yes	Both	Conar	Both Anvisa and Conar
Canada	Health Canada	Legally no/in practice yes	No	RA	ASC and PAAB	Non-profit-making organisations, ASC and PAAB
The Czech Republic	SÚKL	No	Some	Both	MAFS	SÚKL/MAFS
France	AFSSAPS	No, but must be submitted to AFSAAPS within 8 days of publication.	Some	Both	LEEM	AFSSAPS
Germany	HWG	No	No	Both; there are several self-regulatory organisations	FSA	Directly to court system, or by notification of one of the 'self-regulatory' regulatory' organisations
Greece	EOF	No	Yes	RA	SFEE	Industry association/RA or courts
Ireland	IMB	No	No	Mainly self-regulation	IPHA	IPHA industry association
Italy	AIFA	Yes, must be submitted to AIFA 10 days before use	No	Self-regulation	Farmindustria	Depends; usual practice is Farmindustria, but RA also possible

(continued)

TABLE 5.1 Continued

Country	Regulatory authority (RA)	Pre-approval mandatory by RA?	Active monitoring by RA?	Control by RA / self-regulation?	National self-regulatory agency	Complaints handled by
Japan	MHLW	No	Some	Both	JPMA	
Mexico	COFEPRIS	Yes		Both	Code of Ethics of NCPI	COFEPRIS
The Netherlands	MHWS	No	No	Self-regulation	Nefarma	Special commission Medicines Advertising
Norway	NMA	No	No	Self-regulation	LMI	Norwegian Association of Pharmaceutical Manufacturers
Spain		No (yes for over the counter, however)	Yes	Controlled by regional autonomous authorities	Farmaindustria	RA, but also an industry board
Sweden	SMPA	No	Yes	Mainly self-regulatory	LIF	LIF/SMPA
Switzerland	Swissmedic	Yes	No	Both	SSCI	Health Authority and Industry Association
Turkey	Ministry of Health (MoH)	Yes	Unknown	RA	None	MoH
The UK	MHRA	No	Limited	Mainly self-regulation?	PMCPA (part of ABPI)	PMCPA/MHRA
The USA	FDA	Yes	Yes (by DDMAC)	FDA	PhRMA	Appeal to FDA or court

ABPI, Association of the British Pharmaceutical Industry; AFSSAPS, French Drug Agency; AIFA, Italian Medicines Agency; Anvisa, Brazilian Sanitation Agency; ASAI, Advertising Standards Authority for Ireland; ASC, Advertising Standards Canada; COFEPRIS, Federal Commission for Protection against Sanitary Risks (Mexico); Conar, Brazilian Advertising Self Regulation Council; DDMAC, Division of Drug Marketing, Advertising and Communication Agency (the USA); EOF, National Organisation for Medicines (Greece); FPHC, French Public Health Code; FDA, Food and Drug Administration Agency (the USA); FSA, German Code of Conduct; HA, health authority; HC, Health Canada; IAMA, Industry Association Medicines Australia; IMB, Irish Medicines Board; IPHA, Irish Pharmaceuticals Health Authority; JPMA, Japan Pharmaceutical Manufacturers Association; LIF, Swedish Association of the Pharmaceutical Industry; LMI, Norwegian Association of Pharmaceutical Manufacturers; MAFS, International Association of Pharmaceutical Companies (the Czech Republic); MHLW, Ministry of Health, Labour and Welfare (Japan); MHRA, Medicines and Healthcare Regulatory Agency (the UK); MHWS, Ministry of Health Labour and Sports (the Netherlands); NCPI, National Chamber of the Pharmaceutical Industry (Mexico); NMA, Norwegian Medicines Agency; PAAB, Pharmaceutical Advertising Advisory Board (Canada); PMCPA, Prescription Medicines Code of Practice Authority (the UK); SFEE, Hellenic Association of Pharmaceutical Companies; SMPA, Swedish Medical Products Agency; SSCI, Swiss Society of Chemical Industries; SÚKL, State Institute for Drug Control (the Czech Republic); TGA, Therapeutic Goods Administration (Australia).

CHAPTER 6

Basic Principles of the Self-Regulatory Codes

The basic principles of the regulatory codes are to ensure that promotion of medicines is conducted in an ethical manner and that any information is clear, accurate, balanced, fair and objective.

6.1 Substantiation

Substantiation is the verification of claims or statements made in promotional materials. This verification is usually by citing references, which in most countries must be provided to healthcare professionals and sometimes to competitors when requested.

In general terms, substantiation by referencing is required in promotion in the following circumstances:

- When a quotation is used
- When a clinical trial is used
- When graphs, tables, figures and illustrations are used.

It is not normally necessary to substantiate claims that are within the terms of the licence. The type of data allowed to substantiate statements varies from country to country. They are:

1. Published data, e.g. from journals in the public domain
2. Abstracts, e.g. from data presented at international conferences
3. Posters, e.g. presented at international conferences
4. Data on file: data that are not in the public domain, e.g. clinical studies from the pharmaceutical company making the claim.

The quality of the data and its credibility are highest for published data (group 1), especially if the journal is peer reviewed. The credibility decreases, moving down the list from 1 to 4. In some countries data from posters and data on file may not be used to substantiate claims. Table 6.1 summarises the situation in each country with respect to whether posters or data on file are acceptable as a reference and if they are required to be supplied upon reasonable request.

TABLE 6.1 Standards of proof allowed to substantiate promotional claims[6-46]

Country	Data on file	Poster	Abstract	Published papers	Other information
Australia	Yes, but must not rely solely on data on file	Yes	Yes	Yes	
Brazil*	Yes	Yes, provided that there is also a published abstract	Yes	The paper must be published in indexed magazines	Data on file must be made available upon request
Canada	Yes	Yes	Yes	Yes	Data on file must be made available to the PAAB Commissioner and may be classified as 'Confidential' by the advertiser or the author (pending publication). Copies of all reference sources cited in advertising and promotion must be provided to the PAAB Commissioner for verification of claims and quotations
The Czech Republic	Yes, but must not rely solely on data on file	Yes	Yes	Yes	Data on file must be made available to healthcare professionals and industry companies upon request within 10 working days
France	Only in certain circumstances (refer to other information)	No	Yes, provided that they are consistent with the SPC and are less than 12 months old	Yes, provided that the journal is peer reviewed/ refereed	If it is not published it can be used if it is contained in the marketing authorisation file and in compliance with this authorisation OR If it has not been published but has been used by the TC to render its opinion and is in line with the recommendations of the TC
Germany	No	No	Yes	Yes	If a promotional claim cannot be directly substantiated by the text of the SPC, reference should be made to appropriate published material to support the claim
Greece	Yes	Yes	Yes	Yes	
India	Yes	Yes	Yes	Yes	
Ireland	Yes	Yes	Yes	Yes	When promotional material refers to published studies, clear references must be given. Data on file must be provided without delay if it is requested
Italy	No	No	Yes	Yes	Information and data that are not referred to in the SPC may be used for product promotion, provided that such information is not inconsistent with the content of the SPC. However, the supporting reference must be published
Japan	No information found				
Mexico	No information found				
The Netherlands*	No	Yes	Yes	Yes	Any source used in promotion must be verifiable. Claims versus another product must be supported by two peer-reviewed publications
Norway*	No	No – unless abstract is printed on reverse	Yes, if abstract is available on Medline	Yes, if available on Medline	The availability of data on Medline is used in Norway as a measure of acceptability as a reference.
Spain	No	No	Yes	Yes	Information and data that are not referred to in the SPC may be used for product promotion, provided that such information is not inconsistent with the content of the SPC. However, the supporting reference must be published in a peer-reviewed journal
Sweden*	Yes	Yes	Yes	Yes, provided it is of high scientific standard	Data on file must be provided on request. Posters can be used if they are similar to abstracts and selected by a conference organising committee.

Switzerland*	No	No	No	Yes	All statements in promotional material must be in line with the latest Swissmedic-approved prescribing information. Standards of proof must be published
Turkey	Yes	Yes	Yes	Yes	References to congress abstracts, poster presentations of national and international congresses as well as posters accepted to be displayed in such congresses can be used in promotion for 2 years after the congress When promotional material refers to 'data on file', the relevant part must be provided without delay at the request of the members of health professions
The UK	Yes	Yes	Yes	Yes	Information and data that are not referred to in the SPC may be used for product promotion, provided that this information is not inconsistent with the content of the SPC. All promotional statements made must be capable of substantiation
The USA	Yes	Yes	Yes	Yes	

PAAB, Pharmaceutical Advertising Advisory Board (Canada); SPC, summary or product characteristics; TC, Transparency Commission (France).

In countries where data on file are allowed as substantiation in promotional items, but requirements state that they should be supplied on request, the following factors should be taken into account:

- Cite only data that you are prepared to provide. Care must be taken in many instances where data are to be published in the future that revealing the data does not jeopardise the publication. In addition, your company may not wish to provide commercially sensitive data to competitors.
- If your company does not own the data, you must have the owner's permission to use them.
- Data on file can usually be supplied as a summary document, but it must be a stand-alone document and contain enough information so that the reader can adequately assess the validity of any claims or statements made. It is advisable to prepare the data on file with the promotional item, so that this can be reviewed and approved for release at the same time. This avoids the panic of having to prepare data on file when requested to provide because some countries specify that it must be provided within a specified time frame, e.g. 10 days in the Czech Republic and the UK.

6.1.1 IFPMA[6]

Clause 4

Promotion should be capable of substantiation either by reference to the approved labelling or by scientific evidence. Such evidence should be made available on request to healthcare professionals. Companies should deal objectively with requests for information made in good faith and should provide data that are appropriate to the source of the enquiry.

6.1.2 EFPIA[7]

Clause 3

Promotion must be capable of substantiation, which must be promptly provided in response to reasonable requests from healthcare professionals.

In particular, promotional claims about side effects must reflect available evidence or be capable of substantiation by clinical experience. Substantiation need not be provided, however, in relation to the validity of elements approved in the marketing authorisation.

6.1.3 WHO[8]

Clauses 7 and 8

All promotional claims must be reliable, accurate, truthful, informative, balanced, up to date, capable of substantiation and in good taste.

Scientific data in the public domain should be made available to prescribers and any other person entitled to receive it, on request, as appropriate to requirements.

6.1.4 AUSTRALIA[29]

Clause 1

A company will, upon reasonable request, provide healthcare professionals with additional accurate and relevant information about products that it markets, in addition to the information supplied or generally available, including company information.

Data in support of a claim, including 'data on file' or 'in press', must be made available without delay upon reasonable request. Where this material is not available through standard library services, it must be made available without delay.

Any information used to support a medical or promotional claim must include sufficient detail and be of adequate quality to allow evaluation of the validity of results and hence the claim. Such substantiating information must not rely solely on data on file.

6.1.5 BRAZIL[30]

Chapter 15

The quotes, tables or other illustrations extracted from scientific publications used in any advertisement, publicity or promotion should be faithfully reproduced and specify the complete bibliographical reference.

6.1.6 CANADA[31]

Clause 3

Quotes and claims used in advertising and promotion must be consistent with the marketing authorisation:

- Advertising and promotion containing direct or indirect product claims and/or quotations from the scientific literature must include a complete listing of the scientific references.
- Reference materials, published and unpublished (data on file), should be the most recent available and should be consistent with current Canadian medical opinion.
- References cited in advertising and promotion must be available to health professionals on request, in English and/or French, either in their original form or translated.
- Data on file must be made available to the Commissioner and may be classified as 'Confidential' by the advertiser or the author (pending publication).
- A copy of the summary of the data on file must be provided to health professionals upon request.
- Copies of all reference sources cited in advertising and promotion must be provided to the Pharmaceutical Advertising Advisory Board (PAAB) Commissioner for verification of claims and quotations.
- Advertising and promotion must have fair balance, e.g. it cannot emphasise just positive features of a pharmaceutical product while ignoring significant negative findings.
- Quotations from published or unpublished scientific literature must be verbatim as presented in the source and in context. Any deletions should be identified by a series of dots. Deletions of negative findings or other significant information relative to the product and uses are not acceptable.

- Claims or selected quotations must not refer to other products or different formulations of the same active ingredients unless authoritative data, including approved methods, are available to warrant cross-referencing between products.

6.1.7 THE CZECH REPUBLIC[32]

Clause 1

The manufacturer has to provide healthcare professionals with additional accurate and relevant information about its marketed products.

Substantiating information must not rely solely on data on file. Data cited in promotional material in support of a claim, including 'data on file' or 'in press', must be made available to healthcare professionals and industry companies upon request within 10 working days.

6.1.8 FRANCE[33]

Marketing authorisation application (MAA) files and studies used for the Transparency Commission opinion, whether or not published, can be used in a comparative advertisement on the condition that they correspond to the therapeutic indications validated by the marketing authorisation and, if applicable, the conclusions of the Transparency Commission.

Other studies can be used, on the condition that they are within the scope of the indications validated by the marketing authorisation and correspond, if applicable, to the conclusions of the Transparency Commission, provided that they have been published in a peer-reviewed journal.

The use of summaries of congress communications (abstracts) in an advertising document is acceptable when these comply with the summary of product characteristics and existing recent standards (less than 12 months old), and exist in a referenced journal.

'Submitted' or 'accepted for publication' studies cannot be used. Similarly, posters, special editions and special issues released as part of a contractual agreement between a publishing journal and a company are excluded.

Studies referenced must be provided to any practitioner who requests them. All claims must be supported by a complete bibliographic reference clearly showing: title, authors, journal, volume, year, page. The date and study number must be stated when these originate from an unpublished document (MAA files or Transparency files).

Types of studies that can be used:

- Explanatory-type studies are most appropriate for underpinning efficacy or safety of use, especially in comparative advertising. They must be prospective, controlled, randomised and, if possible (and depending on the case), blind, with ample numbers for sufficient power.
- Other methodologies (of the pragmatic type) or other study conditions (of the 'naturalistic' type) that are better adapted to the assessment of therapeutic interest and medical benefit are relevant and can be used when accurate justifications are provided.
- The use of the results of rigorous meta-analysis is allowed.

6.1.9 GERMANY[34]

Section 7

Promotion must be based on sufficient scientific evidence, especially those for advertising claims referring to specific benefits, qualities or properties of a product.

- Promotion about side effects must also reflect all available findings or be capable of substantiation by clinical experience.

- Claims that are already included in the marketing authorisation of the medicinal product do not require further scientific evidence. If requested by healthcare professionals, the relevant scientific evidence must be made directly available to an appropriate extent.

6.1.10 GREECE[35]

Article 7

Companies must provide to healthcare professionals and the competent administrative executives, upon request, accurate information with respect to the medicinal product distributed by each company:

- Information, claims and comparisons must be correct, accurate, objective and clear, and must be based on relevant and comparable aspects of the medicinal products as well as on an updated assessment of all data, reflecting the facts clearly. They must not be misleading, either explicitly or implicitly, and they must not distort the scientific facts.
- It is prohibited to: promote misleading indications; refer to old scientific data if there is newer different information available; make inaccurate or undocumented claims, make misleading comparison with other products and generalise isolated observations.
- Any information, claims or comparisons in promotional materials must be clearly referenced and, including the corresponding section of data on file, must be provided without delay on request by a healthcare professional or a competent administrative executive of the health system. Documentation is not necessary for indications approved in the marketing authorisation.
- Wherever there is a claim based on in vitro studies or studies on guinea-pigs, it must be clearly indicated in the promotional material that these are experimental data.

6.1.11 INDIA[16]

Clause 4

Promotion should be capable of substantiation either by reference to the approved labelling or by scientific evidence. Such evidence should be made available, on request, to healthcare professionals. Companies should deal objectively with requests for information made in good faith and should provide data that are appropriate to the source of the enquiry.

6.1.12 IRELAND[36]

Clause 4

A company must promptly provide health professionals with accurate and relevant information about the medicinal products that it markets:

- Information about medicinal products must be up to date and accurately reflect current knowledge or responsible opinion.
- Information about medicinal products must be accurate, balanced, fair and objective, and must not mislead either directly or by implication.
- Information must be capable of substantiation. Such substantiation need not be provided, however, in relation to the validity of indications approved in the product authorisation.
- Substantiation must be provided without delay at the request of members of the medical, pharmacy and dentistry professions, including the members of those professions employed in the pharmaceutical industry.
- When promotional material refers to published studies, clear references must be given.

6.1.13 ITALY[37]

Information and data that are not referred to in the summary of product characteristics (SPC) may be used for product promotion provided that such information is not inconsistent with the SPC. The supporting references must, however, be published.

Clause 2

The information material prepared by the company on its products and used to provide information to physicians must be based on official documents issued by the Ministry of Health when the drug is registered, or successively approved by the Ministry on the basis of the pertinent laws in force.

The texts, tables and other illustrations taken from medical review or scientific works must be reproduced faithfully and in full, with the exact indication of the source. No citations are admissible that can appear partial and/or contradictory with respect to the author's intentions when separated from the context in which they originally appeared.

6.1.14 JAPAN[38]

Clause 4

The statements contained in promotional materials should be correct, fair and objective, and based on scientific data.

Statements shall not deviate from the approved items.

6.1.15 MEXICO

No information available.

6.1.16 THE NETHERLANDS[39]

Clause V

The advertising statement, when considered in relation to the advertising for the medicinal product as a whole, must be accurate, up to date and truthful, and correct and verifiable in its constituent parts.

All citations of publications must be accurate and must mention their sources; a check must have been performed to ensure that the use of these citations is not in conflict with the tenor of the publication.

The cited publications must be a fair reflection of the current status of science and technology.

6.1.17 NORWAY[40]

Clause 4

All information included in marketing material shall be supported by documentation that can be provided on request. There is, however, no need to provide such documentation concerning information that has been approved in connection with the issue of a marketing authorisation.

6.1.18 SPAIN[41]

Clause 3

Information about medicinal products should be accurate, balanced, fair and objective, and sufficiently complete to enable recipients to form their own opinion of the therapeutic value of the medicine concerned.

It should be based on an up-to-date evaluation of scientific evidence and reflect that evidence clearly. It should not mislead by distortion, undue emphasis or omission, or any other way.

Information, statements or comparisons included in promotional materials should be well founded. This should be provided to physicians and all other healthcare professionals on request. In particular, any comparison made between different medicines must be scientifically verified. This is not necessary for statements related to the indications approved in the SPC.

6.1.19 SWEDEN[42]

Article 32

A pharmaceutical company should be able to substantiate any facts, statements, claims and other presentations made in its drug information. The company shall be prepared, whenever requested by the Information Examiner or the Information Practices Committee, to produce supporting evidence without delay.

6.1.20 SWITZERLAND[43]

Clause 141

Advertising to healthcare professionals for, and information about, medicinal products must be accurate, balanced, objective and fair.

The statements must be substantiated.

6.1.21 TURKEY[44]

Clause 6

A company must promptly provide members of the health professions with accurate and relevant information about the medicines that the company markets.

Information, claims and comparisons must be accurate, provable, balanced, fair, objective and unambiguous, and must be based on an up-to-date evaluation of all the evidence and must reflect that evidence clearly.

Any claim, information or comparison must be substantiated. Substantiation need not be provided, however, in relation to the validity of elements approved in the marketing authorisation.

References to congress abstracts, poster presentations of national and international congresses, as well as posters accepted to be displayed in such congresses, can be used in promotion for 2 years after the congress.

Substantiation for any information, claim or comparison must be provided without delay at the request of the health professional or the competitor against which the product is compared.

When promotional material refers to a published study, clear references must be given. When it refers to 'data on file', the relevant part of the data must be provided without delay at the request of the members of health professions.

6.1.22 THE UNITED KINGDOM[45]

Clause 7

Any information, claim or comparison must be capable of substantiation.

Substantiation for any information, claim or comparison must be provided as soon as possible and certainly within 10 working days, at the request of members of the health professions or appropriate administrative staff. It need not be provided, however, in relation to the validity of indications approved in the marketing authorisation.

6.1.23 THE UNITED STATES OF AMERICA[46]

No guidance within the PhRMA code of conduct.

In the author's experience 'data on file' can be used to substantiate claims, but it is not necessary to provide this information if requested.

6.2 Comparison and hanging comparatives

A hanging comparative is where, for example, product X is said to be better, faster, cheaper, etc. without saying with what it is compared.

The example often used is of the soap powder, brand name Persil, where the statement used is 'Persil washes whiter'. This is a hanging comparative, because the statement does not explain what Persil washes whiter than. If Persil were a medicine this statement would not be allowed in promotional materials.

Further examples of hanging comparatives would be the following if they do not qualify their claim:

- Increased response
- Decreased response
- More effective
- Better tolerability
- Stronger.

6.2.1 IFPMA[6]

Clause 4

Promotional material should not mislead by distortion, exaggeration, undue emphasis or omission, or in any other way.

6.2.2 EFPIA[7]

Clause 3

Any comparison made between different medicinal products must be based on relevant and comparable aspects of the products. Comparative advertising must not be misleading or disparaging.

6.2.3 WHO[8]

No guidance found.

6.2.4 AUSTRALIA[29]

Clause 1

Comparison of products must not be disparaging, but must be factual, fair and capable of substantiation and referenced to its source. In presenting a comparison, care must be taken to ensure that it properly reflects the body of evidence and does not mislead by distortion, by undue emphasis or in any other way.

'Hanging' comparatives are those that merely claim that a product is better, stronger, more widely prescribed, etc. and must not be used.

6.2.5 BRAZIL[30]

Chapter 4

It is forbidden to make comparisons, in a direct and/or insinuating manner, that are not based on information proven through clinical studies published in indexed publications.

6.2.6 CANADA[31]

Clause 5

Pharmaceutical manufacturers are required to observe the following principles:

- The comparison is drawn between drugs under the same conditions of use, e.g. at equivalent part(s) of their authorised dose ranges (e.g. maximum vs maximum dosage) or in a similar population.
- The claim does not conflict with the terms of market authorisation of the compared products.
- The claim is of clinical relevance in humans, i.e. relevant to treatment selection, and, where this is not readily apparent, the sponsor can justify its clinical relevance.
- The evidence generated to substantiate the claim is conclusive and based on:
  - consideration of all relevant data
  - scientifically accurate, unbiased, reproducible data obtained from studies conducted and analysed to current scientific standards using established research methodologies and validated end-points
  - appropriate interpretation of the data.
- The claim and its presentation should:
  - identify the compared entities
  - identify the medicinal use related to the claim where this is not readily apparent
  - not obscure the therapeutic use of the advertised product
  - not attack the compared drug product(s) in an unreasonable manner
  - be expressed in terms, language and graphics that can be understood by the intended audience.
- Comparative claims of efficacy and safety require support of evidence from head-to-head, well-designed, adequately controlled, blinded, randomised, clinical studies. Open label studies are not considered to be a high level of evidence and are not acceptable if subjective end-points are included in the study. Comparative claims should be relevant to current medical opinion and practice.
- To be considered as evidence, clinical studies must use established research methodologies and validated end-points. To aid in the assessment of these study parameters, PAAB looks for evidence that the full study results have been subject to independent review, such as that found by achieving the publishing of study results, including statistical analyses, in a peer-reviewed journal.

Analysis of data To be considered as evidence, results must achieve the statistical significance level of $p < 0.05$, which can also be stated in terms of 95 per cent confidence intervals. Failure of study results to demonstrate a statistically significant difference in the measured effect is not sufficient to support a claim of equivalence between the treatments studied.

All direct and indirect comparisons must not mislead, and be supported by reliable current data.

Disclosure of study parameters The claim should be accompanied in prominent type size (a minimum of 8 point on 9 point) by disclosure of relevant study parameters that would aid the reader in interpreting the data, e.g. study methodology, description of patient type and number, disease severity, dosage range, p value or confidence intervals, study sites. In no circumstances would extrapolation of the claim beyond the actual conditions of the supporting studies be acceptable.

Context Selective data presentations or claims that distort study findings, or that are out of context with study conclusions, are not acceptable.

Equivalence Products cited in comparative claims should be those products actually used in the supporting evidence. Cross-referencing to non-Canadian products is not permitted unless bioequivalence or other authoritative evidence is presented. The reference drug used in the study must be clearly stated in the claim copy.

Scare tactics Advertising that induces fear or uses scare tactics to introduce unwarranted concern will not be accepted.

6.2.7 THE CZECH REPUBLIC[32]

Clause 1

Comparative advertising is advertising that directly or indirectly identifies any other manufacturer or medicinal product of any other manufacturer. It should comply with the following:

- Comparative advertising must not be disparaging, but must be factual, fair and capable of substantiation, and referenced to its source. It must compare only relevant, substantial, verifiable, representative elements and compare in more than one element.
- In presenting a comparison, care must be taken to ensure that it does not mislead by distortion, the scale used, doses selected or undue emphasis, or in any other way.
- 'Hanging' comparatives – those that merely claim that a product is better, stronger, more widely prescribed, etc. must not be used.
- 'Data on file', when used to substantiate comparative statements, must be supplied on request.
- Where a claim of comparative efficacy or safety is made, it must not be based solely on a comparison of product information documents that do not reflect the general literature.
- Claims of comparative efficacy or safety must be substantiated with respect to all aspects of efficacy or safety. Where a comparative claim relates to a specific parameter, any claims must be clearly identified as pertaining to that parameter.
- The accepted level of statistical significance is $p < 0.05$. If comparative data that are not statistically significant are used, such data must comply with the following conditions:
  - the data must be clearly identified as such by statement, not just by a p value
  - the data must not be used to generalise or to indicate superiority or inferiority
  - the statement that the claim is not statistically significant needs to be linked in some manner to the original claim, made on the same page and within a reasonable proximity of the original claim in a manner that is not obscured by other material using a type size of not less than 2 mm.

6.2.8 FRANCE[33]

The comparison must be as exhaustive as possible without emphasising favourable elements. In order to be objective, the comparison must be based on essential, significant, relevant and verifiable characteristics.

At a minimum, efficacy and safety of use criteria must be provided (part of the benefit:risk ratio), but criteria of interest to the practitioner can also be provided: dosage, treatment duration, interactions, acceptability, etc.

Validated pharmacological properties of no clinical consequence are not compared.

However, with respect to generics, price itself can be a comparison criterion, whether the comparison is based on the original product or on generics in the same group.

6.2.9 GERMANY[34]

Section 12

- Any advertising that explicitly or by implication identifies the medicinal products of a competitor shall be deemed to be comparative advertising.
- Any comparative advertising that fails objectively to refer to one or more essential, relevant, verifiable and typical properties of the medicinal products compared is inadmissible.
- Comparative advertising must not be misleading or disparaging with regard to a competitor's medicinal product.

6.2.10 GREECE[35]

Article 7

Information, claims and comparisons must be correct, accurate, objective and clear, and must be based on relevant and comparable aspects of the medicinal products as well as on an updated assessment of all data, reflecting the facts clearly. They must not be misleading, either explicitly or implicitly, and they must not distort the scientific facts.

The direct or indirect promotion of misleading indications of the medicinal product, reference to older scientific data (if there is newer different information available), the promotion of inaccurate or undocumented claims, the misleading comparison with other medicinal products and the generalisation of isolated observations are prohibited.

Any information, claims or comparisons must be scientifically documented.

The documentation of any information, claims or comparison must be provided without delay upon request by a healthcare professional or a competent administrative executive of the health system. However, no documentation is necessary with respect to indications approved in the marketing authorisation.

6.2.11 INDIA[16]

Clause 4

Promotional material should not mislead by distortion, exaggeration, undue emphasis or omission, or in any other way.

6.2.12 IRELAND[36]

Clause 5

Comparisons of medicinal products must be factual, fair and capable of substantiation. Care must be taken to ensure that comparisons do not mislead by distortion, by undue emphasis or omission, or in any other way.

Brand names of products of other companies must not be used in comparison unless the prior consent of the companies concerned has been obtained.

6.2.13 ITALY[37]

No guidance found.

6.2.14 JAPAN[38]

Clause 4

Comparisons with other drugs shall be based on scientific data. Competitors or competitors' drugs shall not be slandered or defamed.

6.2.15 MEXICO[20]

No guidance found.

6.2.16 THE NETHERLANDS[39]

Clause 5

If a comparison is made with another substance or another medicinal product in which a competitor or medicinal product offered by a competitor is expressly or implicitly named, then due care must be taken to ensure the following:

- The comparison is not misleading; the drugs that are being compared meet the same need or are intended for the same purpose.

- The comparison relates objectively to one or more essential, relevant, verifiable and representative characteristics of the medicinal products, e.g. the (clinical) effect.
- The comparison does not harm the value of these other substances or medicinal products.
- The marketing authorisation holder of these other substances or preparations, his or her tradename and/or brand names of these other substances or medicinal products are not bought into discredit.
- The comparison does not give rise to any confusion between the substances or medicinal products being compared with each other and their brand names and/or between the marketing authorisation holders involved and/or their tradenames.
- The comparison does not present medicinal products as an imitation or copy of medicinal products with a protected trademark or protected tradename.
- The comparison does not create any unfair advantage as a result of the reputation of a mark, tradename or other distinguishing characteristics of a competitor.
- The accuracy of the comparison can be scientifically demonstrated and the comparison is in accordance with the latest scientific knowledge.
- The comparison is complete with regard to the effect, undesirable effects, indications, contraindications and other relevant details of the substances or medicinal products being compared.
- In general, due regard has been shown to one's colleagues in the sector and to those at whom the advertising is aimed.

6.2.17 NORWAY[40]

Clause 4

Illustrations used in promotion should clearly indicate the precise source(s). Where adaptation or modification is required it must be clearly stated that the artwork has been adapted and/or modified.

Particular care must be taken to ensure that artwork included in the promotion does not mislead about the nature of a medicine or about a claim or comparison.

Any comparison made between different medicinal products must be based on relevant and comparable aspects of the products. Comparative advertising must not be misleading or disparaging.

6.2.18 SPAIN[41]

Clause 3

Comparative advertising must always comply with the regulations on fair competition. It cannot be disparaging, and comparisons must be based on relevant and comparable aspects.

Care must be taken to ensure that the sources on which statements are based are valid and immediately accessible to the competitor.

Any information, statement or comparison included in promotional materials should be well founded. This should be provided to physicians and all other healthcare professionals on request. In particular, any comparison made between different medicines must be scientifically verified. Such rationale need not be provided for statements related to the approved indications.

6.2.19 SWEDEN[42]

Article 12

Drug information that includes comparisons of effects, active ingredients, costs of treatment, etc. shall be so presented that the comparison as a whole is fair and objectively and truthfully presented. The criteria for correct comparison mean the following:

- The objects included in the comparison should always be clearly specified; thus, if required for clarity, the complete name and generic designation of compared drugs should be stated.

- The facts that the comparison is intended to clarify and the limitations inherent in the comparison shall be stated in such a way that the comparison is not likely to mislead.
- The comparison of properties of synonymous drugs, or of drugs with the same indications, shall give a comprehensive and fair picture of the properties compared.
- The comparison of certain properties should not induce incorrect or misleading conclusions about properties not covered by the comparison.

6.2.20 SWITZERLAND[43]

Clause 145

Comparisons with other medicinal products must be scientifically correct and referenced. Possible references include the latest valid version of the medicinal product's approved information.

6.2.21 TURKEY[44]

Clause 6

The medicines, products and activities of other pharmaceutical companies must not be disparaged. A comparison is permitted in promotional material only if:

- it is not misleading
- medicines or services for the same needs or intended for the same purpose are compared
- relevant, meaningful features that are capable of substantiation are compared
- no confusion is created between compared medicines
- trademarks, tradenames or other distinguishing marks of a competitor are not discredited or denigrated
- no unfair advantage is taken of the reputation of a competitor
- competitor's trademark, tradename or package is not imitated to confuse the purchaser.

6.2.22 THE UNITED KINGDOM[45]

Clause 7

A comparison is only permitted in promotional material if:

- it is not misleading
- medicines or services for the same needs or intended for the same purpose are compared
- one or more materials that are relevant, capable of substantiation and have representative features are compared
- no confusion is created between the medicine advertised and that of a competitor or between the advertiser's trademarks, tradenames, other distinguishing marks and those of a competitor
- the trademarks, tradenames, other distinguishing marks, medicines, services, activities or circumstances of a competitor are not discredited or denigrated
- no unfair advantage is taken of the reputation of a trademark, tradename or other distinguishing marks of a competitor
- medicines or services are not presented as imitations or replicas of goods or services bearing a competitor's trademark or tradename.

6.2.23 THE UNITED STATES OF AMERICA

No guidance found.

6.3 Superlatives

Superlatives are words that imply a special merit, quality or property for a product. Examples of superlatives are claims such as:

- the best
- safe
- the most effective
- the most prescribed
- unique
- the standard for
- the number one
- the drug of choice
- the gold standard.

In some countries these phrases are not allowed at all; in others they are allowed only if they can be substantiated or qualified in some way.

6.3.1 IFPMA

Clause 4

Absolute or all-embracing claims should be used with caution and only with adequate qualification and substantiation. Descriptions such as 'safe' and 'no side effects' should generally be avoided and should always be adequately qualified.

6.3.2 EFPIA[7]

Clause 3

Promotion must encourage the rational use of medicinal products by presenting them objectively and without exaggerating their properties. Claims must not imply that a medicinal product, or an active ingredient, has some special merit, quality or property unless this can be substantiated.

6.3.3 WHO

No guidance found.

6.3.4 AUSTRALIA[29]

Clause 1

Unqualified superlatives must not be used. Claims must not imply that a product or an active ingredient is unique or has some special merit, quality or property unless this can be substantiated.

The word 'safe' must not be used without qualification.

6.3.5 BRAZIL[30]

Chapter 4

It is forbidden to publish messages such as: 'approved', 'recommended by the specialist', 'demonstrated in clinical tests' or 'publicity approved by the sanitary surveillance', by the 'Health Ministry' or by state, municipal or federal district, except in the cases specifically determined by the National Agency of Sanitary Surveillance.

6.3.6 CANADA[31]

Clause 5

Unless substantiation can be provided, advertisers may not claim or imply that a product has a superlative feature or function (e.g. most effective, least toxic), or is accorded special status (e.g. the standard, unique). Similarly, advertisers may not, without substantiation, claim or imply superiority or special status for a company, its personnel, services or product line.

6.3.7 THE CZECH REPUBLIC[32]

Clause 1

Unqualified superlatives must not be used. Claims must not imply that a product or an active ingredient is unique or has some special merit, quality or property unless this can be substantiated. The words 'safe', 'standard', etc. must not be used without qualification.

It must not be stated that a product has no side effects, toxic hazards or risks of addiction or dependency.

6.3.8 FRANCE[33]

Terminology – exclusive terms

Terms that have inappropriate connotations for the brand image of a medicinal product and/or that are derogatory to the competition must be avoided. Included in these terms are particularly those that imply a hierarchy, such as: number 1, the first, the best.

Inflated terms

The use of terms praising safety of use or optimal efficacy is not acceptable. Included in these terms are particularly: optimal tool, perfect or complete tolerance, excellent safety of use.

Reference

The use of the term 'reference' medicinal product is prohibited.

6.3.9 GERMANY[34]

Section 7

Misleading promotion is inadmissible, irrespective of whether it is misleading by distortion, exaggeration, undue emphasis or omission, or in any other way.

6.3.10 GREECE[35]

Article 7

No exaggerated or generalised claims must be made and superlatives must not be used, except in restricted cases where there is a reference to clear facts for a specific medicinal product. Claims must not imply that a medicinal product or active ingredient has a specific advantage, quality or property except in cases where this can be verified.

6.3.11 INDIA[16]

Clause 4

Absolute or all-embracing claims should be used with caution and only with adequate qualification and substantiation. Descriptions such as 'safe' and 'no side effects' should generally be avoided and should always be adequately qualified.

6.3.12 IRELAND[36]

Clause 5

Exaggerated claims must not be made and all-embracing claims and superlatives avoided. Claims must not imply that a medicinal product, or an active ingredient, has some special merit, quality or property unless this can be substantiated.

6.3.13 ITALY[37]

Clause 2

Apart from ministerial authorisations no omni-comprehensive statements are admissible such as 'preferred drug', 'absolutely innocuous' or 'fully tolerated' and similar, and no categorical assertions must be made that a product has no collateral effects or toxicity risks.

6.3.14 JAPAN[38]

Clause 4

No false, exaggerated or misleading expression shall be used regarding efficacy and safety. Advantageous claims relating to safety such as 'there are few adverse reactions' shall not be cited without qualification and must be supplemented with a summary of data on which such claims are based.

6.3.15 MEXICO

No guidance found.

6.3.16 THE NETHERLANDS[39]

Clause 5

In order to encourage the rational use of the medicinal product, an effort must have been made to avoid the use of vague terms or superlatives or any other form of exaggeration of the characteristics of the medicinal product in question.

6.3.17 NORWAY[40]

Clause 4

Pharmaceutical information shall be exact, balanced, truthful and objective, and sufficient to enable the recipient to form an opinion about the therapeutic value of the product in question. The information should be based on the most recent evaluation of scientific material and should clearly reflect this material. The information shall not be misleading as a result of distortions, incorrect assertions, omissions, etc.

6.3.18 SPAIN[41]

Clause 3

Exaggerated or all-embracing statements should not be made. Statements should not imply that a medicine or drug substance has some special merit, quality or property unless this can be substantiated.

6.3.19 SWEDEN[42]

Article 4

Drug information shall be fair and trustworthy and may not contain any presentation in words or pictures that directly or indirectly by implication, omission, exaggeration or ambiguity is misleading. This requires:

- That information about the composition, active ingredients, properties and effects of a drug may not be incorrect, misleading or unverified.
- That information about a drug should not be so scanty or incomplete that it could be misunderstood.
- That exaggerated claims about the properties or effects of a drug should not be made.
- That the presentation must not be deceptive or suggestively misleading.
- That expressions such as 'better', 'more effective', 'cheaper' and the like should not be used unless it is made clear what is being compared.
- That the drug may be described as a 'drug of choice', 'routine preparation' or the like only if most specialists within the area of therapy in question consider the drug a first-line choice.

6.3.20 SWITZERLAND[43]

Clause 145

Claims such as 'better', 'more effective', 'better tolerability' or similar expressions, as well as for superlatives (e.g. 'the best', 'the most effective', 'the most prescribed') or similar expressions (e.g. 'unique', 'at the top of . . .', 'the standard for . . .', 'the number 1', 'the drug of choice', 'the gold standard') are not allowed.

6.3.21 TURKEY[44]

Clause 6

Claims must not, either by implication or directly, mislead by distortion, exaggeration, undue emphasis or omission, or in any other way.

Exaggerated or all-embracing claims must not be made and superlatives must not be used except for those limited circumstances where they relate to a clear fact about the medicine.

6.3.22 THE UNITED KINGDOM[45]

Clause 7

Promotion must encourage the rational use of a medicine by presenting it objectively and without exaggerating its properties. Exaggerated or all-embracing claims must not be made and superlatives must not be used except for those limited circumstances where they relate to a clear fact about a medicine. Claims should not imply that a medicine or an active ingredient has some special merit, quality or property unless this can be substantiated.

6.3.23 THE UNITED STATES OF AMERICA

No guidance found.

6.4 New

'New' in most countries must be used in promotional materials only when referring to a product, presentation or indication that has been available or marketed in that country for a specified period of time. In many countries this is for a period of up to 12 months; the exceptions are Brazil and Spain, which allow up to 2 years' use of the word 'new'. In Canada a 'new product' is defined as any product manufactured or marketed in Canada, by a particular company, for a period of less than 2 years. However, the use of the word 'new' in advertising is restricted to 1 year after initial marketing.

6.4.1 IFPMA
No guidance found.

6.4.2 EFPIA[7]
Clause 3
The word 'new' must not be used to describe any product or presentation that has been generally available, or any therapeutic indication that has been generally promoted, for more than 1 year.

6.4.3 WHO
No guidance found.

6.4.4 AUSTRALIA[29]
Clause 1
The word 'new' must not be used to describe any product, presentation or therapeutic indication that has been available and generally promoted for more than 12 months in Australia.

6.4.5 BRAZIL[30]
Chapter 4
It is forbidden to advertise the same medicine as if new after a 2-year elapse from the date of the start of its commercialisation, except for new presentations or new therapeutic indications registered at the National Agency of Sanitary Surveillance.

6.4.6 CANADA[31]
Clause 11
A new product is defined as any product manufactured and/or marketed in Canada by a company for a period of less than 2 years. Use of the word 'new' in advertising should be restricted to 1 year after initial marketing.

6.4.7 THE CZECH REPUBLIC[32]
Clause 1
The word 'new' must not be used to describe any product, presentation or therapeutic indication that has been available and generally promoted for more than 12 months in the Czech Republic.

6.4.8 FRANCE[33]
The use of the term 'new' must not be for longer than 1 year from the date of marketing.

6.4.9 GERMANY[34]
Section 7
The word 'new' must not be used to describe any medicinal product that has been generally available, or any therapeutic indication that has been generally promoted, for more than 1 year.

6.4.10 GREECE[35]
Article 7
The words 'innovative' or 'new' must not be used for the description of a product or package and form that are already marketed, or for a therapeutic indication that has been promoted for more than 12 months.

6.4.11 INDIA

No guidance found.

6.4.12 IRELAND[36]

Clause 5

The word 'new' must not be used to describe any medicinal product that has been generally available, or therapeutic indication that has been generally promoted, in Ireland for more than 12 months.

6.4.13 ITALY

No guidance found.

6.4.14 JAPAN

No guidance found.

6.4.15 MEXICO

No guidance found.

6.4.16 THE NETHERLANDS

No guidance found.

6.4.17 NORWAY[40]

Clause 4

The word 'new' must not be used to describe any product or presentation that has been generally available, or any therapeutic indication that has been generally promoted, for more than 1 year.

6.4.18 SPAIN[41]

Clause 3

The word 'new' cannot be used to describe any medicine or presentation that has been generally available, or any indication that has been generally promoted, for more than 2 years in Spain.

6.4.19 SWEDEN

No guidance found.

6.4.20 SWITZERLAND[43]

Clause 146

Medicinal products, indications, possible applications, dosages, pharmaceutical forms and packaging may be described as new only within 1 year of their marketing authorisation in Switzerland. From the information, it must be obvious to what the term 'new' refers.

6.4.21 TURKEY[44]

Clause 6

A medicine and/or an indication shall not be promoted before the marketing authorisation has been granted (registration or a grant of permission).

The word 'new' must not be used to describe any product or presentation that has been generally available, or any therapeutic indication that has been generally promoted, for more than 12 months in Turkey.

6.4.22 THE UNITED KINGDOM[45]

Clause 7

The word 'new' must not be used to describe any product or presentation that has been generally available, or any therapeutic indication that has been generally promoted, for more than 12 months in the UK.

6.4.23 THE UNITED STATES OF AMERICA

No guidance found.

6.5 Side effects

It is extremely important that any claims made about the safety and side effects of a product are accurate and reflect the available evidence. In general, the following rules should be adhered to:

- The word 'safe' must never be used to describe a medicinal product without proper qualification.
- It must not be stated that a product has no side effects, toxic hazards or risks of addiction or dependency.

6.5.1 IFPMA

Clause 4

Descriptions such as 'safe' and 'no side effects' should generally be avoided and should always be adequately qualified.

6.5.2 EFPIA[7]

Clause 3

The word 'safe' must never be used to describe a medicinal product without proper qualification. It must not be stated that a product has no side effects, toxic hazards or risks of addiction or dependency.

6.5.3 WHO[8]

Clause 7

The word 'safe' should be used only if properly qualified.

6.5.4 AUSTRALIA[29]

Clause 2

Where a change of clinical significance relating to product safety or the addition of a boxed warning is incorporated into the product information (PI), it should be indicated in all representations of the PI for a period of 12 months from the date of change by an asterisk(s) to a footnote in type size not less than 2 mm: 'Please note change(s) in product information'.

The full text of the changed section should be included in any abridged PI during this period.

Where a company is not actively promoting the product, written advice of the change to PI should be forwarded to the appropriate healthcare professionals.

6.5.5 BRAZIL[30]

Chapter 4

It is forbidden to suggest absence of side or adverse effects or to use expressions, such as 'innocuous', 'safe' or 'natural product', except in the cases registered as such at the National Agency of Sanitary Surveillance.

6.5.6 CANADA[31]

Clause 2

The advertising copy should provide sufficient information to permit assessment of risk/benefit in a prominent manner.

The body copy should include reference to the safety profile and clinically significant adverse effects. For specific details, the advertiser may refer to the prescribing information in a prominent manner.

Special warnings, precautions or use limitations cited in the product monograph should be included in the body copy. Examples include abuse potential for narcotics or central nervous system agents, or specific directions for use in special patient groups such as elderly people, children, pregnant women, nursing mothers, women of childbearing age.

6.5.7 THE CZECH REPUBLIC[32]

Clause 2

Where a change of clinical significance relating to product safety is incorporated into the PI, it should be indicated in all representations of the PI for a period of 12 months from the date of change by an asterisk(s) to a footnote in type size not less than 2 mm: 'Please note change(s) in product information'.

The full text of the changed section should be included in any abridged PI during this period.

6.5.8 FRANCE[47]

Section III Clause 2

In printed promotional aids, information about the use of a product, and particularly the side effects, precautions and contraindications, is clearly referred to so that the relationship with the indication and the expected benefits is clearly shown.

6.5.9 GERMANY[34]

Section 7

General claims that a medicinal product has no side effects, toxic hazards or risks of addiction or dependency are inadmissible. Claims that specific side effects, toxic hazards or risks of addiction or dependency have so far not become known are permitted only if they are based on sufficient scientific evidence.

6.5.10 GREECE[35]

Article 7

Information and claims with respect to adverse reactions must reflect the data available or be verifiable with clinical experience. It must not be declared that a product does not have adverse reactions, interactions with other medicinal products or no risk of toxicity. The term 'safe' must not be used without detailed justification.

6.5.11 INDIA[16]

Clause 4

Descriptions such as 'safe' and 'no side effects' should generally be avoided and should always be adequately qualified.

6.5.12 IRELAND[36]

Clause 5

The word 'safe' must not be used without qualification and it must not be stated categorically that a medicine has no side effects, toxic hazards or risk of addiction

6.5.13 ITALY[37]

Clause 2

No categorical assertions must be made that a product has no collateral effects or toxicity risks.

6.5.14 JAPAN[38]

Clause 4

False, exaggerated or misleading expressions should not be used with regard to efficacy and safety. Advantageous claims relating to safety, such as 'there are few adverse reactions', shall not be cited without qualification and must be supplemented with a summary of data on which such claims are based.

Fair statements should be made, by presenting both efficacy data and safety data, including adverse reactions.

6.5.15 MEXICO

No guidance found.

6.5.16 THE NETHERLANDS[39]

Clause 5

The totality of the advertising material aimed at practitioners must provide a picture of the effect of the medicinal product as complete and accurate as possible. In evaluating this criterion, the indication and the clinical effectiveness according to the registration details, as well as the undesirable effects and contraindications in the prescribing information, must be taken into account in every case.

6.5.17 NORWAY[40]

Clause 4

The word 'safe' must never be used to describe a medicinal product without proper qualification.

It must not be stated that a product has no side effects, toxic hazards or risks of addiction or dependency.

Information about new, serious side effects or contraindications, limitations on indications and decisions to withdraw the medicinal product from the market because of side effects shall be sent out separately to prescribers and pharmacists. The designation 'important notice' shall be used only when sending out information of this kind. The reasons for such withdrawals shall be stated.

6.5.18 SPAIN[41]

Clause 3

Information and statements about untoward reactions should reflect the available evidence or be capable of substantiation by clinical experience. It cannot be stated that a product has no adverse effects, toxicity or addiction risks.

6.5.19 SWEDEN[42]

Article 15

Information relating to new findings about serious side effects, contraindications, or limitations applying to indications or decisions about recall of manufacturing batches or drugs shall be dispatched in the form of a separate communication. The marking 'important message' or similar expressions may be used only for such dispatches.

6.5.20 SWITZERLAND[43]

Clause 148

If companies need to inform healthcare professionals urgently about the safety of a particular medicinal product, e.g. about market recall of a medicinal product, limitations to its distribution or use, this information must be marked as an 'important notice'.

The label, 'important notice', must be added in an easily visible and clearly legible manner both on the envelope of the mailing as well as on the information itself.

This label may only be used for such information. Similarly sounding labels (e.g. 'urgent information') are to be avoided so that attention is not detracted from the important notices.

6.5.21 TURKEY[44]

Clause 6

Information and claims about side effects must reflect available evidence or be provable by clinical evidence. It must not be stated that a product has no side effects, toxic hazards or risks of addiction only because none has been discovered so far.

The words 'safe' or 'effective' must not be used without qualification.

Post-marketing studies should not be carried out and used in order to influence physicians, and should not be disguised as research.

6.5.22 THE UNITED KINGDOM[45]

Clause 7

Information and claims about side effects must reflect available evidence or be capable of substantiation by clinical experience. It must not be stated that a product has no side effects, toxic hazards or risks of addiction or dependency. The word 'safe' must not be used without qualification.

The restrictions on the word 'safe' apply equally to grammatical descriptions of the word such as 'safety'. For example, 'demonstrated safety' or 'proven safety' is prohibited under this clause.

6.5.23 THE UNITED STATES OF AMERICA

No guidance found.

6.6 False or misleading claims

It is important that claims made for medicines do not mislead either intentionally or unintentionally. Therefore, it is important to consider whether the information presented in advertising and promotion can be misconstrued in any way. The way that graphs are presented and statistics are used in promotional items are common causes of false or misleading claims. These are therefore looked at in more detail here.

Graphs

The main principles behind the codes of conduct are that data be presented in a clear, accurate way, so as not to mislead the reader.

Do

- Label axes of graphs with parameter and unit of measurement
- Ensure adequate and accurate referencing
- Include statistical information and ensure that this is accurately presented, e.g. p values where relevant or stating 'not statistically significant' if the data presented do not have statistical significance

- Include all relevant data, e.g. patient numbers
- Make it clear whether the data presented are from different studies. It is misleading to present data from two or more studies in one graph as though they were all from the same study. This is because, for example, there will be differences in study protocols, patient demographics and numbers.

Do not

- Use suppressed zeros when the aim is to convey the message that drug X gives better results than drug Y. The difference between the two is accentuated by shortening the axis. This is illustrated in Figures 6.1 and 6.2.
- Extrapolate the graph into an area where there are no data.
- Select only part of the data for use in a graph if this gives a misleading impression. This is illustrated in Figures 6.3, 6.4 and 6.5.

It can be seen in Figure 6.1, where the X axis starts at 60 per cent response (i.e. a suppressed zero), that the difference between the drugs looks much greater than the difference in Figure 6.2, where the axis starts at zero.

However, suppressed zeros can be used and are not considered misleading if the message is that the two products are similar. In all cases the statistical significance (or lack of it) should be stated.

From Figures 6.3 and 6.4 it can be seen that the pharmaceutical company marketing drug A would be considered to be misleading if they were using the 12-month data alone when the 24-month data were known.

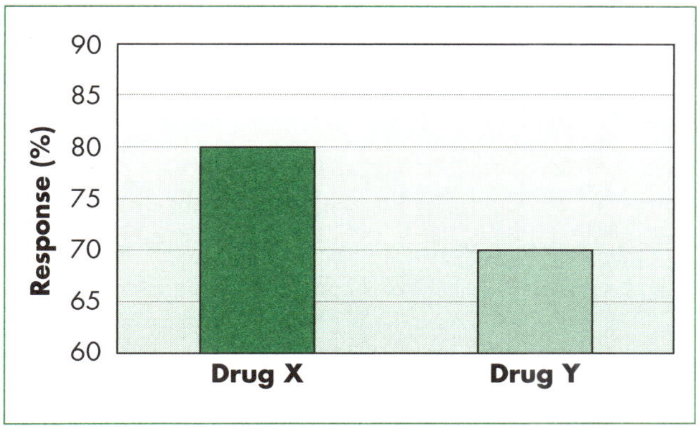

FIGURE 6.1 Drug X gives increased response compared with drug Y.

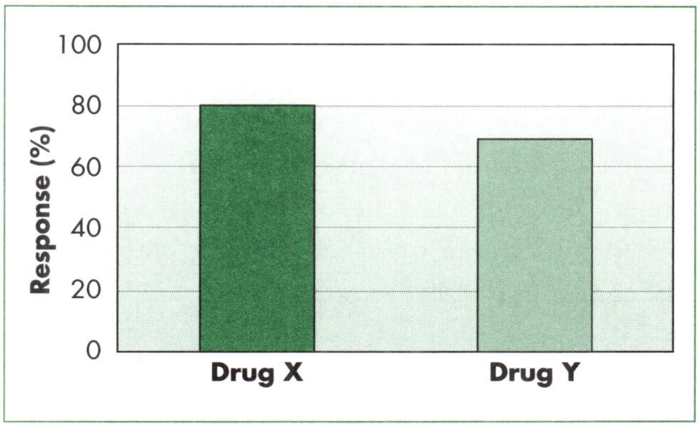

FIGURE 6.2 Drug X gives increased response compared with drug Y.

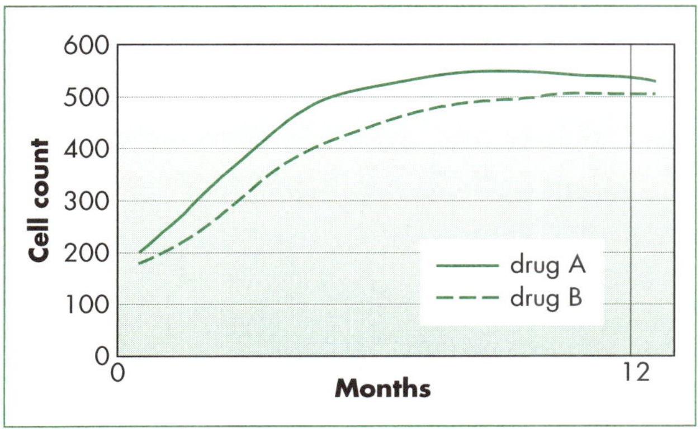

FIGURE 6.3 Increase in blood cell count with drug A compared with drug B after 12 months.

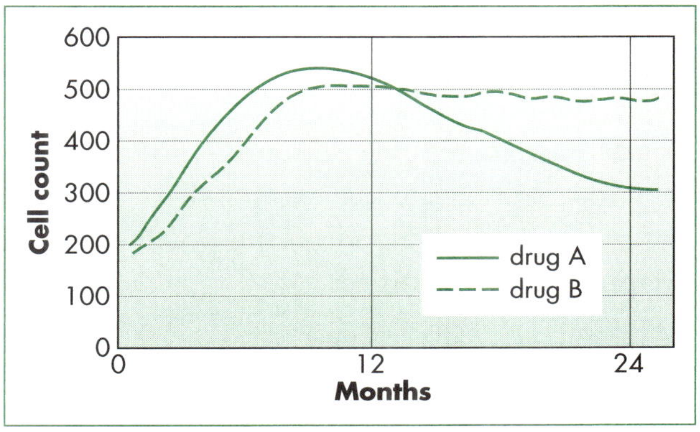

FIGURE 6.4 Increase in blood cell count with drug A compared with drug B after 24 months.

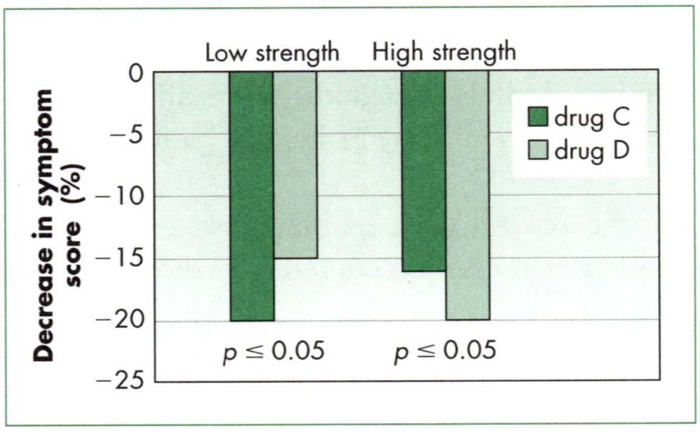

FIGURE 6.5 Percentage decrease in symptoms with drug C compared with drug D.

In Figure 6.5 it can be seen that if the data for just the low strength of the two drugs were used promotionally by the pharmaceutical company marketing drug A, this could be misleading, because there is a better response at the higher dose for drug B. However, selective use of data would be justified and often mandatory if use of all the data is outside the terms of the product licence. For example, it would be justified to omit the data for strengths of product that are not licensed.

6.6.1 IFPMA[6]

Clause 4

Promotional information should be clear, legible, accurate, balanced, fair, objective and sufficiently complete to enable the recipient to form his or her own opinion of the therapeutic value of the pharmaceutical product concerned. Promotional information should be based on an up-to-date evaluation of all relevant evidence and reflect that evidence clearly. It should not mislead by distortion, exaggeration, undue emphasis or omission, or in any other way. Every effort should be made to avoid ambiguity. Absolute or all-embracing claims should be used with caution and only with adequate qualification and substantiation.

6.6.2 EFPIA[7]

Clause 3

Promotion must be accurate, balanced, fair, objective and sufficiently complete to enable the recipient to form his or her own opinion of the therapeutic value of the medicinal product concerned. It should be based on an up-to-date evaluation of all relevant evidence and reflect that evidence clearly. It must not mislead by distortion, exaggeration, undue emphasis, omission or in any other way.

All artwork, including graphs, illustrations, photographs and tables taken from published studies included in promotional material should:

- clearly indicate the precise source(s) of the artwork
- be faithfully reproduced, except where adaptation or modification is required in order to comply with any applicable code(s), in which case it must be clearly stated that the artwork has been adapted and/or modified.

Particular care must be taken to ensure that artwork included in promotion does not mislead about the nature of a medicine (e.g. whether it is appropriate for use in children) or about a claim or comparison (e.g. by using incomplete or statistically irrelevant information or unusual scales).

6.6.3 WHO[8]

Clauses 7 and 8

All promotional claims must be reliable, accurate, truthful, informative, balanced, up to date, capable of substantiation and in good taste.

Scientific data in the public domain should be made available to prescribers and any other person entitled to receive it, on request, as appropriate to requirements.

6.6.4 AUSTRALIA[29]

Clause 1

Advertising and promotion must comply with the following:

- All information, claims and graphic representations provided to healthcare professionals and members of the general public must be current, accurate and balanced, and must not mislead directly, by implication or by omission.
- Claims must be referenced where there is a possibility that a reader may be misled if the source of the reference is not disclosed.
- Products that have not been approved for registration by the Department of Health and Ageing must not be promoted. However, samples of unapproved products may be displayed and educational material made available at international congresses. This restriction also applies to unapproved indications for registered products.

6.6.5 BRAZIL[30]

Chapter 4

It is forbidden:

- to provoke fear or anguish, and/or to suggest that a person's health will be, or can be, affected by not using the medicine
- to suggest risk decrease, in any degree, except for those cases in which such risk decrease is explicitly stated on the indications or properties approved in the registration action at the National Agency of Sanitary Surveillance and, even in those cases, just in publications directed at health professionals
- to ascribe healing properties to the medicine when it is destined, according to registration at the National Agency of Sanitary Surveillance, just for the symptomatic treatment and/or control of chronic diseases.

6.6.6 CANADA[31]

Clauses 2 and 4

Advertising and promotion must comply with the following:

- All advertising and promotion must be accurate, complete and clear, and designed to promote credibility and trust. Statements or illustrations must not mislead.
- All data presented in advertising and promotion, including charts, graphs and tables or other reproductions extracted from reference studies or other sources, or reproduced by artwork, must be accurate, complete and clear. The source(s) must be identified. Each adaptation of data should be so labelled and the source(s) indicated.
- Statistics must be presented so as to reflect their validity, reliability and level of significance accurately.
- Data presentations that are misleading or ambiguous, or that distort the original meaning or interpretation, either directly or by implication, are in violation of the code.

6.6.7 THE CZECH REPUBLIC[32]

Clause 1

Information, medical claims and graphic representations about products must be current, accurate and balanced, and must not mislead directly, by implication or by omission, and must not be able to cause deceptive imagination of an addressee.

All artwork, including graphs, illustrations, photographs and tables taken from published studies included in promotional material should:

- clearly indicate the precise source(s) of the artwork;
- be faithfully reproduced; except where adaptation or modification is required in order to comply with any applicable code(s), in which case it must be clearly stated that the artwork has been adapted and/or modified.

Particular care must be taken to ensure that artwork included in promotion does not mislead about the nature of a medicinal product (for example whether it is appropriate for use in children) or mislead about a claim or comparison (for example by using incomplete or statistically irrelevant information or unusual scales). Information, claims and graphics must be capable of substantiation. Such substantiation must be provided within 10 working days at the request of healthcare professionals or a pharmaceutical company.

Quotations from medical literature or personal communications must accurately reflect the author's meaning and the study's significance (except where adaptation or modification is required in order to comply with any applicable code(s) or laws, in which case it must be clearly stated that the quotation has been adapted and/or modified) and the precise sources identified and they must accurately reflect the meaning of the author and significance of the study or analysis.

6.6.8 FRANCE[33]

When presenting data (tables, figures, diagrams), clear, accurate and balanced information that has been processed consistently must be provided.

This could be either a faithful account of the source document, or a true adaptation of all or part of the document.

When a table, graph or figure has been extracted from a study (the references must be cited), the number of patients and the type of analysis done must be shown in the legend.

The scales must be identical for the products compared, and the choice of scale must not distort the representation of the results, so as wrongly to increase the value of one product over another.

6.6.9 GERMANY[34]

Section 7

Misleading promotion is inadmissible, irrespective of whether it is misleading by distortion, exaggeration, undue emphasis or omission, or in any other way.

A misleading practice is in particular found to exist if:

- medicines are attributed with therapeutic efficiency, effects or an application that they do not possess
- a false impression is given that success is guaranteed
- improper or misleading information concerning the composition or properties of medicinal products is given
- when evaluating the question of whether non-disclosure of a fact is misleading, special regard has to be paid to the potential influence, such as non-disclosure, that it may have on the decision of the healthcare professionals addressed with regard to prescriptions.

6.6.10 GREECE[35]

Article 7

Information, claims and comparisons must be correct, accurate, objective and clear, and must be based on relevant and comparable aspects of the medicinal products, as well as on an updated assessment of all data that reflect the facts clearly. They must not be misleading, either explicitly or implicitly, and they must not distort the scientific facts.

The direct or indirect promotion of misleading indications of the medicinal product, reference to older scientific data (if there is newer different information available), promotion of inaccurate or undocumented claims, misleading comparison with other medicinal products and generalisation of isolated observations are all prohibited.

The overall creative part, including images, graphs and tables, must comply with the letter and spirit of the present code. Graphs and tables must be presented in such a way as to provide a clear, fair and balanced view of the data presented. These must be included only if they are relevant to the claims or comparisons made. Medical information leaflets must not contain misleading information or imply any vague indications for the medicinal product.

6.6.11 INDIA[16]

Clause 4

Promotional information should be clear, legible, accurate, balanced, fair and objective, and sufficiently complete to enable the recipient to form his or her own opinion of the therapeutic value of the pharmaceutical product concerned. Promotional information should be based on an up-to-date evaluation of all relevant evidence and reflect that evidence clearly. It should not mislead by distortion, exaggeration, unnecessary emphasis or omission, or in any other way. Every effort should be made to avoid ambiguity. Absolute or all-embracing claims should be used with caution and only with adequate qualification and substantiation.

6.6.12 IRELAND[36]

Clause 5

Claims for the usefulness of a medicinal product must be based on an up-to-date evaluation of all the evidence and must reflect this evidence accurately and clearly. Such claims must have prior medical review and approval.

6.6.13 ITALY[37]

Clause 2

The information material prepared by the company on its products and used to provide information to physicians must be based on official documents issued by the Ministry of Health, when the drug is registered or successively approved by the Ministry on the basis of the pertinent laws in force:

- The scientific citations must accurately portray the meaning that the author intends to give them.
- The texts, tables and other illustrations taken from medical review or scientific works must be reproduced faithfully and in full, with the exact indication of the source. No citations are admissible that can appear partial and/or contradictory with respect to the author's intentions, when separated from the context in which they originally appeared.

6.6.14 JAPAN[38]

Clauses 4 and 5

Member companies shall fully realise that brochures, advertisements in medical journals, internet web pages for the medical profession, audiovisual materials and other promotional materials are important media in the dissemination of drug information, and shall produce and use those materials in compliance with the Pharmaceutical Affairs Law and relevant self-regulations. The statements contained therein shall be correct, fair and objective, based on scientific data:

- False, exaggerated or misleading expression shall not be used regarding efficacy and safety. Advantageous claims relating to safety, such as 'there are few adverse reactions', shall not be cited without qualification and must be supplemented with a summary of data on which such claims are based.
- Statements must be fair presenting both efficacy data and safety data, including adverse reactions.
- Member companies shall properly recognise the objectives of post-marketing surveillance (PMS), i.e. the establishment of the appropriate usage of marketed pharmaceuticals, and shall conduct such PMS activities on a scientific basis, in strict compliance with laws, regulations and self-regulations. These activities shall not be misused as a means of promotion.

6.6.15 MEXICO

No guidance found.

6.6.16 THE NETHERLANDS[39]

Clause 4

The advertising must not in any way conflict with the officially approved summary of product characteristics (SPC) for the medicinal product.

The advertising must be performed in such a way that the rational use of the medicinal product is encouraged from a pharmacotherapeutic perspective and so that the person to whom the recommendation is made is not misled in any way.

6.6.17 NORWAY[40]

Clause 4

Pharmaceutical information shall be exact, balanced, truthful and objective, and sufficient to enable the recipient to form an opinion about the therapeutic value of the product in question. The information should be based on the most recent evaluation of scientific material and should clearly reflect this material. The information shall not be misleading as a result of distortions, incorrect assertions, omissions, etc.

All illustrations used in promotion should clearly indicate the precise source(s). Where adaptation or modification is required, it must be clearly stated that the artwork has been adapted and/or modified. Particular care must be taken to ensure that artwork included in promotion does not mislead about the nature of a medicine or a claim or comparison.

6.6.18 SPAIN[41]

Clause 3

Information about medicinal products should be accurate, balanced, fair, objective and sufficiently complete to enable the recipient to form his or her own opinion of the therapeutic value of the medicine. It should be based on an up-to-date evaluation of scientific evidence and reflect that evidence clearly. It should not mislead by distortion, undue emphasis or omission, or in any other way. The following should be observed:

- All artwork, including illustrations, graphs and tables, must conform to the letter and spirit of the code. Graphs and tables should be presented in such a way as to give a clear, fair and balanced view of the topics covered, and should not be included unless they are relevant to the claims or comparisons being made. Special care should be taken to ensure that all graphic material included in the promotion is not misleading about the nature of the medicine (e.g. if the product is appropriate for use in children) or because of an argument or comparison (e.g. when incomplete or statistically non-relevant information, or unusual scales, are used).

- When promotional material refers to published studies, these should be faithfully reproduced or a clear reference given as to where they can be found. A 'faithful reproduction' is one that accurately reflects the full meaning and content of the original source, without adding or omitting any information that could mislead or confuse the recipient. As an example of this, when the efficacy, safety or other properties of different drug substances are compared in promotional material, information such as the statistical significance of the results cannot be omitted, nor can the results of different clinical studies or trials be compared in the same table or graph without clarifications, except when the source is a meta-analysis. Statistics, conclusions or any other data from different studies conducted using different methodologies also cannot be mixed or compared, unless they come from systematic reviews or meta-analyses in which homogeneity criteria are specified.
- Adaptations that may introduce bias and be misleading are unacceptable.

6.6.19 SWEDEN[42]

Articles 4 and 11

Drug information shall be fair and trustworthy and may not contain any presentation in words or pictures that directly or indirectly by implication, omission, exaggeration or ambiguity is intended to mislead.

The trustworthiness criterion requires the following:

- Information about the composition, active ingredients, properties and effects of a drug may not be incorrect, misleading or unverified.
- Information about a drug should not be so scanty or incomplete that it could be misunderstood.
- Exaggerated claims about the properties or effects of a drug should not be made.
- The presentation must not be deceptive or suggestively misleading.
- Documentation shall be cited in a balanced and fair way. The criterion for fair and balanced presentation means, among other things, that:
  - the results of a study, which are contradicted by another study, may not be cited without reservation and results that have been refuted must not be used
  - a study should not be cited in such a way that it could convey an incorrect or misleading impression of the nature, scope, implementation or importance of the study
  - a study performed in vitro or one based on animal tests should not be cited in such a way that it could give an incorrect or misleading impression of the clinical value of the investigation
  - statements of comparisons between different drugs or alternative treatments should be expressed in such a way as to make clearly evident their statistical validity
  - the report of a study should not be cited or abstracted in such a way that the citation or abstract gives an inaccurate or misleading impression of the contents of the report and conclusions.

6.6.20 SWITZERLAND[43]

Clause 142

The following are inadmissible, because they are misleading:

- The use of the expression 'safe', except when used in connection with an appropriate qualification.
- Statements indicating that a medicinal product has no adverse reactions, does not evoke addiction, is harmless or risk free, or other statements or expressions that minimise the possible risks.

6.6.21 TURKEY[44]

Articles 3 and 6

The promotion of a product should not be misleading by distortion, exaggeration, undue emphasis, omission or use of unproven claims, or in any other way.

- Claims should not be stronger than scientific evidence warrants. Every effort should be made to avoid ambiguity. They must not, either by implication or directly, mislead by distortion, exaggeration, undue emphasis or omission, or in any other way.
- Substitution rules of an institution cannot be used as a basis for promotion. However, it is allowed to inform prescribers and pharmacists of an institution about the substitution rules implemented in the specific institution.
- All artwork, including illustrations, graphs and tables, must conform to the letter and spirit of the code. They shall be faithfully reproduced and the full source clearly indicated. Graphs and tables must be presented in such a way as to give a clear, fair and balanced view of the matters with which they deal. If an entire graph or table from a publication is not used as published, the graph or table should clearly be labelled as 'adapted'.
- Particular care must be taken to ensure that artwork included in promotion does not mislead about the nature of a medicine (e.g. whether it is appropriate for use in children) or mislead about a claim or comparison (e.g. by using incomplete or statistically irrelevant information or unusual scales).
- Statistics used should be sound. Statistical significance should be watched for because instances have occurred where claims have been based on published papers in which methodology was known to be incorrect. It is the duty of the promotional material maker to appraise the correctness of the statistics used before using it in the document.

6.6.22 THE UNITED KINGDOM[45]

Clause 7

Information, claims and comparisons must be accurate, balanced, fair, objective and unambiguous, and must be based on an up-to-date evaluation of all the evidence and reflect that evidence clearly:

- They must not mislead directly or by implication, or by distortion, exaggeration or undue emphasis.
- Material must be sufficiently complete to enable the recipients to form their own opinion of the therapeutic value of the medicine.
- All artwork, including illustrations, graphs and tables, must conform to the letter and spirit of the code and, when taken from published studies, a reference must be given. Graphs and tables must be presented in such a way as to give a clear, fair and balanced view of the matters with which they deal, and must not be included unless they are relevant to the claims or comparisons being made.

6.6.23 THE UNITED STATES OF AMERICA

No guidance found.

6.7 Company-commissioned articles and papers

In general in most countries, materials commissioned by pharmaceutical companies must clearly indicate the name of the company and the sponsorship even if they are not promotional.

This does not normally include market research material, which need not reveal the name of the company involved but must make it clear that a pharmaceutical company (not necessarily named) sponsored the research.

6.7.1 IFPMA

No guidance found.

6.7.2 EFPIA[7]

Clause 7

Where a company pays for or otherwise secures or arranges the publication of promotional material in journals, such promotional material must not resemble independent editorial matter.

Material relating to medicines and their uses, whether or not promotional in nature, which is sponsored by a company, must clearly indicate that it has been sponsored by that company.

6.7.3 WHO

No guidance found.

6.7.4 AUSTRALIA[29]

Clause 3

Company-commissioned articles must be identified as such in a type size of not less than 1.5 mm, as measured by the font's lower case letter 'e'.

The company that is responsible for the insertion of the company-commissioned article must be clearly identified at either the top or the bottom of the company-commissioned article in a type size of not less than 1.5 mm, as measured by the font's lower case letter 'e'.

Company-commissioned articles must also conform to all other relevant provisions of the Australian code in this chapter, e.g. good taste, comparative statements and unqualified superlatives.

Statements by third parties, which are quoted in company-commissioned articles, must also comply with the requirements of the code as specified above.

6.7.5 BRAZIL[30]

Chapter 20

The sponsorship granted by a producer or distributor of medicines, for any public or private events, symposia, congresses, meetings, conferences and assimilated functions either partial or total, must be contained in all of the circulating documents or the documents resulting from and a consequence of the respective event.

Any support granted to the health professionals, to participate in national or international meetings, should not be linked to any promotion of any type of medicine or institution, and must be clearly stated in the documents referred to in the caput of this chapter.

6.7.6 CANADA[31]

Clauses 2 and 11

For purposes of this code, private/single sponsor journals, newsletters and other publications are defined as any commissioned communication prepared or controlled by the manufacturer or its agent.

All advertising submitted to the PAAB must be approved by the medical/regulatory department of the sponsor before sending it to them.

6.7.7 THE CZECH REPUBLIC[32]

Clause 3

Company-commissioned articles must be identified as such in a type size of not less than 2 mm. The member that is responsible for the insertion of the company-commissioned article must be clearly identified at either the top or the bottom of the company-commissioned article in a type size of not less than 2 mm. Company-commissioned articles must conform to all relevant provisions of the

Czech Republic referred to in this chapter, e.g. good taste, comparative statements and unqualified superlatives.

6.7.8 FRANCE

A warning that something is an advertisement must precede editorial advertisements; this warning must be clear and legible to the reader.

Medical press professionals and advertisers recommend the following wording:

- 'Information provided by laboratory x'.
- 'Information provided in collaboration with laboratory'.

6.7.9 GERMANY[34]

Section 8

Where a company pays for or arranges the publication of promotional material in journals, it must make sure that such promotional material cannot be confused with independent editorial matter.

In the case of any publications made by third parties about medicinal products and their use that are either wholly or partially sponsored by a company, particular care must be taken to ensure that such publications clearly indicate that they have been sponsored by that company.

6.7.10 GREECE[35]

Articles 4, 10 and 22

References to information, contained in tables and representations from publications in medical journal or scientific works used in the informative document, must be faithfully reproduced and the source thereof accurately indicated.

When a pharmaceutical company sponsors or secures in any other way, or regulates the publication of, promotional material in a scientific journal, the said promotional material must not be presented as an independent article.

The material sponsored by a pharmaceutical company that refers to medicinal products and the use thereof, and to whether or not the promotion of these medicinal products is promoted, must not include any deceptive or inaccurate references and must indicate clearly that the pharmaceutical company is the one sponsoring the material.

In all publications, lectures and other presentations of clinical trials, the identity of the sponsor must be known.

6.7.11 INDIA

No guidance found.

6.7.12 IRELAND[36]

Clause 7

All promotional material appearing in journals, the publication of which is paid for or secured or arranged by a company and refers by brand name to any product of that company, must comply with the code, irrespective of the editorial control of the material published.

6.7.13 ITALY[37]

Clause 2

When advertising in newspapers and reviews, companies must comply with the rule of transparency and hence accept the net separation between information and advertising as an essential criterion. This will allow the reader immediately to recognise a promotional message, in whatever form, whether editorial or column format, in which it is presented.

6.7.14 JAPAN
No guidance found.

6.7.15 MEXICO
No guidance found.

6.7.16 THE NETHERLANDS[39]
Clause 5
The researcher concerned must have given prior permission for the use of unpublished research.

6.7.17 NORWAY[40]
Clause 5
Information material sponsored or produced with financial support from the industry must be labelled with the sponsor's company name.

6.7.18 SPAIN[41]
Clauses 4 and 5
All material relating to medicines and their uses that is sponsored by a pharmaceutical company must clearly state this sponsorship.

Whenever a company finances, ensures, or directly or indirectly organises publication of promotional material in newspapers or magazines, it should be expressly stated that such material is not included as an independent editorial topic, and the sponsoring company should be included in a visible place.

Any material related to medicines and their uses, whether or not promotional, that is sponsored by a company should clearly state that it has been sponsored by the company.

6.7.19 SWEDEN
No guidance found.

6.7.20 SWITZERLAND[43]
Clauses 362 and 363
In principle, results of clinical trials should be published. Upon publication, the relevance of the results should be assessed, considering the significance of the disease as well as the clinical effort involved, and the associated financial costs of the procedure or measure investigated. It should be stated in the publication that this was a company-sponsored clinical trial and the sponsor must be mentioned.

When publishing the results of a clinical trial, a statement or footnote that clearly indicates the sponsor of the clinical trial must be made. When presenting the results of a clinical trial during lectures, congresses and the like, sponsorship must also be mentioned; likewise, any possible financial interest of the authors must be clearly indicated.

The interpretation of the results of a clinical trial must be independent of the interests of the sponsors.

6.7.21 TURKEY[44]
Material relating to medicines and their uses, whether or not promotional in nature, must clearly indicate the sponsor, if any.

Market research material, which need not reveal the company name, must state nevertheless that a pharmaceutical company sponsors it.

6.7.22 THE UNITED KINGDOM[45]

Clause 9

Material relating to medicines and their uses, whether or not promotional in nature, that is sponsored by a pharmaceutical company must clearly indicate that it has been sponsored by that company.

The only exception to this is market research material, which need not reveal the name of the company involved but must state that a pharmaceutical company sponsors it.

6.7.23 THE UNITED STATES OF AMERICA

No guidance found.

6.8 Good taste

Promotion should be carried out in such a way that it recognises the special nature of medicines and they must not be promoted in the same way as consumer goods. Companies must maintain high ethical standards and recognise the professional standing of the recipients. The promotion must not cause offence; this can be a difficult area because the subjects and images that may cause offence vary around the world. An example of this may be images of female body parts used in advertising, which may be acceptable in the western world but not in the east. Therefore, if a campaign is to be used globally, this should be taken into account with the images and concepts used.

6.8.1 IFPMA

No guidance found.

6.8.2 EFPIA[7]

Clause 5

Companies must maintain high ethical standards at all times. Promotion must:

- never be such as to bring discredit upon, or reduce confidence in, the pharmaceutical industry
- be of a nature that recognises the special nature of medicines and the professional standing of the recipient(s)
- not be likely to cause offence.

6.8.3 WHO[8]

All promotional claims must be reliable, accurate, truthful, informative, balanced, up to date, capable of substantiation and in good taste.

6.8.4 AUSTRALIA[29]

Clause 1

All promotional and educational material (including graphics and other visual representations) must conform to generally accepted standards of good taste and recognise the professional standing of the recipients.

These materials must not contain anything that would be likely to cause serious or widespread offence taking into consideration prevailing community standards.

6.8.5 BRAZIL[30]

Title 1

Abusive advertising or promotion is not allowed. This is defined as:

Advertising that incites discrimination of any kind, violence, fear, superstitions, takes advantage of children, disrespects environmental values, or that is capable of inducing the user to behave in a harmful or dangerous manner to his or her health or safety.

6.8.6 CANADA[31]

Clause 2

All Advertising/Promotion Systems (APSs) must be accurate, complete and clear, and designed to promote credibility and trust.

The code does not accept APSs that are prejudicial to any sex, race, occupation or patient group, or contravene the ethical values of the health professions.

6.8.7 THE CZECH REPUBLIC[32]

Clause 1

Promotional material (including graphics and other visual representations) must conform to generally accepted standards of good taste and recognise the professional standing of the recipients. Promotion must not be discriminatory, deceptive or disparaging.

6.8.8 FRANCE

No guidance found.

6.8.9 GERMANY[34]

Section 4

When applying the present code of conduct, not only the letter of the individual provisions, but also their spirit and intention, as well as all applicable laws, must be observed, especially the regulations of the German Drugs Act (AMG), the German Advertising in the Health Care System Act (HWG), the German Fair Trade Practices Act (UWG) and the German Penal Code (StGB). In addition, the generally recognised legal principles applicable to healthcare professionals and the conduct recommendations of the participating associations of the pharmaceutical industry must be observed, which are based on these principles by considering their wording as well as their meaning and purpose.

6.8.10 GREECE[35]

Article 9

The overall material and the promotional activities must acknowledge the special nature of medicinal products and the professional position of the scientists to whom it is addressed and who must be respected and protected from any offence. A high standard of ethics must always be ensured.

6.8.11 INDIA

No guidance found.

6.8.12 IRELAND[36]

Clause 7

Promotional material must conform, in both text and illustrations, to canons of good taste and must be expressed so as to recognise the professional standing of the recipients. In addition it must not be likely to cause offence.

6.8.13 ITALY[37]

No specific guidance on advertising and promotion but the following general advice is given.

Clause 1

Observance of the code entails the contribution of each company towards defending the good name of the pharmaceutical industry to the public at large.

6.8.14 JAPAN[38]

Clause 4

Misleading or indecent photos, illustrations, etc., which are not suitable to the socially respected role of drugs, shall not be used.

6.8.15 MEXICO

No guidance found.

6.8.16 THE NETHERLANDS[39]

Clause 4

The advertising must otherwise be in compliance with the Act and must, with regard to both text and presentation, meet the prevailing standards of good taste and conduct, for which due regard must be shown with respect to both the person at whom the advertising is aimed and colleagues in the sector.

A degree of dignity and prudence appropriate to the nature of the product must have been displayed.

6.8.17 NORWAY[40]

Clause 3

Marketing must be in accordance with public regulations and laws.

It must maintain high quality and never be such as to bring discredit upon, or reduce confidence in, the pharmaceutical industry. In addition, it must not be likely to cause offence.

6.8.18 SPAIN[41]

Clause 4

Any promotional activity or material should respect the special nature of the medicinal product and the professional standing of the target audience, and must not be likely to cause any offence or decrease the confidence in the pharmaceutical industry.

6.8.19 SWEDEN[42]

Article 3

Drug information shall conform to professional standards of ethics and good taste. Offensive presentations are not permitted.

6.8.20 SWITZERLAND

No guidance found.

6.8.21 TURKEY[44]

Clause 3

The promotion of a medicinal product must be informative about the characteristics of the product, consistent with scientific facts, reliable, fair and objective, and clear.

It should conform not only to legal requirements but also to high ethical standards, and be in good taste.

6.8.22 THE UNITED KINGDOM[45]

Clause 9

High standards must be maintained at all times.

All material and activities must recognise the special nature of medicines and the professional standing of the audience to which they are directed and must not be likely to cause offence.

6.8.23 THE UNITED STATES OF AMERICA

No guidance found.

6.9 Disguised promotion

Promotion must not be disguised as non-promotional activity. Examples include:

- clinical assessments
- post-marketing surveillance and experience programmes
- post-authorisation studies.

Such assessments, programmes and studies must be conducted with a primarily scientific or educational purpose.

6.9.1 IFPMA

Clause 2

Promotion should not be disguised. Clinical assessments, post-marketing surveillance and experience programmes, and post-authorisation studies must not be disguised promotion. Such assessments, programmes and studies must be conducted with a primarily scientific or educational purpose. Material relating to pharmaceutical products and their uses, whether or not promotional in nature, that is sponsored by a company should clearly indicate by whom it has been sponsored.

6.9.2 EFPIA[7]

Clause 7

Promotion must not be disguised.

Clinical assessments, post-marketing surveillance and experience programmes, and post-authorisation studies must not be disguised promotion. Such assessments, programmes and studies must be conducted with a primarily scientific or educational purpose.

6.9.3 WHO[8]

Promotional material should not be designed so as to disguise its real nature.

6.9.4 AUSTRALIA2[9]

Clause 1

Promotional material must be clearly distinguishable as such.

6.9.5 BRAZIL[30]

Chapter 4

It is forbidden to include verbal and non-verbal messages that disguise the actual indications of the medicines registered at the National Agency of Sanitary Surveillance.

6.9.6 CANADA

No guidance found.

6.9.7 THE CZECH REPUBLIC[32]

Clause 1

Promotion must not be disguised or based on the subliminal perception. Promotion and promotional material must be clearly distinguishable as such. Materials relating to medicinal products and their uses, whether promotional in nature or not, which is sponsored by a member, must clearly indicate that it has been sponsored by that member.

6.9.8 FRANCE

No guidance found.

6.9.9 GERMANY[34]

Section 8

Promotion must not be disguised.

6.9.10 GREECE[35]

Article 10

Promotional material and activities must not be disguised:

- Clinical assessments, post-marketing surveillance, experience programmes and post-authorisation studies must not constitute a disguised promotion. Such assessments, programmes and studies must be performed mainly for a scientific or educational purpose.
- When a pharmaceutical company sponsors or secures in any other way or regulates the publication of promotional material in a scientific journal, the said promotional material must not be presented as an independent article.
- The material sponsored by a pharmaceutical company, which refers to medicinal products and the use thereof, and to the promotion or not of these medicinal products, must necessarily not include any deceptive or inaccurate references and indicate clearly that the pharmaceutical company is the one sponsoring the material.

6.9.11 INDIA[16]

Clause 2

Promotion should not be disguised. Clinical assessments, post-marketing surveillance and experience programmes, and post-authorisation studies must not be disguised promotion. Such assessments, programmes and studies must be conducted with a primarily scientific or educational purpose. Material relating to pharmaceutical products and their uses, whether or not promotional in nature, that is sponsored by a company should clearly indicate by whom it has been sponsored.

6.9.12 IRELAND[36]

Clauses 7 and 16

Promotional material such as mailings and journal advertisements must not be designed to disguise their real nature. Where a pharmaceutical company pays for, or otherwise secures or arranges, the publication of promotional material in journals, such promotional material must not resemble editorial matter.

Market research must not be used as a form of disguised sales promotion.

6.9.13 ITALY

No guidance found.

6.9.14 JAPAN

No guidance found.

6.9.15 MEXICO

No guidance found.

6.9.16 THE NETHERLANDS[39]

Clause 4

The advertising must be in such a form that the promotional nature can be recognised by the person at whom the advertising is aimed.

6.9.17 NORWAY[40]

Clauses 4 and 5

Request for appointments with health professionals must never be presented in such a way that the real intent is disguised.

Marketing material shall not be presented in such a way that its real objective is disguised. Promotion must not be disguised as market research.

Information material sponsored or produced with financial support from the industry must be labelled with the sponsor's company name.

6.9.18 SPAIN[41]

Clause 5

Promotional material and activities should not be designed to disguise their actual purpose or nature.

6.9.19 SWEDEN[42]

Article 5

Information disseminated through media that also contain scientific or other editorial materials shall be so presented that it will be readily recognised as a marketing activity.

6.9.20 SWITZERLAND[43]

Clause 132

Advertising to healthcare professionals may not veil or obscure the actual intention. In professional media, advertisements are to be clearly distinguishable from the contributions for which the editors of the professional medium are responsible. The same applies to information in the edited part (PR texts, reports for the public and similar) that is triggered either directly or indirectly (e.g. via advertisements in the same medium).

6.9.21 TURKEY[44]

Clause 7

Promotional material and activities of pharmaceutical companies must not be disguised.

Post-marketing studies should not be carried out and used in order to influence physicians, and should not be disguised as research.

6.9.22 THE UNITED KINGDOM[45]

Clause 10

Promotional material and activities must not be disguised. Market research activities, post-marketing surveillance studies, clinical assessments and the like must not be disguised promotion and must be conducted with a primarily scientific or educational purpose.

6.9.23 THE UNITED STATES OF AMERICA

No guidance found.

6.10 Imitation of competitor products/tradenames

Companies should not imitate the promotion of competitors in a way that is likely to mislead or confuse, e.g. by using devices, copy, slogans or general layout that has been adopted by other companies and is likely to be associated with that company.

The medicines, products and activities of other pharmaceutical companies must not be disparaged.

6.10.1 IFPMA

No guidance found.

6.10.2 EFPIA

No guidance found.

6.10.3 WHO

No guidance found.

6.10.4 AUSTRALIA[29]

Clause 1

Promotional information should not imitate the devices, copy, slogans or general layout adopted by other manufacturers in a way that is likely to mislead or confuse.

6.10.5 BRAZIL[30]

No guidance found.

6.10.6 CANADA[31]

Clause 5

Copy must acknowledge competitors' trademarks.

6.10.7 THE CZECH REPUBLIC[32]

Clause 1

Promotional information should not imitate the devices, copy, slogans or general layout adopted by other manufacturers in a way that is likely to mislead or confuse. Promotional information must not infringe or be able to infringe intellectual property rights, trademarks, patents or similar rights of other person or entity.

6.10.8 FRANCE

No guidance found.

6.10.9 GERMANY[34]

Section 12

Comparative advertising must not be misleading or disparaging with regard to a competitor's medicinal product.

6.10.10 GREECE[35]

Articles 7 and 9

Tradenames of other companies must not be used without the prior authorisation of the holder of the marketing authorisation for the other medicinal product.

The promotional material must not imitate the methods, prints, slogans (sayings) or general layout adopted by another company in a way that may create deception or confusion.

6.10.11 INDIA

No guidance found.

6.10.12 IRELAND

Clause 7

Promotional material must not imitate the devices, copy, slogans or general layout adopted by other companies in a way that is likely to mislead or confuse.

6.10.13 ITALY

No guidance found.

6.10.14 JAPAN[38]

Clause 4

Competitors or competitors' drugs shall not be slandered or defamed.

6.10.15 MEXICO

No guidance found.

6.10.16 THE NETHERLANDS[39]

Clause 5

- The marketing authorisation holder of these other substances or preparations, and the tradename and/or brand names of these other substances or medicinal products are not brought into discredit.
- The comparison does not give rise to any confusion between the substances or medicinal products being compared with each other and their brand names, and/or between the marketing authorisation holders involved and/or their tradenames.
- The comparison does not present medicinal products as an imitation or copy of medicinal products with a protected trademark or tradename.
- The comparison does not create any unfair advantage as a result of the reputation of a mark, tradename or other distinguishing characteristics of a competitor.

6.10.17 NORWAY[40]

Clause 4

Any comparison made between different medicinal products must be based on relevant and comparable aspects of the products. Comparative advertising must not be misleading or disparaging.

6.10.18 SPAIN[41]

Clauses 3 and 4

Trademarks or tradenames of medicinal products from other companies may be quoted only if their ownership is clearly indicated.

Comparative advertising must always comply with the regulations on fair competition. It cannot be disparaging, and comparisons must be based on relevant and comparable aspects. At any rate, and particularly with regard to comparative advertising, care must be taken to ensure that the sources on which statements are based are valid and immediately accessible to the competitor.

Promotional material should not imitate the products, slogans, presentation or general layout adopted by other companies in a way that is likely to mislead or confuse.

6.10.19 SWEDEN[42]

Article 13

Drug information shall not contain a presentation in words or pictures that is likely to be considered to denigrate another pharmaceutical company. Nor shall it contain a presentation likely to bring another drug into contempt or lay it open to ridicule.

6.10.20 SWITZERLAND

No guidance found.

6.10.21 TURKEY[44]

Clause 7

Promotional material must not imitate the devices, copy, slogans or general layout adopted by other companies in a way that is likely to mislead or confuse.

6.10.22 THE UNITED KINGDOM[45]

Clauses 8 and 9

The medicines, products and activities of other pharmaceutical companies must not be disparaged.

Promotional material must not imitate the devices, copy, slogans or general layout adopted by other companies in a way that is likely to mislead or confuse.

6.10.23 THE UNITED STATES OF AMERICA

No guidance found.

6.11 Discrediting reports and medical ethics

Promotion must not involve discrediting reports about the clinical and scientific opinions of health professionals and must be ethical at all times.

6.11.1 IFPMA

Preamble ii

Industry relationships with healthcare professionals must support, and be consistent with, the professional responsibilities that healthcare professionals have towards their patients. Pharmaceutical companies must maintain high ethical standards when conducting promotional activities and comply with applicable legal, regulatory and professional requirements. Through the promotion of this code, IFPMA seeks to ensure that ethical promotional practices are established worldwide.

6.11.2 EFPIA[7]

Clause 5

Companies must maintain high ethical standards at all times. Promotion must:

- never be such as to bring discredit upon, or reduce confidence in, the pharmaceutical industry
- be of a nature that recognises the special nature of medicines and the professional standing of the recipient(s)
- not be likely to cause offence.

6.11.3 WHO[8]

Clause 3

The interpretation of what is ethical varies in different parts of the world and in different societies. The issue in all societies is what is proper behaviour. Ethical criteria for drug promotion should lay the foundation for proper behaviour concerning the promotion of medicinal drugs, consistent with the search for truthfulness and righteousness. The criteria should thus assist in judging whether promotional practices related to medicinal drugs are in keeping with acceptable ethical standards.

6.11.4 AUSTRALIA[29]

Clause 1

Healthcare professionals' names or photographs must not be used in any way that is contrary to professional ethics.

6.11.5 BRAZIL[30]

Chapter 4

It is forbidden to discriminate as a result of nationality, sex, race, religion or any other reason.

6.11.6 CANADA[31]

Clause 2

The code does not accept advertising that is prejudicial to any sex, race, occupation or patient group, or that contravenes the ethical values of the health professions.

6.11.7 THE CZECH REPUBLIC[32]

Clause 1

Healthcare professionals' names or photographs must not be used in any way that is contrary to medical ethics or provisions on the protection of personal data, privacy and personhood.

6.11.8 FRANCE

No guidance found.

6.11.9 GERMANY[34]

Section 4

The companies must maintain high ethical standards at all times. In particular, their conduct must never be such as to bring discredit upon, or reduce confidence in, the pharmaceutical industry, or to cause offence. Additional regard must be paid to the special nature of medicines and the professional standing of the healthcare professionals addressed.

6.11.10 GREECE[35]

Articles 8 and 9

Medicinal products and activities of other companies must not be mentioned in a discrediting manner. The healthcare professions, clinical practice and their scientific opinions must not be discredited.

The overall material and the promotional activities must acknowledge the special nature of medicinal products and the professional position of the scientists to whom it is addressed and who must be respected and protected from any offence. A high standard of ethics must always be ensured.

The name or the photograph of a healthcare professional must not be used in any way whatsoever contrary to his or her profession's ethics.

6.11.11 INDIA[16]

Preamble ii

Industry relationships with healthcare professionals must support, and be consistent with, the professional responsibilities that healthcare professionals have towards their patients. Pharmaceutical companies must maintain high ethical standards when conducting promotional activities and comply with applicable legal, regulatory and professional requirements.

6.11.12 IRELAND[36]

Clauses 2 and 7

Methods of promotion must never be such as to bring discredit upon, or reduce confidence in, the pharmaceutical industry.

The names or photographs of health professionals must not be used in a prominent manner in promotional material or in any way that is contrary to the ethical code of the appropriate profession.

6.11.13 ITALY[37]

Clause 1

In performing its activities, the companies shall not damage the image of competing companies or their products. The companies, which must issue specific internal directives for their staff, shall also be ethically and professionally responsible for the behaviour of their staff when engaged on corporate business.

6.11.14 JAPAN[38]

Clause 10

Member companies shall proactively and strictly comply with the Fair Competition Code Concerning Restrictions on Premium Offers in the Ethical Pharmaceutical Drugs Manufacturing Industry, based on high ethical standards.

6.11.15 MEXICO

No guidance found.

6.11.16 THE NETHERLANDS[39]

Clause 5

A degree of dignity and prudence appropriate to the nature of the product must have been displayed.

No harm must be done to the reputation of the pharmaceutical industry or its products or the reputation of practitioners.

6.11.17 NORWAY[40]

Clause 3

Marketing must maintain high quality and must never be such as to bring discredit upon, or reduce confidence in, the pharmaceutical industry; it also must not be likely to cause offence.

6.11.18 SPAIN[41]

Clause 4

Any promotional activity or material should respect the special nature of the medicinal product and the professional standing of the target audience, and must not be likely to cause any offence or decrease the confidence in the pharmaceutical industry.

6.11.19 SWEDEN[42]

Article 3

Drug information shall conform to professional standards of ethics and good taste. Offensive presentations are not permitted.

6.11.20 SWITZERLAND

No guidance found.

6.11.21 TURKEY[44]

Clauses 6 and 7

- The health professions and the clinical and scientific opinions of health professionals must not be referred to in a humiliating manner.
- High standards must be maintained at all times.
- All materials and activities must recognise the special nature of medicines and the professional nature of the audience to which they are directed, and must not be likely to cause offence.

6.11.22 THE UNITED KINGDOM[45]

Clauses 8 and 9

The health professions and the clinical and scientific opinions of health professionals must not be disparaged:

- High standards must be maintained at all times.
- All material and activities must recognise the special nature of medicines and the professional standing of the audience to which they are directed, and must not be likely to cause offence.
- The name or photograph of a member of a health profession must not be used in any way that is contrary to the conventions of that profession.

6.11.23 THE UNITED STATES OF AMERICA

No guidance found.

CHAPTER 7

Gifts, Sponsorship and Payments

The aim of code of practice rules about gifts and prizes for competitions is that these should not induce the recipient healthcare professional to prescribe or supply a particular medicine. The specific restrictions in each country vary.

See Table 7.1 on pages 84–86.

7.1 Gifts and promotional aids

7.1.1 IFPMA[6]

Clause 7

Cash Payments in cash or cash equivalents (such as gift certificate) must not be offered to healthcare professionals.

Personal gifts Gifts for the personal benefit of healthcare professionals (including, but not limited to, music CDs, DVDs, sporting or entertainment tickets, electronic items) must not be provided or offered.

Promotional aids Promotional aids or reminder items may be provided or offered to healthcare professionals and appropriate administrative staff, provided that the gift is of minimal value and relevant to the practice of the healthcare professional.

Cultural courtesy gifts In some countries, if allowed under local law and in accordance with local practice, an inexpensive gift not related to the practice of medicine may be given on an infrequent basis to healthcare professionals in acknowledgement of significant national, cultural or religious holidays.

Value of gifts Member associations shall provide guidance, using local currency, on the precise value of gifts and define what constitutes significant national, cultural or religious holidays or events.

TABLE 7.1 Chapter overview: Gifts, sponsorship and payments

Country	Gifts, cash, prizes, financial advantage	Competitions	Charity donations	Medical and education goods and services	Payment for services	Samples
IFPMA	No cash or personal gifts allowed. Promotional aids or reminder items of minimal value and 'cultural courtesy' gifts may be permitted	No guidance found	No guidance found	Permitted if items are of modest value and benefit the patient or the provision of medical services	Reasonable fees and expenses permitted for genuine services on the basis of a written contract	Permitted in accordance with local regulations. Companies must have adequate control and accountability systems in place
EFPIA	No gifts unless they are inexpensive and relevant to the practice of medicine or pharmacy	No guidance found	No guidance found	No guidance found	No guidance found	Limited number permitted under conditions as specified
Australia	No items or offers permitted unless sanctioned by specific sections of the code, e.g. brand name reminders are allowed	Yes, but must fulfil specific criteria defined	Must not be offered as an inducement to visit trade display stands	Yes, but items must include the supplier's name and registered address. Clearly identified and approved promotional statements may be included	No guidance found	Referred to as 'starter packs' in the Australian code and are permitted with very specific guidance
Brazil	Prohibited to offer prizes or financial cash advantage	Prohibited	No guidance found	No guidance found	Any sponsorship of speakers must be declared in circulated material	Only permitted under specific conditions in the code
Canada	Nothing intended for personal/family benefit or pecuniary advantage is permitted	Nothing intended for personal/ family benefit or pecuniary advantage is permitted	Permissible under specific circumstances. See code	Attendance at educational programmes (preceptorships) may be supported. A maximum of five healthcare professionals per year, per brand may be supported to attend a preceptorship	Grants/honoraria may be provided to speakers/ moderators at educational programmes	Referred to as clinical evaluation packages. See code for specific regulations
The Czech Republic	Gifts to a value less than CZK200 may be permitted provided that they are related to healthcare practice	Prize value needs individual assessment and must be specific to medicine or pharmacy. Additional rules apply	No guidance found	Professional activities may be supported by financial or other means. Support must conform to professional standards of ethics and good taste	Remuneration must be commensurate with the service and not linked to prescribing or recommending a product	Distribution must accord with the law and regulations issued by the State Institute for Drug Control. See code
France	Prohibited. The only exceptions are those with little or no value and that are related to a professional activity	Promotional quizzes must be submitted to AFSSAPS for approval	No guidance found	No guidance found	Fees are acceptable only if they strictly relate to a professional activity	A limited number of 10 per year, per recipient, and must be in response to a signed and dated request

Germany	Must be inexpensive and include prescribing information unless it is a 'reminder' item (i.e. only refers to medicinal product, company name and trademark)	Must not be based solely on chance. Those where entry depends on providing a scientific service, and the prize is appropriately proportionate, may be permitted	No guidance found	Healthcare professionals may be invited to company-organised, job-related training events	Reimbursement must be exclusively monetary, based on a written contract for scientific/ medical services. In addition certain expenses are allowed	Only permitted under certain specific conditions. See code
Greece	Allowed in some circumstances, provided that their value does not exceed €20 and they are directly related to the recipient's profession	No guidance found	Monetary donations are allowed provided that it is not an inducement to prescribe and is transparent	Permitted, provided that the item or service indicates no more than the name of the sponsoring company, is not an inducement to prescribe and is transparent	Remuneration must be in accordance with the related legislation and in compliance with the relevant tax provisions	Only permitted under certain specific conditions. See code
India	Must be of minimal value and related to healthcare	No guidance found	No guidance found	Permitted if items are of modest value and benefit the patient or the provision of medical services	Reasonable fees and expenses permitted for genuine services on the basis of a written contract	Permitted but must be clearly identified as a sample, be for the purpose of familiarisation or be directly requested
Ireland	Must be inexpensive and relevant to the practice of medicine or pharmacy	No guidance found	No guidance found	Allowed under certain circumstances provided that they are to improve patient care and are not an inducement	Appropriate honoraria are allowed	Permitted under specific circumstances. See code
Italy	Must be of negligible value and directly related to the practice of medicine or pharmacy. Must be purchased directly by the head office of the company	Not permitted unless any prize is of negligible value and directly related to the activities of physicians or pharmacists	Donations strictly related to medicine to university institutes, hospitals and clinics are allowed	Scientific books and subscriptions to scientific reviews may be offered under certain circumstances. All initiatives must originate from the head office of the company	Scholarships and scientific consultancy may be permitted but must be initiated by the company's top management	No guidance found
Japan	Not permitted for the purpose of potentially influencing the use of drugs	No guidance found	Not permitted for the purpose of potentially influencing the use of drugs	No guidance found	No guidance found	Permitted, but must be supplied in minimum quantity necessary and with related drug information
Mexico	Doctors working for IMSS or ISSSTE are not permitted to accept gifts or donations from pharmaceutical companies	No guidance found	Doctors working for IMSS or ISSSTE are not permitted to accept gifts or donations from pharmaceutical companies	The donation of equipment, etc. by pharmaceutical companies is common practice. There may be tax implications to consider	Permitted, provided that the company acts responsibly	Permitted, with some specific conditions. See code

(continued)

TABLE 7.1 Continued

Country	Gifts, cash, prizes, financial advantage	Competitions	Charity donations	Medical and education goods and services	Payment for services	Samples
The Netherlands	Must be of meagre value and significant to the practice of medicine/pharmacy. Additional guidance on commercial discounts, etc. is provided in code	No guidance found	No guidance found	No guidance found	Permitted, provided that the payment is in reasonable proportion to the service provided	Permitted. Records of individuals receiving samples and the quantity issued need to be maintained for a minimum of 5 years
Norway	Must not exceed a value of NOK1000 and be related to the practice of medicine or pharmacy	No guidance found	No guidance found	Grants/Scholarships may be permitted. Financial support for running medical offices, etc. is not acceptable	Permitted under specific circumstances. See code	A limited number are permitted with some specific conditions. See code
Spain	Must be inexpensive and related to the practice of medicine or pharmacy	No guidance found	No guidance found	No guidance found	Payment of reasonable fees and reimbursement of expenses for speakers is permissible	Permitted with some specific conditions. See code
Sweden	Must be of negligible value and bear the company's name or trademark, or the name of its representative in Sweden, and nothing else	No guidance found	No guidance found	Aids intended to facilitate prescription of drugs should be used with restraint and not be given a more lavish appearance than required for purpose	Financing the costs of planning and executing training meetings, e.g. study materials, speaker fees, may be permitted	Permitted only in conformity with the directives issued by the Medical Products Agency
Switzerland	Must be of modest value and relevant to the professional activity of the recipient. Commercial discounts may be allowed	No guidance found	No guidance found	Support for medical education is permitted with specific conditions attached. See code	Appropriate honoraria for speakers and reimbursement of expenses are permitted	Permitted with some specific conditions. See code
Turkey	Must be of modest value and relevant to the professional activity of the recipient	Prohibited except that certain draws of, for example, rare books at a congress may be allowed. See code	Donations to institutions are not considered gifts. Donations should be limited to state-run and not-for-profit organisations	Permitted, provided that they enhance patient care or benefit, are not inducements to prescribe and bear no more than the name of the company concerned	Payment for attending company-sponsored meetings or time spent in interviews is not permitted	Permitted with some specific conditions. See code
The UK	Must not be an inducement to prescribe, must not exceed a perceived value of £6 and must be related to the practice of medicine	Unacceptable method of promotion	Donations to charities may be made with certain conditions. See code	Not limited in value but must comply with specific rules. See code	Appropriate honoraria for speakers and reimbursement of expenses are permitted	No more than 10 per health professional per year are permitted under specific conditions. See code
The USA	Items for the benefit of patients (valued at $US100 or less) are permitted, as are items of minimal value associated with the practice of medicine	No guidance found	Cannot be offered as an inducement to prescribe	Should not be offered in exchange for prescribing products or for a commitment to continue prescribing	It is appropriate for consultants to be offered reasonable compensation for services and to be offered reimbursement of expenses. For specific guidance, see cod	Acceptable in accordance with the Prescription Drug Marketing Act

7.1.2 EFPIA[7]

Section 10

Gifts, pecuniary advantage or benefit in kind must not be supplied, offered or promised to a healthcare professional as an inducement to prescribe, supply, sell or administer a medicinal product.

Gifts must not be provided to doctors and other healthcare professionals unless they are inexpensive and relevant to the practice of medicine or pharmacy.

Gifts may bear no more than the name of a product, its approved name and logo of the company, and the name of the medicinal product, or its recommended international non-proprietary name (or rINN), where this exists, or the trademark, unless they adhere to the requirements for promotional advertising.

Gifts for the personal benefit of healthcare professionals (such as tickets to entertainment events) should not be offered or provided.

Companies must comply with guidance concerning the meaning of the term 'inexpensive', as defined in any applicable country's code(s).

7.1.3 WHO

No guidance found.

7.1.4 AUSTRALIA[29]

Clause 3

No items or offers shall be offered or given to healthcare professionals, their families or employees unless they are items or activities sanctioned under the following sections of this code:

- brand name reminders
- competitions
- involvement in educational symposia, congresses and satellite meetings
- sponsorship
- hospitality
- medical educational material.

Brand name reminders Brand name reminders must include the following information:

- the brand name of the product
- the Australian approved name(s) of the active ingredient(s)
- where applicable, the notation 'See warning' or 'See boxed warning' drawing attention to the boxed warning in the product information.

Brand name reminders may also include:

- a non-promotional logo, device or graph
- a simple non-qualitative or quantitative description of the therapeutic category or approved indication for the product.

Brand name reminders are not to contain any promotional claims including promotional tag lines and/or statements.

Brand name reminders will be acceptable only if it is possible clearly and legibly to display the product's brand name. Where the nature of a brand name reminder is such that it is demonstrably and obviously impractical to display the Australian approved name(s) of the active ingredient(s), as required in the section, the brand name reminder must be accompanied by a document containing the information specified above.

Where the nature of a brand name reminder is such that it is demonstrably and obviously impractical to display legibly the notation 'See warning' or 'See boxed warning' as required above, a brand name reminder must not be used for that product.

7.1.5 BRAZIL[30]

Chapter 19

It is prohibited to grant, offer or promise, prizes, financial or cash advantages to the health professionals qualified to prescribe or distribute medicines.

7.1.6 CANADA[31]

Clause 7

Members recognise their responsibility to ensure the appropriateness and professionalism of their interactions with healthcare professionals.

Members must not offer to any healthcare professional, or to any member of a healthcare professional's clinical/administrative staff, any gift – in cash or in kind – or any promotional aid, prize, reward or any other item that is intended for personal/family benefit or pecuniary advantage.

7.1.7 THE CZECH REPUBLIC[32]

Clauses 3 and 6

Small gifts (or reminders) of value less then CZK200 may be available at booths. All gifts must be reasonably related to the recipient's work as a healthcare professional. A reminder must:

- contain only the brand name of the product
- not contain any promotional claims
- not have the sole use of a reminder within any one issue of a publication permitted before 12 months from the first advertisement of a new chemical entity.

7.1.8 FRANCE[33,47]

Section III and AFSSAPS Website

The pharmaceutical sales representative must not give the doctor gifts in kind or in cash; nor must he or she respond to any requests in this respect from the healthcare professional. This prohibition also covers gifts that are not covered by a convention (gifts of small items of office equipment, furniture, travel vouchers, gift tokens and discount vouchers).

AFSSAPS website

All gifts to physicians, pharmacists or health professionals are forbidden. The only exceptions are those with little or no value and that are related to a professional activity.

According to the French National Medical board (CNOM) a maximum of 30 Euros per year per healthcare professional may be spent on gifts.

Bonuses or gifts In the context of the promotion of medicinal products to people authorised to prescribe or dispense them, it is forbidden to give, offer or promise a bonus, financial benefit or any type of benefit, including as part of a competitive game, except if they are of little value or related to the practice of medicine and/or pharmacy.

Advertisements for a medicinal product, related to the provision of foodstuffs and confectionery in particular, are not allowed, to the extent that the association of a medicinal product with a current consumer product is likely to cause the recipient to make a mistake and contribute to trivialising the image of the medicinal product, which does not encourage its proper use.

Promotional items of the 'games' type that are not connected to the practice of medicine and/or pharmacy are not allowed.

7.1.9 GERMANY[34]

Section 21

Gifts must be inexpensive and include prescribing information, unless it is intended as a reminder item. It is classed as a reminder if it exclusively refers to the name of the medicinal product or, in addition, to the name, company name and trademark of the pharmaceutical manufacturer, or active substance.

Gifts that are not related to the promotion of specific medicines may be presented on special occasions (e.g. practice openings) as long as the value is a maximum of 35 Euros per year and they are intended for use in professional practice.

7.1.10 GREECE[35]

Article 18

Promotional gifts in the form of promotional aids, related to some specific product, may be distributed to healthcare professionals under the following conditions:

- They are of negligible value and are directly connected with the profession of the recipient. Promotional gifts are considered to be of negligible value when they do not exceed €20 per item. This amount shall be readjusted by resolution of the General Assembly.
- The people authorised to prescribe or to supply medicinal products cannot accept gifts for their personal benefit (i.e. tickets for entertainment events, etc.).

Prescribing information for the medicinal product does not necessarily have to be included, as required in promotional aids, if the aid does not include more than the following information with respect to the medicinal product:

- the name of the medicinal product
- an indication that the name is a registered trademark
- the name of the person responsible for marketing.

7.1.11 INDIA[16]

Clause 7

Cash Payments in cash or cash equivalents (such as gift certificate) must not be offered to healthcare professionals.

Personal gifts Gifts for the personal benefit of healthcare professionals (including, but not limited to, music CDs, DVDs, sporting or entertainment tickets, electronic items) must not be provided or offered.

Promotional aids Promotional aids or reminder items may be provided or offered to healthcare professionals and appropriate administrative staff, provided that the gift is of minimal value and relevant to the practice of the healthcare professional.

Cultural courtesy gifts In some countries, if allowed under local law and in accordance with local practice, an inexpensive gift not related to the practice of medicine may be given on an infrequent basis to healthcare professionals in acknowledgement of significant national, cultural or religious holidays.

Value of gifts Member associations shall provide guidance using local currency, on the precise value of gifts, and define what constitutes significant national, cultural or religious holidays or events.

7.1.12 IRELAND[36]

Clause 14

A person promoting a medicinal product must not supply, offer or promise to health professionals gifts, pecuniary advantage or benefits in kind, unless they are inexpensive and relevant to the practice of medicine or pharmacy.

If the gift/promotional aid incorporates more than the name of the preparation, approved name and company logo then it must also contain abbreviated prescribing information.

Gifts for the personal benefit of health professionals (such as tickets to entertainment events) should not be offered or provided.

7.1.13 ITALY[37]

Clause 2

In the framework of the information and drug presentation activities on the premises of physicians or pharmacists it is forbidden to concede, offer or promise prizes, pecuniary advantages or advantages in nature, unless of negligible value and directly related to the activities conducted by physicians or pharmacists.

Companies must also guarantee that all gifts for physicians or pharmacists are purchased directly by the head office.

Although the code does not give a definition of negligible value the Guidelines on Regional Regulation on Scientific Information relating to Medicinal products January 2005 provides a limit of 20 Euros per health professional per year.

7.1.14 JAPAN[38]

Clauses 8 and 9

Member companies shall not offer to the medical profession any gift that could potentially affect the appropriate use of drugs or any gift that is not in good taste.

Member companies shall not offer, either directly or indirectly, a pecuniary benefit or its equivalent to medical institutions, for the purpose of potentially influencing the appropriate use of drugs. Even where member companies are permitted to offer a pecuniary benefit or its equivalent to medical institutions, care must be taken to ensure that the amount offered does not exceed a socially acceptable level.

7.1.15 MEXICO[20]

The Federal Law of Responsibilities for Government Officers forbids these officers from requesting, accepting or receiving any gifts or donations from people whose commercial or industrial activities are directly linked to or regulated or supervised by the government official.

Doctors working for the Mexican Institute of Social Security (IMSS) or the Institute of Social Security and Services for Government Workers (ISSSTE) are considered to be government officers, and therefore are not allowed to receive gifts or donations from pharmaceutical companies.

7.1.16 THE NETHERLANDS[39]

Articles 18, 19 and 21

Marketing authorisation holders must refrain from the following activities involving practitioners:

- offering or promising gifts in any form whatsoever
- offering or promising discharge for the payment of invoices other than in return for full payment
- making the price of medicinal products dependent on purchasing other medicinal products or other products
- making or promising other special offers or benefits in cash or kind
- making any other act of omission or commission through which dispensers might feel improperly obligated to companies.

Exempted from the above stipulations are gifts or benefits in cash or in kind that are of meagre value and also of significance for the exercise of medicine or pharmacy. The concept of 'meagre value' suggests something modest in size. The value must also be viewed in relationship to the frequency with which the gifts or benefits are offered. It is not the intention that gifts of meagre value be offered so often or in such a volume that the value of them as a totality becomes substantial.

A gift or reminder must not contain more than:

- the composition of the medicinal product
- the name of the pharmacotherapeutic group
- the name and address of the marketing authorisation holder
- practical information for the identification of the medicinal product to be supplied, without this involving any pharmacotherapeutic claims.

Marketing authorisation holders must refrain from offering or providing practitioners with discounts in the form of gifts (including bonus deliveries of other medicinal products or products alien to the sector). This provision does not apply to discounts made in connection with the supply of medicinal products provided that, in the case of discounts either in kind, in the form of bonus deliveries of the same drug, or in cash, these are made expressly in writing (specifically on an invoice or credit note).

7.1.17 NORWAY[40]

Chapter 3

The distribution of free promotional items from the pharmaceutical industry shall take place in compliance with the provisions on promotion.

Professional gifts shall have a value that does not exceed NOK1000. The meaning of professional gifts is professional literature or professional aids related to the practice of the activities of the health personnel in question.

The gift can be intended to serve only as a reminder, provided that it contains just:

- the name of the product
- the generic name of the components
- the name of the marketing agent.

7.1.18 SPAIN[41]

Clause 10

Gifts, bonuses, pecuniary advantages or benefits in kind must not be granted, offered or promised to healthcare professionals involved in the cycle of prescription, purchase, distribution, dispensing and administration, or to administrative staff, as an inducement to prescribe, dispense, supply or administer any medicine, unless they are inexpensive gifts related to the practice of medicine or pharmacy.

The following therefore apply:

- The provision of gifts such as items for professional use in the practice of medicine or pharmacy or office items of insignificant value is permissible. The provision of gifts of higher value, or not of a scientific or technical nature, is not permissible.
- Gifts will be considered to be inexpensive when their cost does not exceed €30. This amount will be regularly updated, based on market criteria.
- Exceptions are the provision of objects such as books or other materials on optical, magnetic, electronic or similar supports to medicine or pharmacy topics sponsored by the company, provided that they comply with applicable legal requirements.

- Gifts must include prescribing information specified. When the medicinal product has been authorised for at least 2 years, reminder advertising is allowed. In this case, the name of the medicinal product must be included and, if this is a brand name or an invented name and the product contains a single drug substance, it must be accompanied by the Spanish official name or, if unavailable, the rINN. The product logo, and the name and logo of the pharmaceutical company, may also be included, but no other information.

7.1.19 SWEDEN[42]

Articles 27 and 28

Promotional gifts may be distributed only with great restraint and may take the form only of articles of negligible value to the recipient. Such articles shall bear the name of the pharmaceutical company or of its representative in Sweden. In addition, or instead of the company or representative's name, a trademark used by the company may be shown. No other marking is permitted.

7.1.20 SWITZERLAND[43]

Preamble, 136–137

It is neither ethically justifiable nor legal to influence, or to try to influence, the therapeutic decisions of healthcare professionals via financial incentives. The exception to this is that, to the extent that they are allowed, discounts in the sale of medicinal products are permissible as long as they are aligned with an economically justifiable purchasing behaviour. Nevertheless, the companies are, in this respect, obligated to obey the respective legislation and its federal enforcement.

Promotional gifts to healthcare professionals are permitted only if they are of modest value and relevant to the professional activity of the recipient or of use to the patient. If such a gift does not bear the information of a free sample, it may bear only the brand name of the pharmaceutical product, its approved name, and name and logo of the manufacturer.

7.1.21 TURKEY[44]

Clause 14

Gifts, pecuniary advantage or benefit in kind must not be given, offered or promised to such persons as an inducement to prescribe, supply, administer, recommend or buy any medicine.

Gifts in the form of promotional aids and prizes, whether related to a particular product or of general utility, may be distributed to members of health professions, provided that the gift or prize is modest in monetary value and relevant to the practice of their profession or employment. Small gift items used as reminders should have 'modest monetary value' (YTL20 per item).

The prescribing information for a medicine does not have to be included on a promotional material if the promotional material includes no more than the following about the medicine:

- the tradename of the medicine
- list of active ingredients
- the name and address of the company responsible for marketing the product.

7.1.22 THE UNITED KINGDOM[45]

Clause 18

Gifts, benefit in kind or pecuniary advantage must not be offered or given to members of the health professions or to administrative staff as an inducement to prescribe, supply, administer, recommend, buy or sell any medicine.

Promotional aids, whether related to a particular product or of general utility, may be distributed to members of the health professions and to appropriate administrative staff, provided that the promotional aids are inexpensive and relevant to the practice of their profession or employment.

The prescribing information for a medicine does not have to be included on a promotional aid if the promotional aid includes no more than the following about the medicine:

- the brand name or the non-proprietary name of the medicine
- an indication that the name of the medicine is a trademark
- the name of the company responsible for marketing the product.

7.1.23 THE UNITED STATES OF AMERICA[46,48]

Clause 7

Items primarily for the benefit of patients may be offered to healthcare professionals provided that they are not of substantial value ($US100 or less). Items should be offered only occasionally, even if the individual item is appropriate.

However, items of minimal value can be offered if they are primarily associated with a healthcare professional's practice (e.g. pens, notepads bearing company or product logos).

Items intended for the personal benefit of the healthcare professionals or cash/cash equivalents may not be offered except where the cash is compensation for bona fide services such as consultancy.

The federal anti-kickback statute[48] provides that any individual or entity that knowingly or wilfully offers, solicits, pays or receives, directly or indirectly, covertly or overtly, in cash or in kind, anything of value to influence or reward the referral of any good, item or service reimbursable under any federal healthcare programme can be charged with a felony. This law prohibits direct or indirect payments that are intended to induce or reward someone to purchase, prescribe, or even endorse or recommend a product that is reimbursed under a federal healthcare programme. For example, the law prohibits provision of a gift to a doctor or pharmacist to influence the selection or prescribing of a pharmaceutical company's products. The distribution of drug samples may fall into this category. A healthcare provider's decisions about the treatment of his or her patients must not be tainted or appear to be tainted by motives of personal gain or enrichment.

7.2 Competitions

7.2.1 IFPMA

No guidance found.

7.2.2 EFPIA[7].

No guidance found

7.2.3 WHO

No guidance found.

7.2.4 AUSTRALIA[29]

Clause 3

Competitions must fulfil all of the following criteria:

- The competition is based entirely on medical knowledge or the acquisition of medical knowledge.
- The prize is directly relevant to the practice of medicine or pharmacy.
- Individual prizes offered are to be of low monetary value or an item of educational material.

- Entry into a competition must not depend on prescribing, ordering or recommending a product, and no such condition shall be made or implied.
- The conduct of competitions shall comply in all respects with relevant state and federal regulations.

7.2.5 BRAZIL[30]

Chapter 19

It is prohibited to grant, offer or promise prizes or financial or cash advantages to the health professionals qualified to prescribe or distribute medicines, as well as to those who exercise consumer direct sales activities.

7.2.6 CANADA[31]

Clause 7

Members must not offer to any healthcare professional, or to any member of a healthcare professional's clinical/administrative staff, any gift, in cash or kind, or any promotional aid, prize, reward or any other item that is intended for personal/family benefit or pecuniary advantage.

7.2.7 THE CZECH REPUBLIC[32]

Clause 3

The value of prizes permitted in competitions needs to be assessed on an individual basis.

Prizes that might be useful in the practice of medicine but are not specific to medicine or pharmacy must not be offered.

Promotional competitions must fulfil all of the following criteria:

- The competition is based on medical knowledge or the acquisition of medical knowledge, which must correspond to the healthcare professionals' background.
- The prize is directly relevant to the practice of medicine or pharmacy.
- Individual prizes offered are to be of low monetary value (up to CZK1500) and be reasonably related to the recipient's work as a healthcare professional.
- Entry into a competition must not depend on prescribing or recommending a product and no such condition shall be made or implied.
- The conduct of competitions shall comply in all respects with relevant Czech legislation.

7.2.8 FRANCE[33]

AFSSAPS website

In accordance with article L.5122–1 of the Code of Public Health, quizzes are of a promotional nature when they refer, even indirectly, to a medicinal product and must be submitted to the AFSSAPS. When a quiz contains questions just about the environment and diseases, it is not of an advertising nature.

Quizzes are games with questions and answers aimed at testing the knowledge of health professionals. These questionnaires can be in several forms: multiple choice questionnaires (MCQs), open and short question questionnaires, and yes/no questionnaires.

There can be several distribution methods – medical representative visits, conference stands, press, internet, etc. – and they can be either paper or electronic.

In the case of MCQs, wrong answers can be suggested. Questions and answers do not have to be expressed in a negative or interrogative way.

Corrections to a questionnaire must be provided in a separate document, in an equivalent font size to that of the questions and in the same order. In a correction, attention must be drawn to the correct answers and, if applicable, be referenced and supported by clinical results, in accordance with the legislation for the advertising of medicinal products to health professionals.

The wording outlined in article R.5047 of the Code of Public Health must be shown after the questionnaire.

7.2.9 GERMANY[34]

Section 23

Winning solely as a result of chance, e.g. sweepstakes, must not be advertised to healthcare professionals. However, those with an entry that depends on a scientific or expert service of the participating healthcare professionals, and for which the promised prize is appropriately proportionate to the scientific or expert service rendered by the entrants, are permissible.

7.2.10 GREECE

No guidance found.

7.2.11 INDIA

No guidance found.

7.2.12 IRELAND

No guidance found.

7.2.13 ITALY[37]

Clause 2

In the framework of the information and drug presentation activities on the premises of physicians or pharmacists, it is forbidden to concede, offer or promise prizes, pecuniary advantages or advantages in nature, unless of negligible value and directly related to the activities conducted by physicians or pharmacists.

7.2.14 JAPAN

No guidance found.

7.2.15 MEXICO

No guidance found.

7.2.16 THE NETHERLANDS

No guidance found.

7.2.17 NORWAY

No guidance found.

7.2.18 SPAIN

No guidance found.

7.2.19 SWEDEN

No guidance found.

7.2.20 SWITZERLAND

No guidance found.

7.2.21 TURKEY[44]

Clause 14

Promotion or service shall not be provided to members of the health professions through the use of games of luck or as prizes for such games.

In the case of certain materials (e.g. rare reference books, their electronic equivalents, illustrated medical gift items or medical gismos) that are not available in sufficient quantity, their distribution during a congress or the like can be made with a draw. Such events are strictly restricted and avoided as much as possible, and should not be linked with any promise to prescribe, recommend or buy medicines.

7.2.22 THE UNITED KINGDOM[45]

Clause 18

The use of competitions, quizzes and such like, and the giving of prizes, are an unacceptable method of promotion.

7.2.23 THE UNITED STATES OF AMERICA

No guidance found.

7.3 Charity donations and grants

7.3.1 IFPMA

No guidance found.

7.3.2 EFPIA

No guidance found.

7.3.3 WHO

No guidance found.

7.3.4 AUSTRALIA[29]

Clause 6

Gifts, cash payments and/or donations to charities or societies must not be offered to healthcare professionals to visit trade display stands.

7.3.5 BRAZIL

No guidance found.

7.3.6 CANADA[31]

Clause 6

As a demonstration of good corporate citizenship, members recognise their responsibility to support worthwhile activities both within and outside their communities:

- Donations, including donations in kind, may be provided to organisations involved in promoting artistic, charitable, cultural, community, educational, humanitarian, health, philanthropic and sporting activities.
- Members must ensure that such support is not undertaken for product promotional reasons, and is not directed to product promotion purposes. Acknowledgement by the recipient organisation of

such support must be restricted to an appropriate statement of support, and the corporate name and logo of the donating member.

- Where members provide financial support to a charity and/or non-profit-making organisation through such avenues as the purchase of a table(s) at a dinner or other social event, or through the purchase of a foursome(s) at a golf tournament, or similar activity, individuals invited to sit at the corporate table(s), or to play golf as part of the foursomes, should not be healthcare professionals.
- Members must never provide a donation, directly or indirectly, in order to have access to a healthcare professional.

7.3.7 THE CZECH REPUBLIC

No guidance found.

7.3.8 FRANCE

Grants for medical research or training of health professionals may be provided to legal entities, not to individuals. Prior declaration must be made to the government representative the 'Préfet du Département' where the head office of the legal entity receiving the grant is located.

7.3.9 GERMANY

Employees of medical institutions must obtain permission from their employer prior to receiving any grant or donation from a pharmaceutical company. Donations must be paid to medical institutions and not to individuals. Grants and donations must not be used for social occasions.

7.3.10 GREECE[35]

Article 18

It is permitted to offer to legal entities directly connected with the provision of healthcare, medical and training goods and services that improve patients' healthcare and benefit the national health system. These must be made in accordance with the legislation and with complete transparency, publicity and includes:

- medical or diagnostic equipment, scientific publications and electronic aids
- sponsorship of independent scientific and research programmes of hospital institutions, as well as prizes and scholarships to healthcare professionals.

It is allowed to indicate the name of the company on the objects donated to hospital institutions, but not the name of a medicinal product.

The donation of articles and services must not be effected in a way that constitutes an inducement to prescribe or purchase the medicinal product.

The donation or sponsorship must be transparent, public and comply with relevant regulations and provisions of tax legislation.

With the reservation of the previous paragraphs of the present article, any other grant, offer or promise of any kind in exchange, monetary donation or benefit to people authorised to prescribe medicinal products is absolutely prohibited.

7.3.11 INDIA

No guidance found.

7.3.12 IRELAND[36]

Clause 14

The Code does not preclude a pharmaceutical company from giving educational or employment grants or donating or sponsoring equipment for the betterment of patients, provided that the following conditions are complied with:

- the company must be in receipt of a written request from a health professional or institution (for example, a practice, medical centre, clinic or hospital) for the grant or equipment. Sufficient information must be obtained to establish that there is a genuine need for the grant or equipment;
- educational, equipment or employment grants must be paid directly to an institution rather than to an individual health professional;
- equipment provided by a company must be relevant to the practice of medicine or pharmacy and must be given to an institution rather than to an individual health professional. The equipment must be intended solely for use in the institution;
- the giving of the grant or equipment must not be linked in any way with product promotion. No commitment must be sought or given in relation to the prescribing, supply or use of the company's products; and
- any such donations or grants must be reasonable, modest and in proportion to the scale and scope of the recipient institution and must be likely to appear so to independent third parties.

7.3.13 ITALY[37]

Clause 2

Donations, free use loans and gratuities involving instrumentation strictly related to the medical profession may be made only in favour of university institutes, hospitals and clinics and in compliance with the administrative procedures of the entity concerned.

Pharmaceutical companies in Italy also often provide study grants. Farmaindustria has established a certification procedure for donations and grants that may be audited.

7.3.14 JAPAN[38]

Clause 9

Member companies shall not offer, either directly or indirectly, a pecuniary benefit or its equivalent to medical institutions, for the purpose of potentially influencing the appropriate use of drugs. Even where member companies are permitted to offer a pecuniary benefit or its equivalent to medical institutions, care must be taken to ensure that the amount offered does not exceed a socially acceptable level.

7.3.15 MEXICO[20]

Mexican Health Law and its Regulations do not provide for donations to medical practitioners. Therefore, following the principle that every activity that is not expressly forbidden is permitted, it is possible to give gifts or donations of money to medical practitioners subject to the general provisions of the civil law.

However, Article 47 of the Federal Law of Responsibilities for Government Officers expressly forbids these officers from requesting, accepting or receiving any gifts or donations from people whose commercial or industrial activities are directly linked to or regulated or supervised by the government official.

Doctors working for the Mexican Institute of Social Security (IMSS) or the Institute of Social Security and Services for Government Workers (ISSSTE) are considered to be government officers, and are not allowed to receive gifts or donations from pharmaceutical companies.

The code of ethics of the National Chamber of the Pharmaceutical Industry states that companies must act responsibly with regard to sponsorship and donations.

7.3.16 NETHERLANDS

No guidance found.

7.3.17 NORWAY

No guidance found.

7.3.18 SPAIN

There are no monetary limits established in Spanish law or Code and the responsibility for proper use of funds lies with the donor and receiver of the grant or donation.

7.3.19 SWEDEN

No guidance found.

7.3.20 SWITZERLAND

No guidance found.

7.3.21 TURKEY[44]

Clause 14

Donations to institutions, in line with laws and regulations of the country, are not considered gifts. Donations should be limited to state-run or not-for-profit institutions.

7.3.22 THE UNITED KINGDOM[45]

Clause 18

Donations to charities may be made in return for attendance at a stand or completion of a quiz card, provided that:

- the donation is modest
- the donation is to a reputable charity
- the action required by the health professional is not inappropriate and must not place undue pressure on the health professional to fulfil that condition
- any donation to a charity must not constitute a payment that would otherwise be unacceptable under the code
- it is not an inducement to prescribe or grant an interview.

7.3.23 THE UNITED STATES OF AMERICA[46]

Clause 8

Grants, scholarships, subsidies, support, consulting contracts, or educational or practice-related items should not be provided or offered to a healthcare professional in exchange for either prescribing products or a commitment to continue prescribing products. Nothing should be offered or provided in a manner or on conditions that would interfere with the independence of a healthcare professional's prescribing practices.

7.4 Medical and educational sponsorship, goods and services

7.4.1 IFPMA[6]

Clause 7

Items of medical utility may be offered or provided free of charge, provided that such items are of modest value and beneficial to the provision of medical services and for patient care.

7.4.2 EFPIA

No guidance found.

7.4.3 WHO

No guidance found.

7.4.4 AUSTRALIA[29]

Clause 10

Materials supplied for medical education must include the name of the supplier and city, town or locality of the registered office.

Material supplied with medical education may include promotional claims and/or statements, but must comply with the relevant sections of the code of conduct. This accompanying material should be clearly identified as promotional material.

7.4.5 BRAZIL

No guidance found.

7.4.6 CANADA[31]

Clause 4

Healthcare professionals' preceptorships are educational programmes that should facilitate learning and transfer of skills and knowledge from one healthcare professional to another. These programmes allow a local healthcare professional to spend time with a qualified expert in the field, to gain better understanding and insight into a therapeutic area or disease state.

To facilitate the transfer of knowledge and skills among qualified healthcare professionals, pharmaceutical companies may support educational programmes. Reimbursement for the expert's travel and accommodation, if necessary, and honoraria are acceptable. Participants in the programme may not be reimbursed for any costs or provided honoraria. As an exception to the general principle, a maximum of five healthcare professionals per calendar year, per brand, may participate in these programmes in a recognised centre of excellence. In this instance, travel and accommodation may be reimbursed.

7.4.7 THE CZECH REPUBLIC[32]

Clauses 8 and 10

Sponsorships are not to be based upon the number of prescriptions written, nor are to be used to influence a healthcare professional's judgment.

Equipment or durable items cannot be provided to individual physicians or other healthcare professionals. Equipment or durable items (e.g., TV sets, printers, PCs, furniture) are appropriate forms of sponsorship for hospitals or institutions when the equipment or item is used as a means of diagnosis/evaluation, or improves medical quality or patient care. In the case of equipment or durable items, such equipment must remain within property/site of the hospital or institution at all times, and must not be used for personal use at any time.

All requests for sponsorship must be unsolicited, and based on a written request by hospital or institution. Each member should establish internal procedures to review sponsorship requests for appropriateness.

Members may choose to support professional activities, by financial or other means. Such support must be able successfully to withstand public and professional scrutiny, and conform to professional standards of ethics and of good taste.

Materials supplied for medical education must include the name of the manufacturer and its mailing address in the Czech Republic.

Material supplied for medical education may include promotional claims and/or statements, but must comply with the code of conduct regarding promotional material.

7.4.8 FRANCE

A company who organises a continuing medical education (CME) event may choose the programme provided it is listed as an official accredited CME programme in the Official Annual Medical Educational programme. The Company may provide the content and select speakers in relation to the CME. Company support for CME must be disclosed and specific forms are available on the CNOM's website: www.conseil-national.medecin.fr

In general equipment and/or service can be provided to an institution but not to an individual subject to the rules on grants. The provision of a subscription to a medical journal for the collective use of a hospital department would be considered as a grant. The provision of an individual subscription to a medical journal or book is allowed for the purpose of medical education but this must be declared to and approved by CNOM or CNOP.

7.4.9 GERMANY[34]

Section 20

Member companies are allowed to invite health professionals to company-organised, job-related training events. (Further information is available in Chapter 8.)

Pharmaceutical companies may provide proposals for continuing medical education (CME) programme, content, venue and speakers. The programme organisers must disclose financial support to the relevant medical association as well as in the programme and in invitations to the participants. Companies must select a health professional as "scientific officer responsible" who applies for the CME status to the relevant medical association. This application must state that all the presentations are objective and free from undisclosed economic interests. The requirements concerning the "scientific officer responsible" vary from one medical association to another in the different German federal states. In some states this responsible person must be independent from the company. The names of the participants and programme content must be documented.

The fact that a CME programme is approved does not mean that the arrangements are acceptable under the national codes and compliance with the code must also be ensured.

7.4.10 GREECE[35]

Article 18

It is also permitted to offer, to legal entities directly connected with the provision of healthcare, medical and training goods and services that improve patients' healthcare and benefit the national health system. These must be made in accordance with the legislation with complete transparency and made public and include:

- Medical or diagnostic equipment, scientific publications and electronic aids
- Sponsorship of independent scientific and research programmes of hospital institutions, as well as prizes and scholarships to healthcare professionals.

It is allowed to indicate the name of the company on objects donated to hospital institutions, but not the name of a medicinal product.

The donation of articles and services must not be effected in a way that constitutes an inducement to prescribe or purchase the medicinal product.

The donation or sponsorship must be transparent and public, and comply with relevant regulations and provisions of tax legislation.

With the reservation of the previous paragraphs of the present article, any other grant, offer or promise of any kind in exchange, monetary donation or benefit to persons authorised to prescribe medicinal products is absolutely prohibited.

7.4.11 INDIA[16]

Clause 7

Items of medical utility may be offered or provided free of charge, provided that such items are of modest value and beneficial to the provision of medical services and for patient care.

7.4.12 IRELAND[36]

Clause 14

The code does not preclude a pharmaceutical company from giving educational or employment grants or donating or sponsoring equipment for the betterment of patients, provided that the following conditions are complied with:

- The company must be in receipt of a written request from a health professional or institution (e.g. a practice, medical centre, clinic or hospital) for the grant or equipment. Sufficient information must be obtained to establish that there is a genuine need for the grant or equipment.
- Educational, equipment or employment grants must be paid directly to an institution rather than to an individual health professional.
- Equipment provided by a company must be relevant to the practice of medicine or pharmacy and must be given to an institution rather than to an individual health professional. The equipment must be intended solely for use in the institution.
- The giving of the grant or equipment must not be linked in any way to product promotion. No commitment must be sought or given in relation to the prescribing, supply or use of the company's products.
- Any such donations or grants must be reasonable, modest, and in proportion to the scale and scope of the recipient institution and must be likely to appear so to independent third parties.

7.4.13 ITALY[37]

Clause 2

For the exclusive purpose of the professional and scientific updating of physicians in general, scientific books and subscriptions to scientific reviews may be offered on condition that the initiatives have high scientific value and are aimed at enhancing therapeutic services. The decision to introduce such initiatives, in strictly decisional and contractual terms, shall be reserved exclusively for the head office of the company. The foregoing material must be acquired by the head office and distributed directly to the physician either by the head office or through a branch office, and in the second case the company must notify the physician in advance.

Similarly, medical initiatives may also be undertaken in the form of information technology software (software programs, links to databanks, CD ROMs, etc.) in the same spirit and with the same arrangements as indicated in the preceding point.

Applications for continuing medical education events are reviewed by a national commission (part of the Ministry of Health) and authorised by AIFA. Companies are allowed to partially or totally sponsor a CME event in collaboration with an accredited sponsor e.g. a hospital or national research institute.

7.4.14 JAPAN

No guidance found.

7.4.15 MEXICO[20]

The code of ethics of the National Chamber of the Pharmaceutical Industry indicates, in general terms, that companies must act responsibly with regard to sponsorships and donations.

There are also no specific restrictions in Mexican law about donations or gifts to institutions (such as the cost of a nurse or of laboratory analyses), and the donation of equipment by pharmaceutical companies is common practice. However, there are tax issues that must be considered before making these types of donations or gifts.

7.4.16 THE NETHERLANDS

No guidance found.

7.4.17 NORWAY[40]

Clause 7

The industry may contribute grants/scholarships alone or in cooperation with the medical association. The donors must not be represented on the board or have any influence in deciding who will receive the grant/scholarship.

Financial or practical support for the running of medical offices, etc. is not acceptable.

7.4.18 SPAIN

Medical equipment and services are considered as donations. In general medical equipment and services are considered acceptable if they are delivered to the institution rather than an individual and the delivery and receipt of this equipment is documented.

7.4.19 SWEDEN[42]

Article 27

Aids intended to facilitate the proper administration or use of a drug by healthcare personnel or patients, e.g. dietary guides for people with diabetes, instructions for drug use, applicators, dosage containers, may be distributed to the extent required by therapeutic considerations.

Aids intended to facilitate the prescription of drugs, e.g. rubber stamps for prescriptions, prescription pads, should be distributed with restraint, and only on order from people licensed to prescribe. If sent by mail, the package should be sent by recorded delivery.

Aids must not be given a more lavish appearance than is necessary for the required purpose.

7.4.20 SWITZERLAND[43]

Clauses 251–256

Companies are allowed to give financial support to events for postgraduate medical training or continuing medical education that are offered or carried out under the aegis of professional societies, universities, clinics, healthcare professionals or other institutions, but they must observe, in particular, the following:

- When an event is announced, at this event itself, and in publications concerning this event, the fact of the financial support must be clearly recognisable, and, similarly, which companies support the event. The financial support for the event is specified in a written contract between the organiser and the company.
- Financial contributions for support by the companies should be transferred into an account of the event organiser that has been specifically bound for this purpose. The speakers, as well as all expenditures for the organisation and implementation of the event, must be paid from this account.
- The event organiser is charged with the responsibility of overseeing the finances. Upon request, the budget and the bills are to be presented to the supporting companies and the professional societies.
- The organiser determines the topics of the event. These should be treated in an objective manner based on the current state of scientific knowledge. In principle, when medicinal products are mentioned in the lectures, they should be referred to with the internationally acknowledged active ingredient description (DCI) or recommended international non-proprietary name (rINN).
- If there are several medicinal products, medical devices or processes available for the diagnosis under discussion, these should be mentioned.

7.4.21 TURKEY[44]

Clause 14

Medical and educational goods and services to state-run insurance systems that will enhance patient care or benefit are allowed. The provision of these goods and services must not be done in such a way as to be an inducement to prescribe, supply, administer, recommend or buy any medicine. They must not bear the name of any medicine but may bear the corporate name.

7.4.22 THE UNITED KINGDOM[45]

Clause 18

Medical and educational goods and services are not limited in value provided that:

- they enhance patient care or benefit the National Health Service (NHS) and do not provide personal benefit to the recipient
- there is no actual or apparent association with a particular product
- they do not bear a product name or promotion
- they are referred to in promotional material for a product
- they are not used as inducement to prescribe, supply or purchase.

7.4.23 THE UNITED STATES OF AMERICA[46]

Clauses 1, 6 and 8

Relationships with healthcare professionals are intended to benefit patients and to enhance the practice of medicine. Interactions should be focused on informing healthcare professionals about products, providing scientific and educational information, and supporting medical research and education.

Financial assistance for scholarships or other educational funds to permit medical students, residents, fellows and other healthcare professionals in training to attend carefully selected educational conferences may be offered, so long as the selection of individuals who will receive the funds is made by the academic or training institution. 'Carefully selected educational conferences' are generally defined as the major educational, scientific or policy-making meetings of national, regional or specialty medical associations.

Grants, scholarships, subsidies, support, consulting contracts, or educational or practice-related items should not be provided or offered to a healthcare professional in exchange for prescribing products or for a commitment to continue prescribing products. Nothing should be offered or provided in a manner or on conditions that would interfere with the independence of a healthcare professional's prescribing practices.

7.5 Payment for services

7.5.1 IFPMA[6]

Clause 7

Payment of reasonable fees and reimbursement of out-of-pocket expenses, including travel and accommodation, may be provided to healthcare professionals who are providing genuine services as speakers or presenters on the basis of a written contract with the company at the event.

Healthcare professionals cannot be compensated for time spent in attending an event, e.g. a company-sponsored meeting or scientific congress, unless they are providing bona fide services as detailed above.

7.5.2 EFPIA

No guidance found.

7.5.3 WHO

No guidance found.

7.5.4 AUSTRALIA

No guidance found.

7.5.5 BRAZIL[30]

Chapter 20

No specific guidance except that lecturers should declare their sponsors' names in material circulated for the event.

7.5.6 CANADA[31]

Clauses 4 and 13

Grants and honoraria may be provided to healthcare professionals who speak at or moderate continuing health education programmes. Such grants and/or honoraria do not apply to other healthcare professionals attending the programme.

Advisory boards/consultants Members seek advice and guidance from healthcare professionals in the conduct of their business operations, e.g. in product development, research programmes, and medical/scientific and marketing issues. In these instances the healthcare professional is acting as a consultant.

Advisory boards/consultant panels may be constituted at the regional, provincial and national levels in order to ensure the selection of individuals who have recognised expertise in the areas in which the advice is needed, and that such advice reflects any geographical differences in attitudes/medical practice, procedures, etc.

When entering into such consultancy/advisory agreements, pharmaceutical companies must be guided by the following:

- The purpose and objectives of the interaction must be clearly defined by the pharmaceutical company in its initial correspondence on the event.
- There must be a written contractual agreement confirming the purpose and objectives of the consultation, outlining the nature of the services to be provided. Documentation relevant to the consultation and its identified objective should be attached to the contractual agreement.
- Remuneration must be in the form of an honorarium (fair and reasonable). Travel, accommodation and out-of-pocket expenses in providing the consulting service, where warranted, may be reimbursed.
- The number of advisory board/consultant meetings must be limited. Members may attend only a limited number of advisory board/consultant meetings consistent with the need to gather scientific input or commercial guidance.
- An advisory board/consultant panel may not include more than 20 healthcare professionals per meeting.
- Involvement of any field-based sales personnel is prohibited.
- Meetings of advisory board/consultant panels must be held in Canada. The only exception is that they may be held in conjunction with international congresses provided that no travel or accommodation expenses are to be paid by the pharmaceutical company convening the meeting. If the advisory board meeting occurs before or after the international event ends, the member may reimburse the healthcare professional for room accommodation in conjunction with the advisory board.
- No social activity should be organised in conjunction with advisory board/consultant panels other than providing refreshments or a modest meal. The guidelines with respect to travel and hospitality also apply to travel and hospitality related to advisory board/consultant panels.
- As the purpose of the activity is to seek consultation, at least one person from the head office (a non-sales individual) must be present to guide the meeting discussion.
- An advisory board/consultant panel may be organised by international affiliates. These meetings, if held outside Canada, may include a maximum of 10 Canadian healthcare professionals, per brand, per year, who should be experts in their fields. Honoraria and reimbursement of travel and accommodation expenses may be provided as indicated above, provided that a consultancy agreement is in place.

7.5.7 THE CZECH REPUBLIC[32]

Clause 10

Any remuneration for services rendered must not exceed that which is commensurate with the services supplied. The remuneration must not depend on prescribing or recommending a product, and no such condition shall be made or implied.

Appropriate amounts of remuneration must be determined, based on amount of time expended by the recipient in providing the services, and the amount of pay that the recipient would ordinarily earn for this amount of time in routine medical practice. Remuneration to national or international opinion leaders must be reasonable and in keeping with the service provided.

7.5.8 FRANCE[47]

Section III Clause 12

Fees are acceptable only if they strictly relate to a professional activity.

Consultancy agreements should be submitted to CNOM and CNOP for prior review.

Additionally the French authorities have implemented specific regulations in order to prevent non-declared taxable activities. According to French law any person or entity that executes a services agreement providing for financial compensation of €3000 or more per year must verify that the service provider (e.g. doctor or pharmacist) complies with tax and social security obligations. The beneficiary of this service (e.g. the pharmaceutical company) must request evidence of compliance with these regulations every six months for the duration of the contract. The documentation required is listed in Article R.324–4 of the French Labor Code. If a beneficiary of a service (e.g. the pharmaceutical company) fails to do this they may themselves be liable for the payment of these taxes.

7.5.9 GERMANY[34]

Clause 18

The following conditions apply to payment for services:

- Physicians may render services for companies (e.g. lectures, consulting, clinical trials, drug monitoring projects) based only on written agreements that clearly state both the nature of the service and the remuneration.
- The contractually stipulated service to be rendered by the physician in question to the company must be scientific or medical in nature, including educational purposes (prohibition of 'fictitious contracts').
- Clinical studies and drug monitoring projects, as well as any other studies or data collections, must not be misused with a view to influencing therapeutic or procurement decisions or for mere promotional purposes.
- The remuneration must be exclusively monetary and must be proportionate to the service rendered. When judging the appropriateness of the intended remuneration, the physician's fee schedule may serve as a reference guide. To take into account the physician's time expended, appropriate hourly rates may also be arranged.
- In addition, physicians may be reimbursed for their out-of-pocket and travel expenses while rendering the contractual services.
- Physicians or third parties must not be granted payment of any fees for their willingness to meet with pharmaceutical consultants or receive information from other members of the pharmaceutical company.

7.5.10 GREECE

Article 21

Pharmaceutical companies can ask physicians to provide counselling or expert services or other similar services, with the reservation of the regulations in force, for physicians of the national health system and university physicians:

- Provision of such services must not jeopardise the counsellor's or the collaborating physician's clinical autonomy, who must at all times be bound to the ethical obligation to take independent medical decisions and exercise his or her medical profession in patients' best interests.
- The provided collaboration/service shall be performed on the grounds of a special agreement signed between the company and the collaborating healthcare professional. Remuneration shall be set in accordance with the related legislation and, in any case, in accordance with compulsory compliance with the relevant tax provisions.
- Whenever physicians/counsellors present opinions or results to third parties, concerning the medical/pharmacological part of their counselling services, a declaration of interest must be presented in order to ensure transparency towards all parties.

7.5.11 INDIA[16]

Clause 7

Payments of reasonable fees and reimbursement of out-of pocket expenses, including travel and accommodation, may be provided to healthcare professionals who are providing genuine services as speakers or presenters on the basis of a written contract with the company at the event.

Healthcare professionals cannot be compensated for time spent in attending an event, e.g. a company-sponsored meeting or scientific congress, unless they are providing bona fide services as detailed above.

7.5.12 IRELAND[36]

Clause 15

Honoraria can be paid to speakers if appropriate.

Consultancy agreements are permitted as long as the compensation is reasonable for the service provided.

7.5.13 ITALY[37]

Clause 4

Scientific cooperation between pharmaceutical companies and the scientific establishment may also include scholarships and scientific consultancy, provided that it is documented and carried out in an appropriate manner. Decisions on such initiatives must be reserved for the company's top management.

Payment for services rendered by doctors who are employed full time by public entities such as hospitals or universities must be previously notified to and receive permission from the employer. It is not necessary to gain these permissions for reimbursement of expenses already incurred e.g. for travel to seminars and congresses.

7.5.14 JAPAN

No guidance found.

7.5.15 MEXICO[20]

Mexican law does not restrict payment of a doctor for both expenses and time invested in scientific meetings. However, the code of ethics of the National Chamber for the Pharmaceutical Industry has general provisions that require companies to act responsibly in donations and sponsorships.

7.5.16 THE NETHERLANDS[39]

Clause 20

Holders of marketing authorisations must ensure that reward of practitioners is in reasonable proportion to the work done, irrespective of whether this is in cash or kind for advice or services rendered. Also the advisory work or the services rendered must not give rise to any connection between the marketing authorisation holders and the practitioners, other than the direct relationship with the advisory work or services rendered.

7.5.17 NORWAY[40]

Clause 5

Payments to healthcare professionals must follow these rules:

- Payment shall not be made for the part of a research assignment that is carried out during the doctor's normal working hours (duty roster). Nor may fees be accepted for assignments for which either reimbursement is made or payment is made in some other manner.

- The employer or owner of a health service may enter into an agreement with the pharmaceutical industry concerning assignments and fees.
- Payment for extra work/use of leisure time in connection with such research assignments shall be made according to an agreement.
- The preparation of an original lecture, etc. shall be paid for according to an agreement.
- The preparation of manuscripts for symposium booklets, etc. shall be paid for according to an agreement.
- The payment of fees and other remuneration shall take place in accordance with good accounting practice.
- The payment must be commensurate with the service. No fees may be paid for services for which either public reimbursement is available or payment is made in some other manner.
- The payment of fees and other remuneration shall take place in accordance with good accounting practice.
- Payment is not allowed in order to get access to the doctor's time.
- Rent must not be paid for meeting rooms in medical offices.

7.5.18 SPAIN[41]

Clause 11

Payments may not be made to doctors, either directly or indirectly, for rental of rooms to be used for meetings, unless it is certified that such payments are made for meetings of a scientific or professional nature.

The payment of reasonable fees and reimbursements of out-of-pocket expenses, including travel for speakers at meetings, is permissible.

7.5.19 SWEDEN[42]

Guidelines

In guidelines for planning and executing training in therapies and scientific meetings, a company may finance the costs for the conference locale, speakers' fees, study material and other material necessary for the execution of the meeting.

7.5.20 SWITZERLAND[43]

Regulation 2

The speakers' honoraria must be appropriate to the extent of work carried out. The speakers may, in addition, be compensated for expenses associated with participating in the event, including travel costs.

7.5.21 TURKEY[44]

Clause 15

Payments or funding may not be made to doctors or groups of doctors, either directly or indirectly, for time spent attending company-sponsored meetings.

No fee should be offered or paid for interview times to health professionals.

7.5.22 THE UNITED KINGDOM[45]

Clause 19

Speakers, advisory board members and the providers of other professional services may receive reasonable payment, together with reimbursement for associated expenses such as travel and subsistence.

7.5.23 THE UNITED STATES OF AMERICA[46]

Clause 4

It is appropriate for consultants who provide services to be offered reasonable compensation for those services and to be offered reimbursement for reasonable travel, lodging and meal expenses incurred while providing those services. Token consulting or advisory arrangements would not justify such reimbursements. The following support the existence of a bona fide consulting arrangement (not all are relevant to any particular arrangement):

- A written contract specifies the services to be provided and the payment.
- A legitimate need for the services has been clearly identified in advance of requesting the services.
- The criteria for selecting consultants are directly related to the identified purpose and the person making this selection has the expertise necessary to evaluate whether the healthcare professional meets those criteria.
- The number of healthcare professionals retained is not greater than the number reasonably necessary to achieve the identified purpose.
- The retaining company maintains records concerning, and makes appropriate use of, the service provided by consultants.
- The venue and circumstances of any meeting with consultants are conducive to the consulting services, and activities related to the services are the primary focus of the meeting. Any social or entertainment is subordinate in terms of time and emphasis.
- It is also appropriate for healthcare professionals who are recruited as speakers for company-sponsored events to be trained and offered reasonable compensation for their time, travel and lodgings during this training, provided that the participants meet the above criteria.

7.6 Samples

7.6.1 IFPMA[6]

Clause 8

In accordance with local laws and regulations, free samples of a pharmaceutical product may be supplied to healthcare professionals in order to enhance patient care. Samples should not be resold or otherwise misused.

Companies should have adequate systems of control and accountability for samples provided to healthcare professionals. including how to look after such samples while they are in the possession of medical representatives

7.6.2 EFPIA[7]

Article 12

A limited number of free samples of a particular medicinal product may be supplied to healthcare professionals who are qualified to prescribe that medicinal product in order to familiarise them with the product, provided that the following conditions are met:

- Samples can be provided only in response to a written request, signed and dated, from the recipient.
- Companies must have adequate systems of control and accountability for samples that they distribute and for all medicines handled by its representatives.
- Each sample shall be no larger than the smallest presentation on the market.
- Each sample must be marked ‘free medical sample – not for resale’ or words to that effect, and must be accompanied by a copy of the summary of product characteristics (SPC).

- Samples of the following medicinal products must not be supplied:
  - medicinal products that contain substances defined as psychotropic or narcotic by international convention, such as the United Nations Conventions of 1961 and 1971
  - any other medicinal products for which the supply of samples is inappropriate, as determined by the competent authorities.

7.6.3 WHO[8]

Clause 20

Free samples of legally available prescription drugs may be provided in modest quantities to prescribers, generally on request.

7.6.4 AUSTRALIA[29]

Clause 5

Samples are referred to as starter packs in the Australian code.

Pharmaceutical companies must ensure that the distribution of starter packs is carried out in a reasonable manner and is compliant with a number of federal and state laws and product registration conditions that control the supply and storage conditions of products.

Starter packs should be supplied only to medical practitioners, dentists and hospital pharmacists, and then only when required for any of the following reasons:

- Immediate use in the surgery for relief of symptoms
- The use of alternative treatments, before a prescription is written
- After-hours use
- Gaining familiarisation with products.

Product information should be offered at the time of distribution or included in the product pack. The size of starter packs is specified in the Australian code and in general this is one-third the size of a normal trade pack.

The maximum quantity of starter packs to be supplied to a medical practitioner, dentist or hospital pharmacist must be at the discretion of health professionals:

- It should reflect their needs until the next visit by their representative.
- It should conform to any relevant federal or state regulations.
- The medical practitioner, dentist or hospital pharmacist must write the quantity requested and sign the request/receipt form as required by federal and state legislation.
- Starter packs can be left with a receptionist only on receipt of a signed request from the medical practitioner.
- The healthcare professional must state the amount required but it is not mandatory for the company to supply that quantity. However, the company must not supply in excess of that stated.
- Companies must keep all records of the request for and supply of starter packs for a period compliant with federal and state legislation, in a way that they are available for inspection by appropriate authorities.

The following rules must be adhered to with regard to samples:

- Representatives must take adequate precautions to ensure the security of starter packs in their possession.
- Companies should develop an appropriate recording system so that, if a product recall is necessary, relevant starter packs will be included in the recall.

- Starter packs, when sent by mail or courier, must be packed so as to be reasonably secure against the package being opened by young children.
- When mail is used to forward starter packs, registered mail (or its equivalent) must be used.
- There must be nothing on the packaging to indicate the nature of the contents.
- Distribution of starter packs in hospitals must comply with individual hospital requirements.
- On request, companies must promptly accept the return of starter packs of their products.
- Primary labelling of all starter packs distributed must comply with the current therapeutic goods order on labelling.
- Where practical, the primary label should allow sufficient space for the medical practitioner, dentist or hospital pharmacist to write or label patient details and dosage instructions.

7.6.5 BRAZIL[30]

Chapter 21

The distribution of free samples will be permitted only under the following conditions:

- If the packaging is presented with at least 50 per cent of the content of the approved original packing.
- If offered exclusively to professionals qualified to prescribe or distribute medicines.
- The packaging contains the words 'FREE SAMPLE', highlighted with the font not less than 70 per cent of the size of the tradename.
- The lot number must be printed on the labelling of the free sample.
- The company must keep its distribution programme updated and available to the National Agency of Sanitary Surveillance for a minimum period of 2 years.
- The distribution of free samples of medicines based on substances subject to special control will be made according to the provisions as ruled by the current sanitary legislation.

7.6.6 CANADA[31]

Clause 3

In Canada samples are referred to as clinical evaluation packages (CEPs): a package containing a limited quantity of a pharmaceutical product sufficient to evaluate clinical response, distributed to authorised healthcare professionals free of charge, for patient treatment.

In addition to the Food and Drugs Act and Regulations governing the manufacture, packaging, storage and distribution of CEPs, the following regulations also apply:

- CEPs shall be given only to authorised healthcare professionals who have filled out a request form for the CEP.
- The request form must be fully completed by the healthcare professional before being passed on to authorised company personnel; prescribing information must be supplied to the healthcare professional. This must be shared with the patient.
- The member should also provide full prescribing information on the CEP for a minimum of 2 years after the introduction of a product to the Canadian market. A shorter version of the disclosure may be provided 2 years after the product is first introduced.
- All free goods (or CEPs) given to a healthcare professional as part of an order must be included on the invoice.
- If no order is made when the free goods are supplied, the goods must be documented on a separate NO CHARGE invoice.
- The number of CEPs provided to a healthcare professional will not be considered excessive, as long as the healthcare professional believes that amount is required for the proper evaluation of clinical response.

- CEPs provided to hospitals must conform to hospital regulations. The hospital's chief pharmacist must authorise the acceptance of CEPs before any CEP distribution begins.
- It is not appropriate to distribute CEPs at conventions.
- It is unethical, and may be cause for dismissal, for a member representative to sell, trade or give away CEPs or stock packages to anyone, for any reason that is not set out in the members' policy.
- Rules and safeguards to prevent theft and/or unauthorised distribution of CEPs must be in place at all times.

7.6.7 THE CZECH REPUBLIC[32]

Clause 5

Care should be exercised by members that the distribution of samples is carried out in accordance with the law and regulations issued by the State Institute for Drug Control (SÚKL). Samples may be supplied to physicians only for becoming familiar with products. Representatives must take adequate precautions to ensure the security of samples in their possession. Members must develop an appropriate recording system so that, if a product recall is necessary, relevant samples will be included in the recall. On request, members must promptly accept the return of samples of their products.

7.6.8 FRANCE[13,47]

Article L.5122–10 of the Code of Public Health stipulates

> Free samples can only be given to persons authorised to prescribe or dispense medicines in internal pharmacies upon their request.

Article R.5122–17 of the Code of Public Health particularly states

> . . . all samples must be in response to a written, dated and signed request from the recipient . . . .

Section IV Clause 13

Samples The Pharmaceutical Companies Association should ensure that providing samples is not wasteful and conforms with the law (article R.5048).

For every medicine, only a limited number of samples can be provided, limited to 10 per year and per recipient, which is determined depending on the type of medicine and the need for the prescribers to be familiar with it.

Every sample must be in response to a dated and signed request from the recipient.

7.6.9 GERMANY[34]

Section 15

Pharmaceutical manufacturers may supply samples of a medicinal product to healthcare professionals who are qualified to prescribe such a product in order to familiarise them with the product, but only under the following conditions:

- If it is in response to a written request, signed and dated, from the recipient.
- Companies must have adequate systems of control and accountability for samples that they distribute.
- Each sample shall be no larger than the smallest presentation of the relevant pharmaceutical being available on the market and no more than two samples of a medicinal product shall be provided within 1 year.

- Each sample must be marked 'unverkäufliches Muster' (free medical sample not for resale) and must be accompanied by the SPC.
- Samples must not contain any substances or preparations within the meaning of Section 2 of the German Narcotics Act (BtMG), listed as such in Annex II or III.

7.6.10 GREECE[35]

Article 17

The production, importation and free distribution of medical samples to physicians and dentists in view of their information, irrespective of the packaging thereof, is permitted only pursuant to special permission from the National Organisation for Medicines (EOF). The permission, granted in exceptional cases, determines the packaging, overall quantity, time and mode of distribution, and any other information necessary.

The following conditions apply:

- Companies must have suitable control and calculation systems for the samples that they distribute and for all the medicinal products that they are handling through their representatives.
- Each sample cannot be larger than the smallest marketed package.
- Each sample must bear the indication 'Free medical sample – not for sale' or a similar phrase and must be accompanied with a copy of the SPC.
- No samples can be given of the following medicinal products:
  - medicinal products containing substances that are defined (by an international convention such as the 1961 and 1971 UN Conventions) as psychotropics or narcotics
  - any other medicinal product for which distribution of samples is improper, as determined by the competent authorities.

7.6.11 INDIA[16]

Clause 8

In accordance with local laws and regulations, free samples of a pharmaceutical product may be supplied to healthcare professionals in order to enhance patient care. Samples should not be resold or otherwise misused.

Companies should have adequate systems of control and accountability for samples provided to healthcare professionals, including how to look after such samples while they are in the possession of medical representatives.

7.6.12 IRELAND[36]

Clause 13

Free samples of medicinal products shall not be supplied to any person who is not a registered medical practitioner or registered dentist. The supply of a sample means the supply of a medicinal product made other than in connection with a clinical trial notified or authorised under the Control of Clinical Trials Act 1987 (No. 28 of 1987).

Of samples of products distributed by a medical representative, the sample must be handed directly to the doctor or dentist or to a person authorised to receive the sample on their behalf.

The following conditions shall be observed in the provision of a sample to a registered medical practitioner or a registered dentist:

- Such samples in respect of a medical preparation concerned shall not exceed six in number per year.
- Any supply of such samples must be in response to a signed and dated request from the recipient.

- An adequate system of control and accountability must be maintained in respect of the supply of such samples.
- Each sample shall be no larger than the smallest presentation on the market, provided that such presentation does not exceed an amount that provides a single treatment in the ordinary course of medical practice.
- Each sample shall be marked 'Free medical sample – not for re-sale' or bear another legend of analogous meaning.
- Each sample shall be accompanied by a copy of the SPC relating to that product. This requirement does not apply where the SPC relating to the product in question appears in the IPHA Medicines Compendium and this fact is drawn to the attention of the doctor or dentist.
- A person shall not supply a sample of a medicinal product that is a controlled drug under Section 2 of the Misuse of Drugs Act 1977, or that is an antidepressant, hypnotic or tranquilliser.
- Samples sent by post must be packed so as to be reasonably secure against the package being opened by young children.
- Distribution of samples in hospitals must also comply with individual hospital regulations.

7.6.13 ITALY

No guidance found.

7.6.14 JAPAN[38]

Clause 6

Samples are a way of providing drug information and may be supplied to the medical professional to show the physical appearance of drugs or to help them evaluate and confirm the quality, efficacy, safety and other claims. Member companies shall always supply clinical samples only in the minimum quantity necessary, together with related drug information.

7.6.14 MEXICO[20]

Providing samples of products is allowed under Article 49 of the Regulations of the Health Law regarding Advertising. Samples do not require authorisation as advertising, as long as they comply with the provisions for the product and contain a smaller number of units.

Sampling of products that require a prescription is not allowed when directed to the general public.

The restrictions for samples are the same as applicable to the original product, and samples of medications cannot be given out to minors.

Product samples should be strictly controlled to avoid re-sales.

7.6.16 THE NETHERLANDS[39]

Clause 15

Marketing authorisation holders must maintain adequate records of the samples of medicinal products provided by them and of the prescribing practitioners to whom they have furnished the samples, as well as the quantities involved. These records must be retained for 5 years.

7.6.17 NORWAY[40]

Clause 9

In accordance with public regulations, a limited number of free samples of a particular medicinal product may be supplied to healthcare professionals who are qualified to prescribe that medicinal product, to familiarise them with the product. The following conditions apply:

- The supply must be in response to a written request, signed and dated, from the recipient.
- Only one of the smallest packages can be distributed to each doctor per year.
- The package must be marked with 'Free medicinal product sample – not for sale'.
- Samples of medicines in the categories A and B cannot be distributed.
- Receivers of free medicinal product samples must be registered and the lists kept for a minimum of 2 years.

7.6.18 SPAIN[41]

Clause 13

In accordance with national law, a limited number of free samples may be supplied to healthcare professionals qualified to prescribe medicinal products, to familiarise them with new medicines, provided that they are requested by the professionals.

The following conditions apply:

- Samples can be provided for a maximum of 2 years from the date of marketing authorisation of the medicinal product.
- A sample of a medicine should be no larger than the smallest presentation of the medicine available on the national market.
- Each sample must bear the statement 'Free sample – sale forbidden', and the coupon of the medicinal product must be suppressed or cancelled.
- Whenever samples are provided, a copy of the current SPC must always be given, together with updated price information, conditions of reimbursement in the national health system, if applicable, and, when feasible, an estimate of the cost of treatment.
- No samples of medicinal products containing psychotropic or narcotic substances, as defined in international agreements, medicines that may cause dependency or give rise to public health problems from improper use, or any other medicinal products as determined by the relevant authorities may be given.
- Samples distributed through medical representatives will be directly provided to healthcare professionals qualified to prescribe medicinal products who have requested them or individuals authorised to receive them on their behalf.
- Sample distribution in hospitals must comply with individual hospital requirements and procedures.
- Companies must have adequate systems for the control and accountability of samples that they distribute.

7.6.19 SWEDEN[42]

Article 26

Drug samples shall be offered in conformity with the directives issued by the Medical Products Agency.

7.6.20 SWITZERLAND[43]

Clause 147

Samples may be supplied to the prescribing and dispensing professions to familiarise them with the corresponding pharmaceutical product and enable them to gain experience with the product in practice. The following conditions apply:

- The smallest commercial packages or especially manufactured sample packages with even smaller contents are permissible as samples.
- Samples must be clearly identified as such by a readily visible, obvious and permanent label 'Free sample – not for sale'.
- Samples may be supplied only upon written request or in exchange for a receipt.

7.6.21 TURKEY[44]

Clause 13

Free samples shall be provided to health professionals who are qualified to prescribe that medicinal product, to familiarise them with the product under the conditions described below:

- Companies shall establish a suitable recording and control system for the production, importation and distribution of free product samples and appoint people responsible for samples, in order to transmit and document to the Ministry officials on request.
- Each sample should be smaller than the smallest presentation in Turkey, except for those products that cannot be reduced as a result of their pharmaceutical form.
- The packaging must bear a label indicating 'Free promotional sample – not for sale'.
- The promotional sample shall be presented with the product leaflet.
- The samples of the products containing psychotropic and narcotic substances, within the framework of the 1961 UN Single Convention on Narcotic Drugs and the 1971 UN Convention on Psychotropic Substances, shall not be distributed.
- Samples should be handed directly to the health professional requesting them, or to a qualified person authorised to receive them.
- Companies must have adequate systems of control and accountability for distributed samples.

7.6.22 THE UNITED KINGDOM[45]

Clause 17

Samples of a product may be provided only to a health professional qualified to prescribe that product. They must not be provided to administrative staff:

- No more than 10 samples of a particular medicine may be provided to an individual health professional during the course of a year.
- Samples may be supplied only in response to written requests that have been signed and dated.
- Samples of medicine must be no larger than the smallest presentation of the medicine on the market in the UK.
- Each sample must be marked 'Free medical sample – not for re-sale' or words to that effect and must be accompanied by a copy of the SPC.
- The provision of samples is not permitted for any medicine that contains a substance listed in any of Schedules I, II or IV to the Narcotic Drugs Convention (where the medicine is not a preparation listed in Schedule III to that Convention) or a substance listed in any of Schedules I–IV of the Psychotropic Substances Convention (where the medicine is not a preparation that may be exempted from measures of control in accordance with Paragraphs 2 and 3 of Article 3 of that Convention).
- Samples distributed by representatives must be handed direct to the health professionals requesting them or persons authorised to receive them on their behalf.
- The provision of medicines and samples in hospitals must comply with individual hospital requirements.
- Companies must have adequate systems of control and accountability for samples that they distribute and for all medicines handled by representatives.
- Medicines that are sent by post must be packed so as to be reasonably secure against being opened by young children. No unsolicited medicine must be sent through the post.
- Medicines may not be sold or supplied to members of the general public for promotional purposes.

7.6.23 THE UNITED STATES OF AMERICA[46,48]

Clause 7

Providing product samples for patient use in accordance with the Prescription Drug Marketing Act is acceptable.

However, the federal anti-kickback statute[48] must be taken into account because this prohibits direct or indirect payments that are intended to induce or reward someone to purchase, prescribe, or even endorse or recommend a product that is reimbursed under a federal healthcare programme. For example, the law prohibits providing a gift to a doctor or pharmacist to influence the selection or prescribing of a pharmaceutical company's products. The distribution of drug samples may fall into this category. A healthcare provider's decisions about the treatment of his or her patients must not be tainted or appear to be tainted by motives of personal gain or enrichment.

CHAPTER 8

Events and Hospitality

Most of the codes agree that, in terms of hospitality at meetings and events, whether these are company organised or externally organised, the hospitality must not be out of proportion to the educational content of the meeting. The following is a general summary, although there are variations in the codes and therefore, for more specific advice, the relevant country section of the book should be consulted.

Accommodation

- It should first of all be considered if this is necessary.
- It should not be lavish, e.g. in five-star venues, unless these are the only ones available with the capacity to accommodate the delegates.
- The pharmaceutical company must not pay for spouses/partners or accompanying people unless they qualify as delegates in their own right.

Travel

For bona fide educational meetings, this can usually be reimbursed under the terms of the country codes, but there may be restrictions on the class of travel that is allowed to be reimbursed.

Food and drink

This should be:

- appropriate to the occasion
- no more than the attendees would pay for themselves.

In addition, alcohol should be provided only in small amounts with the meal.

Entertainment

According to the codes of most countries, pharmaceutical companies should not pay for entertainment, and this includes:

- sporting events
- live music
- other non-educational events.

8.1 Hospitality in general

8.1.1 IFPMA[6]

Clause 7

The following guidance is given with regard to hospitality:

- Events should be held in an appropriate venue that is conducive to the scientific or educational objectives and the purpose of the event or meeting. Companies should avoid using renowned or extravagant venues.
- Hospitality should be limited to refreshments and/or meals incidental to the main purpose of the event and should be provided only to participants in the event and not their guests; the meals should be moderate and reasonable as judged by local standards.
- Member associations should give guidance with regard to what is meant by 'modest', 'moderate' and 'reasonable' As a general rule, the hospitality provided should not exceed what healthcare professional recipients would normally be prepared to pay for themselves.
- No stand-alone entertainment or other leisure or social activities should be provided or paid for by member companies. At events, entertainment of a modest nature, secondary to refreshments and/or meals, is allowed.

International events Pharmaceutical companies should not organise or sponsor events for healthcare professionals (including sponsoring individuals to attend such events taking place outside their home country) unless it is appropriate and justified to do so from the logistical or security point of view. International scientific congresses and symposia that involve participants from many countries are therefore justified and permitted.

8.1.2 EFPIA[7]

Article 9

All promotional, scientific or professional meetings, congresses, conferences, symposia and other similar events (each an 'event') organised or sponsored by a company must be held in an appropriate venue that is conducive to the main purpose of the event and may offer hospitality only when such hospitality is appropriate and otherwise complies with the provisions of any applicable code(s).

Hospitality should comply with the following:

- Hospitality extended in connection with promotional, professional or scientific events shall be limited to travel, meals, accommodation and genuine registration fees.
- Hospitality may be extended only to individuals who qualify as participants in their own right.
- All forms of hospitality offered to healthcare professionals shall be reasonable in level and strictly limited to the main purpose of the event. As a general rule, the hospitality provided must not exceed what healthcare professional recipients would normally be prepared to pay for themselves.
- Hospitality shall not include sponsoring or organising entertainment (e.g. sporting or leisure) events. Companies should avoid using venues that are renowned for their entertainment facilities.

International events Pharmaceutical companies must not organise or sponsor events that take place outside its home country (an 'international event') unless:

- most of the invitees are from outside its home country and, given the countries of origin of most of the invitees, it makes greater logistical sense to hold the event in another country.
- given the location of the relevant resource or expertise that is the object or subject matter of the event, it makes greater logistical sense to hold the event in another country.

8.1.3 WHO[8]

Clause 24

The fact of sponsorship by a pharmaceutical manufacturer or distributor should clearly be stated in advance, at the meeting and in any proceedings. The latter should accurately reflect the presentations and discussions.

Entertainment or other hospitality, and any gifts offered to members of the medical and allied professions, should be secondary to the main purpose of the meeting and should be kept to a modest level.

Any support to individual health practitioners to participate in any domestic or international symposia should not be conditional upon any obligation to promote any medicinal product.

8.1.4 AUSTRALIA[29]

Clause 6

Hospitality provided by companies either directly or by sponsorship or assistance to the meeting organisers of educational meetings must be secondary to the educational purpose.

For educational meetings directly organised by, and the responsibility of companies, all hospitality must be simple and modest and no entertainment should be provided.

8.1.5 BRAZIL[30]

Chapter 20

The sponsorship granted by a producer of medicines for any public or private events, symposia, congresses, meetings, conferences and assimilated functions, either partial or total, must be stated in all the documents resulting from and consequent on the respective event.

Any support granted to the health professionals, to participate in meetings, national or international, should not be linked to any promotion of any type of medicine or institution.

8.1.6 CANADA[31]

Clause 7

To facilitate greater interaction around our business, members may provide modest meals/refreshments to healthcare professionals. The primary objective of the hospitality should be to create the appropriate venue and interaction.

Hospitality should not be used as the primary access to meet with healthcare professionals, but as an opportunity to expand the business discussions:

- During interactions with healthcare professionals, members may provide participants only with refreshments/meals that are modest in content and cost. In all instances, the provision of refreshments/meals must be clearly incidental. No other form of hospitality or entertainment must be provided.
- A maximum of three healthcare professionals is permitted per interaction (there may be more than one member representative in attendance). This number cannot be increased to larger groupings.
- Under no circumstances can refreshments/meals be extended to spouses/companions of healthcare professionals unless the spouse/companion is him- or herself a healthcare professional.
- As the interpretation of 'modest' can clearly vary across the country according to the city or province, the onus is on members to ensure that the venue is not excessive and/or 'five star' Acceptable examples would be a meal/refreshment at any of the national 'mid-range' hotel chains (e.g. Marriott, Hyatt, Sheraton) or similar types of local venues.
- Although hospitality in the form of modest refreshments/meals may be offered during interactions, providing tickets or vouchers, or defraying the costs of this or any other event, is not permitted.

8.1.7 THE CZECH REPUBLIC[32]

Clause 7

Members may only support events for purely professional and scientific purposes, such as scientific meetings, scientific congresses within or outside the Czech Republic (the "Meetings"). Sponsorship of Meetings, that do not satisfy this principle, are not allowed. This support must comply with the following principles:

- purposes of the Meetings must be purely professional and scientific.
- sponsors must be publicly disclosed and mentioned in all documents relating to the Meetings and proceedings.

Sponsorship cannot be undertaken by any Member to the exclusion of any other Member willing to sponsor the particular Meeting.

Sponsorship of Healthcare Professionals attending Meetings organized by third parties (e.g. International Congresses) These must comply with the following principles:

- Sponsorship must be reasonable in level and strictly limited to the main scientific purpose of the meeting.
- The meeting must be directly related to the Healthcare Professional's area of expertise.
- Sponsorship cannot be extended to spouses or traveling companion(s).
- Sponsorship cannot be linked to prescribing behavior or volume of sales.
- Costs for travel, accommodation, meals and registration can be covered by the sponsor. Hospitality provided by Members cannot include sponsoring or organizing entertainment (e.g., sporting or leisure) events.
- Arrival at the venue of the meeting can occur within 24 hours before start of the Meeting and departure must occur within 24 hours after the Meeting finishes. If attendees elect to arrive earlier or stay longer, any expenses associated with the additional time must be paid by the attendee and may not be reimbursed by the sponsoring Member.

Member sponsored Meetings/Stand alone Meetings These must comply with the following principles:

- Members can organize Member sponsored Meetings/Stand alone Meetings for Healthcare Professionals in accordance with the MAFS Code.
- Approved Medicinal Products in accordance with marketing authorization can only be promoted at these Meetings.
- Hospitality at the Meetings must be reasonable in level and strictly limited to the main purpose of the Meetings.
- Costs for travel, accommodation, meals can be covered by the sponsor. Hospitality shall not include sponsoring or organizing entertainment (e.g., sporting or leisure) events. Members should avoid using venues that are renowned for their entertainment facilities.
- Hospitality at promotional meetings cannot be extended to persons other than Healthcare Professionals.
- No spouses, other family members or friends of Healthcare Professionals can be sponsored.
- Domestic Meetings cannot take more than 3 days including travel. At least 75% of usual working hours must be allocated to the scientific program. Invitation to the event cannot be linked to an agreed level of prescriptions.
- No member may organise or sponsor a Meeting or other event that takes place outside its home country unless: Venue must be located in: Major corporate, manufacturing, or research sites of the sponsoring company within Europe (with exception of visit to HQ site if located outside of Europe). This rule does not apply to stand alone meeting organized by the HQ function. Invitation

to the event must not be linked to an agreed level of prescriptions. At least 75% of usual working hours must be allocated to the scientific program. The Meeting cannot last more than 4 days including travel.

- Investigator meetings can be held only for participants of clinical trials which are conducted consistent with Good Clinical Practice and which were either approved by or notified to SÚKL.
- Lunch/dinner meetings can be held for maximum 10 physicians. The hospitality is limited to lunch or dinner. No travel and accommodation should be provided.
- Reimbursement for expenses associated with Member-sponsored Meeting or travel must be made by cheque, bank transfer or money order and not by cash or other cash equivalent, and must be associated with itemized receipts for all reimbursed expenses.

This section applies also to cases when a Meeting or other event is organized by a third party but is funded wholly or partially by a Member.

8.1.8 FRANCE[47]

Section III Clause 11

The hospitality offered by the Pharmaceutical Companies Association to health professionals must be of secondary importance to professional or scientific events. The standard of accommodation must be reasonable and appropriate to the event and the expenses incurred should not exceed what participants would have paid for themselves. Specific requests from a physician for the total or partial covering of his or her travel/accommodation expenses should be submitted to the National Medical Association, the Conseil National de L'Ordre des Médecins (CNOM) if it relates to a national/ international conference, or to the Regional Medical Association for regional conferences.

An application for opinion (letter inviting the physician, conference programme, amount to be covered, etc.) must be sent to the authorities within a reasonable timescale (1 month is recommended) before the date of the event.

The hospitality offered by the Pharmaceutical Companies Association to health professionals must be of secondary importance to professional or scientific events.

The standard of accommodation must be reasonable and appropriate to the event and the expenses incurred should not exceed what participants would have paid for themselves.

Only health professionals who have a connection to the event are invited, but not partners.

Requests for travel, subsistence and hospitality for pharmacists should be submitted to the Conseil National de L'Ordre des Pharmaciens (CNOP).

The opinion of the relevant board verifying that the level of hospitality offered or the amounts paid by the pharmaceutical company is reasonable and justified must be sent to the relevant healthcare professional before the event if the opinion is negative, and in the case of a positive opinion these may be sent before or after the event.

CNOM recommends that the hospitality provided should not cover all the expenses.

8.1.9 GERMANY[34]

Sections 20 and 22

Hospitality is permissible only during in-house training events and work lunches/dinners to a reasonable and socially acceptable extent. Hospitality must comply with the following:

- The job-related, scientific character of the in-house training event clearly takes centre stage.
- The occasion for such a work lunch/dinner must be documented.
- Accommodation, hospitality and travel costs must not exceed reasonable limits.

- The selection of the conference location and venue, as well as the invitation of healthcare professionals, must be made exclusively based on factual criteria, e.g. the leisure offerings of the conference venue do not qualify as such a reason.
- If the organiser is a member of the medical profession, the nature, content and presentation of the training event must be determined solely by the medical organiser.
- Healthcare professionals should be invited only to training events related to their work.
- The invitation of healthcare professionals to the job-related training events of any third party (external training events) may include only reasonable travel expenses, necessary accommodation and registration fees.
- Within appropriate limits, financial support for the organisers of external training events is permissible. However, entertainment programmes must be neither supported financially or in the form of donations nor organised. Member companies supporting external training events must request that the financial support be officially disclosed by the organiser when the event is announced.
- Invitation and assumption of the costs for in-house and external training events must not include companions. This also applies to any hospitality offered.

International events International events are in-house or external training events in which the company organising, holding or supporting the event or supporting its participants is not domiciled in the country where the relevant event takes place. Member company must not organise, hold and/or sponsor international events or pay for the costs of the participants unless, in view of the following factors, it makes greater logistical sense to hold the event in another country:

- Most of the participants are from outside its home country.
- The relevant resource or expertise is available at the venue (e.g. for recognised medical congresses with international lecturers).

The pharmaceutical company must be aware of the following:

- The organisation, holding and/or sponsoring international events, as well as the invitation of healthcare professionals to, and the support of their participation in, such events are subject to the code of both the country where the company organising, holding or supporting the international event is domiciled and the country in which the international event takes place.
- The company must notify any activities in advance to its affiliated company, if there is one, domiciled in the country where the event takes place or obtain appropriate advice for the due and proper implementation of such activities.

8.1.10 GREECE[35]

*Under Greek rules, events are classified into three different categories:

1. Congresses of exclusively scientific content (e.g. congresses, seminars etc. organised by governmental institutions such as universities and hospitals.
2. Events of a scientific nature aimed at providing medical education. This type of event would often be organised by a pharmaceutical company in collaboration with health professionals' associations or scientific councils of hospitals.
3. Events organised by pharmaceutical companies to promote their products.

The sponsorship of 1 and 2 is allowed but an application, together with a detailed programme must be submitted to the Greek National Organisation of Pharmaceuticals (EOF) by the organizers of the event or by the pharmaceutical company sponsoring it. Sponsorship funds must be deposited in an accredited bank and according to Greek tax legislation posted to the chart of accounts.*

Clause 19

Hospitality may be extended only to healthcare professionals:

- All forms of hospitality offered to healthcare professionals must be reasonable in terms of the level and cost, and stringently restricted to the main purpose of the event. As a general rule, hospitality granted must not exceed the level that healthcare professionals would be ready to pay if they were bearing the cost themselves.
- Hospitality must not include events organised by the sponsor or entertainment programmes (i.e. involvement in sports or leisure time). Companies must avoid using establishments known for their leisure facilities.
- Companies must comply with the criteria governing the selection and provision of sponsorship to healthcare professionals in order to attend events organised in accordance with the relevant regulations provided for in any applied code(s). Sponsoring must not be offered merely as a compensation for the time spent by healthcare professionals attending the events.
- Meetings outside Greece are allowed, provided that there are valid reasons for this such as most of the invitees are from outside Greece.

8.1.11 INDIA[16]

Clause 7

The following guidance is given with regard to hospitality:

- Events should be held in an appropriate venue that is conducive to the scientific or educational objectives and the purpose of the event or meeting. Companies should avoid using renowned or extravagant venues.
- Hospitality should be limited to refreshments and/or meals incidental to the main purpose of the event and should be provided only to participants in the event and not their guests; in addition it must be moderate and reasonable as judged by local standards.
- Member associations should give guidance with regard to what is meant by 'modest', 'moderate' and 'reasonable' As a general rule, the hospitality provided should not exceed what healthcare professional recipients would normally be prepared to pay for themselves.
- No stand-alone entertainment or other leisure or social activities should be provided or paid for by member companies. At events, entertainment of modest nature, which is secondary to refreshments and/or meals, is allowed.

International events Pharmaceutical companies should not organise or sponsor events for healthcare professionals (including sponsoring individuals to attend such events that take place outside their home country) unless it is appropriate and justified to do so from the logistical or security point of view. International scientific congresses and symposia that include participants from many countries are therefore justified and permitted.

8.1.12 IRELAND[36]

Clause 15

The following principles apply to any hospitality offered to healthcare professionals:

- It must be reasonable in level and likely to appear, to independent third parties, to be reasonable.
- It must be secondary and strictly limited to the main purpose of the event at which it is offered.
- It must not exceed the level that recipients would normally be prepared to pay for themselves.
- Hospitality and travel must not be extended to spouses/partners or other accompanying individuals, unless they are health professionals who qualify as participants in their own right.

- It must not include sponsoring, securing, or organising directly or indirectly any entertainment, sporting or leisure events.
- Payment of health professionals, to compensate them for the time spent in attending the event, is not permitted.

8.1.13 ITALY[37]

Clause 3

Free travel or hospitality shall be restricted to participants with specific qualifications and may not be extended to individuals accompanying them:

- Hospitality can be offered to GPs or pharmacists only if the meeting qualifies for continuing education credits.
- Events organised directly or indirectly by pharmaceutical companies must be held in the towns and offices chosen for logistic, scientific and organisational reasons and be characterised by an appropriate participation of physicians and an expert scientific programme. Towns with an exclusively tourist vocation must not be used as venues. The participants invited to meetings must be chosen on an international, national or, at least, regional basis.
- It is forbidden to arrange autonomous initiatives with social, cultural or tourist purposes that fall outside the remit of the congress or that are not organised by the congress itself.
- Hospitality should not overshadow the technical and scientific purposes of the event.
- Meetings where the attendees are mainly Italian must not be organised outside Italy.

8.1.14 JAPAN[38]

Clause 7

When social events and gifts incidental to such seminars and study meetings are offered, the events and gifts shall not be luxurious or expensive and shall be in good taste.

8.1.15 MEXICO[20]

It has not been possible to obtain the code of ethics of the National Chamber of the Pharmaceutical Industry, but according to the Global Legal Group Ltd[20] there are no specific rules that forbid hospitality.

8.1.16 THE NETHERLANDS[39]

Clause 12

Marketing authorisation holders must ensure that, when offering hospitality to practitioners, this hospitality remains within reasonable bounds and is subordinate to the objective of the gathering.

8.1.17 NORWAY[40]

Clause 7

Events organised or sponsored by the pharmaceutical industry must comply with the following:

- The pharmaceutical company may cover travel expenses for round-trip travel by the main means of transport and for connecting travel. The pharmaceutical company may also pay for accommodation and meals.
- Meals may be provided outside the hotel and paid for by the pharmaceutical company if this seems appropriate. Alcoholic beverages shall not be served, except beer and wine with meals.
- Non-professional activities are not to be paid for by the pharmaceutical company, neither directly nor indirectly. The above, however, is no impediment for health personnel themselves to pay in full the costs of non-professional activities in connection with the professional event.

- When attending events sponsored by the pharmaceutical industry, the participant cannot be accompanied by a spouse/companion.
- In case of travel paid by a pharmaceutical company, the ticket should not be used for holiday/leisure purposes.

8.1.18 SPAIN[41]

Clause 11

Hospitality must be reasonable in level and its cost must not exceed what recipients would normally be prepared to pay for themselves in the same circumstances:

- Hospitality includes the payment of actual travel and subsistence expenses by the company, which must be reasonable and not out of proportion, and be limited to the days on which the scientific meeting is planned.
- Hospitality must not be extended beyond a reasonable period after the event. It must always be secondary to the main purpose of the meeting, which is the scientific goal. The presence of accompanying individuals shall not be permitted. In no case shall social or cultural aspects predominate over scientific issues.
- Hospitality must not be extended other than to health professionals where these are only those individuals qualified to prescribe or supply medicines.
- Payments may not be made to doctors either directly or indirectly for rental of rooms to be used for meetings, unless it is certified that such payments are made for meetings of a scientific or professional nature.

*Pharmaceutical companies must give prior notification to the Spanish Code of Practice Surveillance Unit of meetings and events (including continuing medical education accredited events) of a scientific or promotional nature which meet any of the following criterion:

- organised, directly or indirectly, or sponsored by a pharmaceutical company;
- includes an overnight stay; or
- involves the participation of at least 20 health professionals.

Failure to provide this notification is an infringement of the Code.*

8.1.19 SWEDEN[42]

Guidelines

Guidelines for planning and executing training in therapies and scientific meetings:

- A company may finance the costs for the conference locale, speakers' fees, study material and other material necessary for the execution of the meeting.
- The participants shall normally receive compensation for travel, board and lodging according to the agreement made in each individual case.
- Pharmaceutical companies may not, with respect to these training sessions/meetings, offer to pay compensation for participation or for expenses in connection with these, if agreements have not been made with the healthcare principal in each individual case. Nor may participants request such compensation, other than to the degree that the participant's principal has granted permission in each individual case.
- The company may arrange group trips for the participants, which include board and lodging, and may charge the participants a fee for this, equivalent to the company's costs for the arrangements.

8.1.20 SWITZERLAND[43]

Regulation 2

Scientific objectives should be the primary focus when arranging such meetings, but this does not preclude entertainment and hospitality features.

The expenditure thereby incurred should be approximately equal to the cost that most guests would be prepared to pay if they had to pay for the event themselves.

8.1.21 TURKEY[44]

Clause 15

Certain basic principles apply:

- Hospitality associated with the meeting must be secondary to the nature of the meeting, appropriate and not out of proportion to the occasion.
- Hospitality provided must not extend to a spouse/partner or other such person unless that person is a member of a health profession or appropriate administrative staff and qualifies as a proper delegate or participant at the meeting in his or her own right.
- Spouses/partners and other accompanying individuals may not attend the actual meeting and may not receive any associated hospitality at the company's expense; the entire costs that their presence incurs are the responsibility of those whom they accompany.

8.1.22 THE UNITED KINGDOM[45]

Clause 19

Hospitality at meetings must comply with the following:

- The meeting must have a clear educational content.
- The venue must be appropriate and conducive to the main purpose of the meeting. Luxury venues should not be used and nor should those renowned for their entertainment facilities.
- Subsistence must always be secondary to the educational element of the meeting.
- Subsistence should be in proportion to the educational element.
- Hospitality should not be separated in time from the event.
- Hospitality must not be extended to spouses/partners or other accompanying individuals unless they qualify as delegates in their own right.
- The costs should not exceed the level that the recipients would normally pay if paying for themselves.
- Hospitality must not include pre-paid sporting activities.
- Sponsorship should be clearly stated.

Meetings outside the UK are acceptable under the following circumstances:

- There are valid reasons for holding it outside the UK, which are that most of the invitees are from outside the UK and, given their countries of origin, it makes logistical sense to hold the meeting outside the UK.
- The main purpose and attraction of the meeting are the educational programme.
- The venue is not the main attraction of the meeting.
- The venue is appropriate to the meeting and audience.
- The cost is appropriate.

8.1.23 THE UNITED STATES OF AMERICA[46]

Clause 2

Hospitality such as meals may be offered in connection with informal presentations and discussions with industry representatives (but no entertainment /recreational events). This is allowed provided that the meals are:

- modest as judged by local standards
- occur in a venue and manner conducive to communication of information and provide scientific or educational value
- only for healthcare professionals.

8.2 Hospitality-permitted individuals

8.2.1 IFPMA[6]

Clause 7

Pharmaceutical companies should not pay any costs associated with individuals accompanying invited healthcare professionals.

8.2.2 EFPIA[7]

Article 9

Hospitality may be extended only to individuals who qualify as participants in their own right.

8.2.3 WHO

No guidance found.

8.2.4 AUSTRALIA[29]

Clause 6

Travel costs and expenses for family or travelling companions must not be paid for or subsidised by the sponsoring company.

8.2.5 BRAZIL

No guidance found.

8.2.6 CANADA[31]

Clause 7

Under no circumstances can refreshments/meals be extended to a spouse/partner/companion of a healthcare professional unless he or she is him- or herself a healthcare professional.

8.2.7 THE CZECH REPUBLIC[32]

Clause 7

Hospitality at promotional meetings cannot be extended to individuals other than healthcare professionals. No spouses/partners, other family members or friends can be sponsored.

8.2.8 FRANCE[47]

Section III, Clause 11

Only health professionals who have a connection to the event are invited, but not partners.

8.2.9 GERMANY[34]

Section 20

The invitation and assumption of the costs for in-house and external training events must not include companions. This also applies to any hospitality offered.

In order to ensure transparency when employees of medical institutions are invited to pharmaceutical company sponsored events the employer must consent in writing that the employee can attend and that the pharmaceutical company can bear the costs.

8.2.10 GREECE[35]

Clause 19

Hospitality may be extended only to healthcare professionals.

8.2.11 INDIA[16]

Clause 7

Pharmaceutical companies should not pay any costs associated with individuals accompanying invited healthcare professionals.

8.2.12 IRELAND[36]

Clause 15

Hospitality and travel must not be extended to spouses/partners or other accompanying individuals, unless they are health professionals who qualify as participants in their own right.

8.2.13 ITALY[37]

Clause 7

This must be restricted to healthcare professionals and cannot under any circumstances be offered to accompanying individuals.

8.2.14 JAPAN

No guidance found.

8.2.15 MEXICO

No guidance found.

8.2.16 NORWAY[40]

Clause 7

The pharmaceutical firm can cover expenses in connection with events aimed at health personnel only if the purpose of the event is to provide professional updating of the participants.

8.2.17 THE NETHERLANDS

No guidance found.

8.2.18 SPAIN[41]

Clause 11

Hospitality should not be extended to individuals other than healthcare professionals.

8.2.19 SWEDEN[42]

No guidance found.

8.2.20 SWITZERLAND[43]

Regulation 2

Travel or hotel expenses can be paid only for healthcare professionals attending the event and must not be paid for accompanying individuals.

8.2.21 TURKEY[44]

Clause 15

Hospitality must not extend beyond members of the health professions or appropriate administrative staff.

8.2.22 THE UNITED KINGDOM[45]

Clause 19

Spouses or other accompanying individuals may also attend social elements but they are not eligible for hospitality. Accompanying delegates must pay their costs.

8.2.23 THE UNITED STATES OF AMERICA[46]

Section 2 and Qs&As

Appropriate hospitality must be provided only to healthcare professionals. It is not appropriate to include a spouse/partner or other accompanying person, regardless of who pays, unless that person would independently qualify as a healthcare professional.

8.3 Hospitality and sponsorship: travel and accommodation

8.3.1 IFPMA

Clause 7

Member companies may sponsor healthcare professionals to attend events, provided that such sponsorship is in accordance with the following requirements:

- The event complies with the hospitality requirements of this code.
- Sponsorship to healthcare professionals is limited to the payment of travel, meals, accommodation and registration fees.
- No payments are made to compensate healthcare professionals for time spent attending the event.
- Any sponsorship provided to individual healthcare professionals must not be conditional upon an obligation to prescribe, recommend or promote any pharmaceutical product.
- Companies should not pay any costs associated with individuals accompanying invited healthcare professionals.

8.3.2 EFPIA[7]

Article 11

Companies must comply with the following criteria governing the selection and sponsorship of healthcare professionals to attend events:

- The event must comply with any applicable codes.
- Funding must not be offered to compensate merely for the time spent by healthcare professionals in attending events.
- Hospitality extended in connection with promotional, professional or scientific events shall be limited to travel, meals, accommodation and genuine registration fees.

8.3.3 WHO[8]

Clause 24

Any support to individual health practitioners to participate in any domestic or international symposia should not be conditional upon an obligation to promote any medicinal product.

8.3.4 AUSTRALIA[29]

Clause 6

The following applies to companies sponsoring delegates travelling to, from and within Australia to symposia and/or congresses:

- Travel may be subsidised provided that the meeting is directly related to the healthcare professional's area of expertise.
- Travel within Australia should be by economy class unless there are circumstances where business class travel may be appropriate. For international travel, only economy or business class should be used.
- A reasonable level of accommodation expenses may be covered.
- Travel costs and expenses for family or travelling companion(s) must not be paid for or subsidised by the sponsoring company.

8.3.5 BRAZIL[30]

No specific guidance on travel and accommodation; general guidance on hospitality is given in Section 8.1.3.

8.3.6 CANADA[31]

Clause 4

Members have a role to play in ensuring that Canadian physicians are educated and kept informed on developments in health research, the health sciences and clinical practice at an international level. To that end, they may receive and consider requests from individual physicians, specialty societies and/or academic institutions for financial assistance to participate in international continuing health education events (CHEs).

The requirements are as follows:

- The request for sponsorship must be received in writing, and must include all details of the programme, as well as the specifics of the educational programme(s) to be delivered by the participant(s) on their return to Canada.
- The member providing the support must respond to the request in writing, outlining the conditions/requirements underpinning the financial support.
- The member must require the individual to advise whether or not he or she has requested support from more than one member company to attend the same event.
- The individual(s)/organisation(s) requesting the support must be required to share with Canadians the benefit of knowledge gained through: (1) submission of a report or paper to the supporting company; (2) a written report to the specialty society/academic institution; or (3) a verbal presentation to healthcare professionals. Such papers and/or presentations must include a statement by the author/presenter acknowledging that financial support to attend the international CHE was received, and such acknowledgement must identify the company from which the support was received.
- Members may provide financial support for a maximum of five individuals to any one international CHE.

8.3.7 THE CZECH REPUBLIC[32]

Clause 7

The sponsor can cover costs for travel, accommodation and meals. No other costs can be reimbursed. This support must comply with the following principles:

- Purposes of the meetings must be purely professional and scientific.
- Sponsors must be publicly disclosed and mentioned in all documents relating to the meetings and proceedings.

Pharmaceutical companies are permitted to support events for purely professional and scientific purposes, such as scientific meetings and congresses outside the Czech Republic. Sponsorship of meetings that do not satisfy this principle is not appropriate.

The purpose of the meetings must be purely professional and scientific.

Sponsors must be publicly disclosed and mentioned in all documents relating to the meeting and proceedings.

Sponsorship cannot be undertaken by any company to the exclusion of any other company willing to sponsor the meeting.

8.3.8 FRANCE

Section III, Clause 3

Specific requests from a physician for the total or partial covering of his/her travel/accommodation expenses should be submitted to the National Medical Association if it relates to a national/international conference or to the Regional Medical Association for regional conferences.

8.3.9 GERMANY[34]

Section 20

Accommodation and hospitality must not exceed reasonable limits and must be of minor importance in relation to the job-related, science-oriented purpose of the in-house event. The selection of the conference location and conference venue, as well as the invitation of healthcare professionals, must be made exclusively based on factual criteria, e.g. the leisure offerings of the conference venue do not qualify as such a reason.

The invitation of healthcare professionals to the job-related training events of any third party (external training events) may include only reasonable travel expenses, necessary accommodation and participation fees charged by said third party, if the scientific character of these events clearly takes centre stage and the company has a relevant interest in such participation. The company may assume the costs only if the event provides a link to the member company's field of activities, as well as a link to the expertise of the event participant.

8.3.10 GREECE[35]

Clause 19

Pharmaceutical and other companies are allowed to cover the hospitality expenses of physicians participating in congresses. Hospitality expenses include, exclusively, expenses for the registration in the corresponding event, food and accommodation of the physician during the event, and transportation from the seat of his professional practice to the location of the event; it must be reasonable with respect to the main scientific purpose of the event.

8.3.11 INDIA[16]

Clause 7

Member companies may sponsor healthcare professionals to attend events provided that such sponsorship is in accordance with the following requirements:

- The event complies with the hospitality requirements of this code.
- Sponsorship to healthcare professionals is limited to the payment of travel, meals, accommodation and registration fees.
- No payments are made to compensate healthcare professionals for time spent in attending the event.
- Any sponsorship provided to individual healthcare professionals must not be conditional upon an obligation to prescribe, recommend or promote any pharmaceutical product.
- Companies should not pay any costs associated with individuals accompanying invited healthcare professionals.

8.3.12 IRELAND[36]

Clause 15

Where appropriate, and depending on the time, location and length of the meeting, support to health professionals may cover actual travel expenses, meals, refreshments, accommodation and registration fees.

It should be the programme that attracts delegates and not the associated venue or hospitality. Companies must not organise meetings to coincide with sporting, entertainment, or other leisure events or activities in venues that are renowned for their sporting, entertainment or leisure facilities.

Any hospitality offered to healthcare professionals must:

- be reasonable in level and likely to appear, to independent third parties, to be reasonable
- be secondary and strictly limited to the main purpose of the event at which it is offered
- not exceed the level that recipients would normally be prepared to pay for themselves
- not include sponsoring, securing, organising directly or indirectly any entertainment, sporting or leisure events.

8.3.13 ITALY[37]

Clause 3

According to the Italian code:

- A company must be able to provide the monitoring committee, in the course of any investigation, good scientific, organisational and logistic reasons for the choice of the venue for meetings organised directly by themselves.
- In no circumstance may the organisation of scientific initiatives be used for tourist purposes.
- Hospitality shall not be offered for more than 12 hours before the congress and 12 hours after its conclusion.

8.3.14 JAPAN

No guidance found.

8.3.15 MEXICO

No guidance found.

8.3.16 NORWAY[40]

Clause 7

Events organised or sponsored by the pharmaceutical industry must comply with the following:

- In case of international travel the event must have a real professional connection to the travel destination.
- Pharmaceutical companies may not provide financial support for attendance at such events if the destination causes the event to be clearly associated with something other than its professional content.
- The combined Norwegian participation at events abroad shall account for a reasonable proportion of the total participation at the event.
- Prior approval must be obtained from the Committee for Drug Information for events abroad. This also applies to events in connection with clinical trials.

The programme, etc. for other events with contributions from the pharmaceutical industry shall be submitted to the Committee for Drug Information in advance.

8.3.17 THE NETHERLANDS[39]

No guidance found.

8.3.18 SPAIN[41]

Clause 11

Pharmaceutical companies established in Spain, which belong to international corporations with headquarters or affiliates or other associated companies located in other countries, shall be responsible for compliance by these associated companies with this code; this is with regard to promotional activities directed at health professionals practising in Spain, when they are invited to events held in either other countries or Spanish territory. Pharmaceutical companies should comply with the following:

- The place where the meeting is to be held should convey an appropriate image.
- Places of a solely tourist nature or associated solely with leisure, recreational or sporting activities should be avoided.
- The locations should be selected taking into account ease of travel for the participant, cost, appropriateness and appearance of the place.
- Travel times to the location should be adjusted to the duration and scientific content of the meeting.
- Events organised at venues outside Spanish territory, in which the participants are solely or mainly health professionals practising in Spain, are unacceptable.

Sponsorship by a pharmaceutical company of meetings, congresses, symposia must be disclosed in any materials or published proceedings that result from the meeting.

The scientific content of congresses and meetings must be the main part of the event and occupy at least 60% of each day (based on an 8-hour working day), this does not include travel time.

8.3.19 SWEDEN[42]

Guidelines

These are guidelines for planning and executing training in therapies and scientific meetings.

Therapy-oriented training meetings shall normally take place in the same city or town as the participants' place of work or as near to this as possible. There must be special circumstances – educational, practical, economic or other – for producing an event that requires participants to travel domestically or internationally.

8.3.20 SWITZERLAND[43]

Regulation 2

The costs must not exceed the level that recipients might be willing to spend if paying themselves.

8.3.21 TURKEY[44]

Clause 15

- Meetings organised by pharmaceutical companies that involve mainly Turkish health professionals at venues outside the country are acceptable if there are valid and justifiable reasons for holding meetings at such venues.
- In all meetings, held in or out of the country, consideration must be given to the educational programme, overall cost, facilities offered by the venue, nature of the audience, hospitality provided and the like.
- It should be the programme that attracts delegates and not necessarily the associated hospitality or venue.

8.3.22 THE UNITED KINGDOM[45]

Clause 19

- The venue must be appropriate and conducive to the main purpose of the meeting. Luxury venues should not be used and nor should those renowned for their entertainment facilities.
- Pharmaceutical companies can pay for reasonable travel, accommodation and subsistence for delegates sponsored to attend educational meetings.
- Economy air travel only may be provided to delegates sponsored to attend meetings.
- Travel or accommodation must not be extended to spouses or other accompanying individuals unless they qualify as delegates in their own right.

8.3.23 THE UNITED STATES OF AMERICA[46]

Clause 4

This is allowed only for bona fide consultants.

It is appropriate for consultants who provide services to be offered reasonable compensation for those services and to be offered reimbursement for reasonable travel, lodging and meal expenses incurred as part of providing those services. Compensation and reimbursement that would be inappropriate in other contexts can be acceptable for bona fide consultants in connection with their consulting arrangements. Token consulting or advisory arrangements should not be used to justify compensating healthcare professionals for their time or travel, lodging and other out-of-pocket expenses. The following factors support the existence of a bona fide consulting arrangement (not all factors may be relevant to any particular arrangement):

- A written contract specifies the nature of the services to be provided and the basis for payment of those services.
- A legitimate need for the services must have been clearly identified in advance of requesting the services and entering into arrangements with the prospective consultants.
- The criteria for selecting consultants are directly related to the identified purpose and those responsible for selecting the consultants must have the expertise necessary to evaluate whether the particular healthcare professionals meet those criteria.
- The number of healthcare professionals retained is not greater than the number reasonably necessary to achieve the identified purpose.
- The retaining company maintains records concerning, and makes appropriate use of the services provided by, consultants.

- The venue and circumstances of any meeting with consultants are conducive to the consulting services; activities related to the services are the primary focus of the meeting, and any social or entertainment events are clearly subordinate in terms of time and emphasis.

It is not appropriate to pay honoraria or travel or lodging expenses to attendees at company-sponsored meetings who are neither teaching staff nor consultants, including attendees who participate in interactive sessions.

8.4 Purpose of attendance

8.4.1 IFPMA[6]

Clause 7

The purpose and focus of all symposia, congresses and other promotional, scientific or professional meetings (an 'event') for healthcare professionals, organised or sponsored by a company, should be to inform healthcare professionals about products and/or to provide scientific or educational information.

8.4.2 EFPIA[7]

No specific guidance, although Article 9 states:

> All promotional, scientific or professional meetings, congresses, conferences, symposia, and other similar events (each, an 'event') organised or sponsored by a company must be held in an appropriate venue that is *conducive to the main purpose of the event.*

The implication is that the main purpose of the event is scientific or educational, although this is not stated.

8.4.3 WHO[8]

Clause 22

Symposia are useful for disseminating information. The objective scientific content of such meetings should be paramount, and presentations by independent scientists and health professionals are helpful to this end.

Their educational value may be enhanced if scientific or professional bodies organise them.

8.4.4 AUSTRALIA[29]

Clause 6

The primary objective of the meeting must be the enhancement of medical knowledge and the quality use of medicines in Australia.

8.4.5 BRAZIL[30]

No guidance found.

8.4.6 CANADA[31]

Clause 4

Symposia, congresses and other continuing health education programmes are vital ways for members to dispense knowledge, and for healthcare professionals to share their experiences with each other. The main goal of such meetings must be to enhance the healthcare of all Canadians. For this reason, the educational programme must be the main focus of, and reason for, sponsoring or participating in an event.

These requirements apply to all types of continuing health education programmes, including events organised by the member and events organised through a third party.

8.4.7 THE CZECH REPUBLIC[32]

Clause 7

Pharmaceutical companies support events for purely professional and scientific purposes.

8.4.8 FRANCE

No guidance found.

8.4.9 GERMANY[34]

Section 20

The scientific character of these events must clearly take centre stage.

8.4.10 GREECE

No guidance found.

8.4.11 INDIA[16]

Clause 7

The purpose and focus of all symposia, congresses and other promotional, scientific or professional meetings (an 'event') for healthcare professionals, organised or sponsored by a company, should be to inform healthcare professionals about products and/or to provide scientific or educational information.

8.4.12 IRELAND[36]

Clause 3

It should be the programme that attracts delegates and not the associated venue or hospitality. Companies must not organise meetings to coincide with sporting, entertainment, or other leisure events or activities in venues that are renowned for their sporting, entertainment or leisure facilities.

8.4.13 ITALY[37]

Clause 3

The primary objective of the participation in or organisation of international, national and regional conferences and congresses must be to promote the development of scientific cooperation with physicians.

8.4.14 JAPAN[38]

Clause 7

Seminars and study meetings organised by member companies to present their drugs to the medical profession shall be academic events where scientific information is provided to attendees.

8.4.15 MEXICO

No guidance found.

8.4.16 NORWAY[40]

Clause 7

The purpose of the event should be to provide professional updating of the participants.

8.4.17 THE NETHERLANDS

No guidance found.

8.4.18 SPAIN[41]

Clause 11

The scientific goals must represent the main focus in the organisation of such meetings. Social or cultural aspects must not predominate and on no account must sponsorship or organisation of entertainment events include sport or leisure activities.

8.4.19 SWEDEN[42]

Guidelines

Therapy-oriented training and/or scientific meetings can be arranged by a company or in collaboration with a company with the aim of providing training within specific treatment areas. The information shall provide healthcare personnel with current and important knowledge about the state of affairs, both general and specific, within the therapy field in question. These meetings shall be problem oriented and not centred on a product.

8.4.20 SWITZERLAND[43]

Regulation 2

Communication of scientific or professional information is the main purpose of these events.

8.4.21 TURKEY[44]

Clause 15

The meeting must have a clear scientific content.

8.4.22 THE UNITED KINGDOM[45]

Clause 19

The main purpose of the meeting must be the educational content.

8.4.23 THE UNITED STATES OF AMERICA[46]

Clause 3

The gathering should be primarily dedicated, in both time and effort, to promoting objective scientific and educational activities. The main incentive for bringing attendees together is to further their knowledge on the topics presented.

8.5 Promotion at booths (licensed and unlicensed)

8.5.1 IFPMA

Clause 7

Promotional information that appears on exhibition stands or is distributed to participants at international scientific congresses and symposia may refer to pharmaceutical products that are not registered in the country where the event takes place, or registered under different conditions, provided that the following conditions are observed:

- The meeting should be a truly international, scientific event with a significant proportion of the speakers and attendees from countries other than the country where the event takes place.

- Promotional material (excluding promotional aids) for a pharmaceutical product, not registered in the country of the event, should be accompanied by a suitable statement indicating the countries in which the product is registered and making clear that such a product is not available locally.
- Promotional material that refers to the prescribing information (indications, warnings, etc.) authorised in a country or countries other than that in which the event takes place, but where the product is also registered, should be accompanied by an explanatory statement indicating that registration conditions differ internationally.
- An explanatory statement should identify the countries in which the product is registered and make it clear that it is not available locally.

8.5.2 EFPIA

No guidance found.

8.5.3 WHO

No guidance found.

8.5.4 AUSTRALIA[29]

Sections 1 and 6

Trade display must include, in a prominent position, the name of the sponsoring company:

- Exhibitors must comply with all requirements of the sponsoring organisation when setting up and conducting a trade display.
- Product information (PI) for products being promoted must be available from the trade display stand.
- Starter packs must not be made available for collection from unattended trade display stands, nor be supplied to unauthorised or non-qualified individuals.
- Competitions that are held as part of a trade display must be consistent with the requirements of the code.
- All promotional materials used at trade displays must be consistent with the requirements of code.
- To encourage healthcare professionals to attend a trade display a company may offer brand name reminders, involvement in complying competitions, or an item of medical educational material or hospitality, provided that these meet the requirements of the code.
- Any activities of a company in relation to its trade display must be able successfully to withstand public and professional scrutiny, and conform to professional and community standards of ethics and good taste.

Products that have not been approved for registration by the Department of Health and Ageing must not be promoted in Australia. However, educational material and samples for unapproved products and unapproved indications may be displayed and made available at International Congresses and Australasian Congresses provided that the following is adhered to:

- Information about products not approved for registration in Australia or non-approved indications of a product registered in Australia must be consistent with the approved PI in the country where the product is registered. This PI must be available and distributed in accordance with this code of conduct.
- Products not approved for registration in Australia must be approved for marketing in an overseas country from which there are delegates registered at the conference.
- All promotional materials used at the trade displays must be consistent with the requirements of the Australian code.

- An appropriately worded label, predominantly located, must state that the product or indication is unapproved in Australia.

8.5.5 BRAZIL

No guidance found.

8.5.6 CANADA[31]

Clause 5

Convention booths or clinic displays allow for enhanced interaction between healthcare professionals and the pharmaceutical industry. The following rules apply:

- The main purpose of such displays must be the presentation of accurate information about the product(s) on display.
- Promotional and educational material available at the display shall not present information or claims that differ in any way from the official product monograph(s).
- Reprints of scientific and medical papers may be distributed at the display, provided that they are reprinted verbatim, and are not presented in a manner that differs in any way from the official product monograph(s).
- Giving out clinical evaluation packages, often termed 'samples', at convention/clinic displays is not permitted.
- Member representatives who are looking after a display must abide by all standards of behaviour.
- The fee that a member pays for exhibit space must not include additional donations to the association holding the convention. Additional donations must be reported as such.
- If a member sponsors a public relations event associated with a convention, the cost of that event must not exceed the cost of a single exhibit.
- Sponsorship of member-specific social functions is not permitted.
- Members must not pay for or make a donation to displays set up on an ongoing basis at clinics/hospitals.

8.5.7 THE CZECH REPUBLIC[32]

Clause 6

Trade displays are important for the dissemination of knowledge and experience to the healthcare professions. The prime objective in organising such displays must be the enhancement of medical knowledge:

- Trade displays must comply with the law.
- A trade display must include, in a prominent position, the name of the sponsoring company.
- PI for products being promoted must be available from the display stand. This information must be consistent with the approved PI registered in the Czech Republic.
- No alcohol and games of chance are accepted at trade display.
- Small gifts of value less then CZK200 may be available at the trade display.
- All gifts must be reasonably related to the recipient's work as a healthcare professional.
- Gifts of professional/medical nature (e.g. books) of the value of up to CZK1500 for draws/quizzes are acceptable.

8.5.8 FRANCE[33]

Promotion of products not licensed in France is not allowed.

8.5.9 GERMANY[34]

Section 9

Medicinal products, subject to a marketing authorisation, must not be promoted before the grant of such marketing authorisation. Any promotion going beyond the indications or pharmaceutical forms approved in the marketing authorisation is inadmissible.

8.5.10 GREECE

No guidance found.

8.5.11 INDIA[16]

Clause 7

Promotional information that appears on exhibition stands or is distributed to participants at international scientific congresses and symposia may refer to pharmaceutical products that are not registered in the country where the event takes place, or registered under different conditions, provided that the following conditions are observed:

- The meeting should be a truly international, scientific event with a significant proportion of the speakers and attendees from countries other than the country where the event takes place.
- Promotional material (excluding promotional aids) for a pharmaceutical product not registered in the country of the event should be accompanied by a suitable statement indicating the countries in which the product is registered, and make clear that such a product is not available locally.
- Promotional material that refers to the prescribing information (indications, warnings, etc.) authorised in a country or countries other than that in which the event takes place, but where the product is also registered, should be accompanied by an explanatory statement indicating that registration conditions differ internationally.
- An explanatory statement should identify the countries in which the product is registered and make it clear that it is not available locally.

8.5.12 IRELAND[36]

Clauses 1 and 3

Promotional material that appears on exhibition stands or is distributed to participants at international congresses or symposia in Ireland can refer to products that are not licensed in Ireland, provided that it is licensed in at least one member state of the EU, and the following conditions are observed:

- The meeting is a truly international scientific event with a significant proportion of the speakers from other countries.
- The promotional material does not promote the prescription, supply, sale or consumption of the product in Ireland. A clearly visible and legible statement must be included to the effect that the product is not licensed in Ireland or that it is licensed for different indications in Ireland.
- Promotional material, which refers to prescribing information authorised in other countries, must contain a statement that the licensing conditions differ internationally.

Promotional material for products not licensed in any country cannot be displayed or distributed. However, scientific papers may be given, provided that this is in accordance with the Irish code of marketing practice as a means of exchange of medical and scientific information during the development of a preparation.

8.5.13 ITALY

*At international congresses held in Italy it is permitted to distribute information regarding products or indications that are not licensed in Italy provided that:

- the information is in the language of the country where the product is licensed
- physicians from the country where the product is licensed are attending the congress
- the distribution is with the prior authorisation of AIFA.*

8.5.14 JAPAN
No guidance found.

8.5.15 MEXICO
No guidance found.

8.5.16 NORWAY
No guidance found.

8.5.17 THE NETHERLANDS
No guidance found.

8.5.18 SPAIN[41]
Clause 1
A medicinal product cannot be promoted before the marketing authorisation allowing its sale or supply has been granted. This prohibition also covers medicines, authorised in another country, that have not obtained marketing authorisation in Spain. This regulation, however, does not imply a limitation to the right of the scientific community to be fully informed about medical and scientific progress, nor is it intended to restrict complete and adequate exchange of scientific information related to medicines or drug substances, including appropriate and objective dissemination of research findings in the scientific communication media and scientific congresses.

8.5.19 SWEDEN
No guidance found.

8.5.20 SWITZERLAND[43]
Clause 133
If products have not yet received marketing authorisation from Swissmedic, no advertisements for these medicinal products are allowed. The same applies for new indications, possible applications, dosages, and pharmaceutical forms and packaging of a medicinal product. The brand name may be used; however, it must always be accompanied by the official abbreviated designation of its active ingredients.

8.5.21 TURKEY[44]
Clause 3
Promotion of products and indications that do not have a marketing authorisation in Turkey are not permitted at international congresses organised in Turkey. In such events scientific presentations or poster presentations are not considered promotion and are therefore permitted.

8.5.22 THE UNITED KINGDOM[45]
Clause 3
The normal rules of promotion of medicines apply to trade booths at company-organised meetings that are not recognised international meetings, i.e. medicines can be promoted only within the terms of their marketing authorisation.

The promotion of a product or indication without a UK licence at international meetings held in the UK is allowed, provided that the following conditions are met:

- The meeting is truly international and of a high scientific standing.
- The product is authorised in another major, industrialised country.
- A significant proportion of the delegates are from outside the UK.
- The product is relevant to the purpose of the meeting.
- It is clearly stated on all promotional materials that the product is not licensed in the UK.
- If the product is licensed in the UK, but not for the indication being promoted, then prescribing information approved in the UK must be available at the booth.
- Promotional material is still certified, but only that the material is a truthful presentation of the facts.

8.5.23 THE UNITED STATES OF AMERICA[50]

The Healthcare Conventions and Exhibitions Associations (HCEA) has established guidelines for exhibits of drug products at meetings and conventions. These guidelines incorporate Food and Drug Administration (FDA) regulations and as such must be followed carefully (especially 21 C.F.R. §§ 202.1 for marketed products and 312.6–312.7 for investigational products).

Investigational products

Any investigational product that is graphically depicted on a commercial exhibit must adhere to the following rules as per FDA regulations:

- contain only objective, non-indication statements about the product
- must not contain claims of safety, effectiveness, or reliability
- must not contain comparative claims to other marketed products
- exist solely for the purpose of obtaining investigators
- must be accompanied by directions for becoming an investigator and a list of investigator responsibilities
- contain a statement that the product candidate is for investigational use only.

Marketed products

Exhibit advertisements must include the following:

- the established name
- the brand name (if any)
- the formula showing quantitatively each ingredient
- a brief summary of side effects, contraindications, and effectiveness.

Advertisements or product promotions

According to FDA regulations, advertisements or promotions for drugs must be truthful and not misleading, give a balanced presentation of benefits and risks, include full prescribing information or at least a brief summary, and not promote off-label uses.

Furthermore, any comparisons or superiority claims must be supported by proper evidence, generally consisting of two adequate and well-controlled investigations.

Giveaways Unless otherwise stated in the prospectus, such items as containers (bags) and giveaways should be allowed if approved for distribution through the convention manager.

Financial support of venues The HCEA has gone on record stating that it is improper for commercial manufacturers to finance health care meetings, either singly or in combination with other firms, for the purpose of influencing the choice of subject matter or speaker's presentations.

Professional communication at exhibits

Off-label information Scientists and health care professionals may engage in scientific exchange of information not contained in approved labelling, but care must be taken to ensure that no statements are made that might be construed as promoting an off-label use of any approved drug product. These discussions should not occur at the exhibition booth.

Records Records of conversations at exhibits should be kept. Information should include name and affiliation of contact, topics discussed, any materials disseminated, and information for follow-up contact.

False claims The False Claims Act provides for any instances when a drug is promoted for an off-label (unapproved) indication, whereby a company can be held responsible for inciting the submission of false claims for drugs that have not been approved to treat the condition for which they were actually prescribed due to the company's promotional activities.

The FDA's mission is to protect the health and safety of the American people by approving new medicinal products and regulating how they are manufactured, marketed, and sold. The FDA acts under the authority of the Federal Food, Drug, and Cosmetic Act and implements regulations codified in 21 C.F.R. § 202.1. Under this regulation, information that is presented on drug product labels and packaging (such as ingredients, dosage, side effects, contraindications, and effectiveness), and advertising materials are strictly controlled. Because of the FDA regulations, all items distributed at exhibit booths, including but not restricted to promotional materials, must be limited to FDA-approved (on-label) uses and may not solicit, encourage, or promote unapproved (off-label) uses of a product or unapproved products with specific limitations. *Therefore, the following are recommendations to ensure legal compliance:

- All materials should undergo internal legal and regulatory review within the pharmaceutical company.
- Unapproved or homemade materials (notes, papers, etc.) should not be distributed.
- Booth staff may not encourage, solicit, promote or discuss unapproved (off-label) uses of a product.*

Unsolicited requests for information The FDA prohibits the promotion of investigational drugs in 21 C.F.R. § 312.7. *For unapproved products, 'coming soon' advertisements can be used to announce the name of a new product; however, such advertisements cannot make any written, verbal or graphic representations or suggestions regarding the safety, efficacy or intended use of the product. Moreover, if the unapproved product is expected to have a black box warning, 'coming soon' advertisements may not be used. In scientific exhibits, information regarding unapproved drugs may be displayed if the exhibit is clearly separated from the sales area, staffed only by scientists, and if there are no commercial materials or distributions made (i.e., in the Scientific or Medical Information Booth).*

Because the FDA recognizes the need for scientific exchange between a healthcare provider and the pharmaceutical company, it has indicated that pharmaceutical company personnel may respond to unsolicited requests and questions even if such questions pertain to unapproved uses of commercially available products (off-label information) or unapproved products if certain guidelines are followed. A distinction is made between a legitimate scientific exchange conducted in a proper setting and the promotion of an unapproved product or the off-label use of an approved product. Off-label discussions must be fair and balanced, i.e. the scientific information must be presented with an accurate representation of a product's side effects, contraindications, and effectiveness. If medical/scientific staff participate in off-label discussions it is recommended that they provide a complete range of results and views, regardless of whether it is favourable to the product, in order that healthcare providers can make their own risk-versus-benefit decisions.

Approved reprints may be provided at trade booths provided certain conditions are met.

CHAPTER 9

Printed Promotional Materials

Printed promotional materials include journal advertisements, stand panels, etc.

9.1 Full advertisements

In most countries such materials must include prescribing information compatible with the summary of product characteristics (SPC) but the requirements for these vary widely from country to country. Table 9.1 on pages 148–149 summarises these requirements but further details can be found in Section 9.4 (p. 158).

9.2 Reminder advertisements

As an exception to the general rule that all promotional material must include information compatible with the SPC, however, some countries allow 'reminder advertisements', e.g. promotional aids such as pens and notepads. This type of advertising usually must not contain more than the brand or generic name and trademark but the rules vary from country to country. Table 9.2 summarises these requirements.

TABLE 9.1 Summary by country of specific information requirements relating to full advertisements

Country	Brand name	Active ingredient and/or approved name	Company name/address	Dose/form and/or regimen	Approved indications	Side effects, contraindications, precautions or interactions	Last revision date of product information	Legal classification	Other
IFPMA	Yes	Yes	Yes	Yes	Yes	Yes			Date of production of ad
EFPIA							Yes	Yes	Selling price and conditions of reimbursement
WHO	Yes	Yes	Yes	Yes	Yes	Yes			Content/strength of active ingredient. Reference to appropriate scientific literature
Australia	Yes	Yes	Yes	Yes	Yes	Yes			Full disclosure information must not be less than 1 mm as measured by the font's letter 'e'
Brazil	Yes	Yes		Yes	Yes	Yes		Yes	
Canada	Yes		Yes	Yes	Yes			Yes	Prescribing information must not be less than 6 or 7 point. Any special storage information. Availability. Where full prescribing information can be found. Symptoms and treatment of overdose
The Czech Republic	Yes	Yes	Yes	Yes	Yes	Yes			Type size not less than 2 mm. Registration number and storage conditions
France	Yes	Yes	Yes		Yes	Yes	Yes	Yes	
Germany	Yes	Yes	Yes		Yes	Yes	Yes	Yes	
Greece	Yes	Yes	Yes		Yes	Yes		Yes	Marketing authorisation number and details. Reimbursement status
India	Yes	Yes	Yes	Yes	Yes	Yes			Date of production of ad
Ireland	Yes	Yes	Yes	Yes		Yes		Yes	Marketing authorisation number and details. A statement that additional information is available on request
Italy	No specific guidance found								
Japan	No specific guidance found								
Mexico	No specific guidance found								
Norway	No specific guidance found								
The Netherlands	Yes	Yes	Yes	Yes	Major indication	Yes in order of importance			If relevant, the pharmacotherapeutic group

Spain	Yes			Yes			Yes		All essential information compatible with the SPC. Price and reimbursement information
Sweden	Yes	Yes		Yes	Yes	Yes			
Switzerland	Yes	Yes	Yes		Yes			Yes	
Turkey	Yes	Yes	Yes	Yes	At least one authorised indication	Yes	Yes, licence date and number	Yes	Quantity of active ingredients. A notice to contact the company for detailed information. Price. Date of preparation of ad. Follow-up code number
The UK	Yes	Yes – a list	Yes	Yes	At least one authorised indication	Yes	Yes	Yes	Cost Typeface of not less than 2 mm

9.3 Basic principles for printed materials

9.3.1 IFPMA[6]

Clause 4

Promotional information should be clear, legible, accurate, balanced, fair, objective and sufficiently complete to enable the recipient to form his or her own opinion of the therapeutic value of the pharmaceutical product concerned.

Promotional information should be based on an up-to-date evaluation of all relevant evidence and reflect that evidence clearly. It should not mislead by distortion, exaggeration, undue emphasis, omission, or in any other way. Every effort should be made to avoid ambiguity.

Absolute or all-embracing claims should be used with caution and only with adequate qualification and substantiation.

Descriptions such as 'safe' and 'no side effects' should generally be avoided and should always be adequately qualified.

9.3.2 EFPIA[7]

Article 3

A medicinal product must not be advertised before the marketing authorisation allowing its sale or supply is granted.

All parts of the advertising must be consistent with the particulars listed in the SPC and be restricted to approved indications. Promotional material must:

- be of a nature that recognises the professional standing of the recipient and not be likely to cause offence
- not be designed to disguise its real nature.

Information about medicinal products must:

- be accurate, balanced, fair, objective and sufficiently complete to enable the recipient to form his or her own opinion of the therapeutic value of the medicinal product concerned
- be based on an up-to-date evaluation of scientific evidence and reflect that evidence clearly
- not mislead by distortion, undue emphasis or omission, or in any other way.

9.3.3 WHO[8]

Clauses 6 and10

Active promotion within a country should take place only with respect to drugs legally available in the country. Promotion should be in keeping with national health policies and in compliance with national regulations, as well as with voluntary standards where they exist.

All promotion making claims concerning medicinal drugs should have the following features:

- It must be reliable, accurate, truthful, informative, balanced, up to date, capable of substantiation and in good taste.
- Comparison of products should be factual, fair and capable of substantiation.
- The wording and illustrations in advertisements to physicians and related health professionals should be fully consistent with the approved scientific data sheet for the drug concerned or other source of information with similar content.
- The text should be fully legible.

They should not contain:

- misleading or unverifiable statements or omissions likely to induce medically unjustifiable drug use or give rise to undue risks
- the word 'safe' should be used only if properly qualified.

Promotional material should not be designed so as to disguise its real nature.

TABLE 9.2 Summary by country of information relating to 'reminder advertisements' where product information (PI) may be omitted

Country	1. Brand name	2. Trademark	3. rINN/generic name or composition	4. Approved therapeutic use/indication	5. Side effects, contraindications, precautions or interactions	6. Company name/address	Comment
IFPMA	Permitted			Permitted (simple statement only)			
EFPIA	Permitted	Permitted	Permitted				1, 2 or 3 permitted
WHO	Required		A list of ingredients and rINN/generic name required			Required	1, 3 and 6 required
Australia	Required		Required	Permitted, up to five words describing therapeutic class		Required	A statement required that further information is available on request. May contain graphics, website address. Available dose forms
Brazil	No information found about reminder advertising						
Canada	Required		rINN/generic name required List of ingredients allowed	Permitted	'Important' contraindications must be mentioned and special restrictions in use and distribution	Required	Not allowed until 2 years after launch Only allowed when no new adverse drug reactions reported over previous 2 years Must state where full PI is available from Must not contain graphics or text
The Czech Republic	Only the brand name is permitted						Not allowed until 12 months after the first advertisement for a new product
France	Promotional aids without P1 are not allowed in France, therefore reminder ads are not allowed						
Germany	Permitted	Permitted	Permitted	No	No	Name only	See code for exhaustive list of forbidden content of reminder advertisements
Greece	Permitted		No	No	No	Permitted	
India	Permitted			Permitted (simple statement only)			
Ireland	Required			Permitted (but no claims of merit, etc.)		Required	Must state 'full PI is available on request' Must include product authorisation number
Italy	Permitted		Permitted			Permitted	

(continued)

TABLE 9.2 Continued

Country	1. Brand name	2. Trademark	3. rINN/generic name or composition	4. Approved therapeutic use/ indication	5. Side effects, contraindications, precautions or interactions	6. Company name/address	Comment
Japan	No information found about reminder advertising						
Mexico	No information found about reminder advertising						
The Netherlands	Name of pharmacothera-peutic group only		List of ingredients allowed			Permitted	Practical information to identify product but no claims, etc.
Norway	No information found about reminder advertising						
Spain	Required	Permitted	Required	No	No	Name and logo permitted	Not allowed until 2 years after launch
Sweden	No information found about reminder advertising						
Switzerland	Required		Required			Required	
Turkey	Required		Required			Required	Must state where full PI is available
The UK	Permitted	An indication that the name of the product is a trademark				Name of company	A promotional aid may bear the names of more than one medicine
The USA	No information found about reminder advertising.						

rINN, recommended international non-proprietary name.

9.3.4 AUSTRALIA[29]

Clause 1

Promotional material must be clearly distinguishable as such. Advertisements in a journal should not be designed to resemble editorial matter and should be clearly identified as an advertisement.

9.3.5 BRAZIL[30]

Chapters 4–8

It is forbidden to do the following:

- To advertise medicines not registered by the National Agency of Sanitary Surveillance in the cases demanded by law.
- To make comparisons, in a direct and/or insinuating manner, that are not based on information proven through clinical studies published in indexed publications.
- To advertise the same medicine as if new, after a 2-year elapse of the date of the start of its commercialisation, except for new presentations or new therapeutic indications registered at the National Agency of Sanitary Surveillance.
- To provoke fear or anguish, and/or to suggest that a person's health will, or can, be affected by not using the medicine.
- To discriminate by nationality, sex, race, religion or other.
- To publish messages such as: 'Approved', 'Recommended by the specialist', 'Demonstrated in clinical tests' or 'Publicity approved by the Sanitary Surveillance', or publicity approved by the Health Ministry, or by the state, municipal or federal district, except in the cases specifically determined by the National Agency of Sanitary Surveillance.
- To suggest decrease in risk, to any degree, except for the cases where such a decrease is explicitly stated on the indications or properties approved in the registration action at the National Agency of Sanitary Surveillance and, even in those cases, just in publications directed at health professionals.
- To include verbal and non-verbal messages that disguise the actual indications of the medicines registered at the National Agency of Sanitary Surveillance.
- To ascribe healing properties to the medicine when it is licensed for symptomatic treatment and/or the control of chronic diseases.
- To suggest absence of side or adverse effects or to use such expressions as 'innocuous', 'safe' or 'natural product', except in cases registered as such at the National Agency of Sanitary Surveillance.

9.3.6 CANADA[31]

Clause 1

All product information provided to healthcare professionals must be accurate and well balanced.

9.3.7 THE CZECH REPUBLIC[32]

Clause 1

It is the responsibility of members, their employees and their medical/technical advisers to ensure that medical content included in all promotional materials is correct, fully supported by the valid version of the Czech summary of product information (PI), literature or 'data on file', where the last do not conflict with the first:

- Information, medical claims and graphic representations about products must be current, accurate and balanced, must not mislead directly, by implication or by omission, and must not be able to induce deceptive imagination of an addressee.

- Information, claims and graphics must be capable of substantiation. Such substantiation must be provided within 10 working days at the request of health professionals or a pharmaceutical company.
- Quotations from medical literature or from personal communications must accurately reflect the meaning of the author and the significance of the study.

9.3.8 FRANCE[47]

Section III, Clause 1

Information made available to physicians is outlined in article R.5047–3 and particularly includes the SPC:

- basic information about medicines (name, active ingredients, legal classification, approved indications and contact details)
- information about the use of the medicine (therapeutic use, dose, side effects, precautions, contraindications, drug interactions, etc.)
- promotional items comply with a marketing authorisation and the latest recommendations from competent authorities and must show the date on which the information was issued or updated
- information about the use of a product, and particularly side effects, precautions and contraindications, is clearly referred to so that the relationship with the indication and the expected benefits are clearly shown
- the use of audio, video or interactive aids must be accompanied by a document given to physicians.

9.3.9 GERMANY[34]

Sections 7, 8 and 9

Medicinal products subject to a marketing authorisation must not be promoted before such marketing authorisation is granted. Any promotion going beyond the indications or pharmaceutical forms approved in the marketing authorisation is inadmissible.

Promotion must not be disguised. Advertisements must be designed in such a manner as to be immediately and clearly identifiable as advertising by the readers and not be confused with editorial coverage.

In the case of any publications made by third parties about medicinal products and their use, which are either wholly or partially sponsored by a company, particular care must be taken to ensure that such publications clearly indicate that they have been sponsored by that company.

Misleading advertising is unlawful:

- if certain therapeutic effects are attributed to pharmaceuticals unable to produce such effects
- if the impression is wrongfully created that success is guaranteed
- when improper or misleading information is provided about the composition or other properties of pharmaceuticals.

9.3.10 GREECE[35]

Clauses 9, 10 and12

It is prohibited to promote any medicinal product for which a marketing authorisation has not been granted or to promote indications that are not covered by the marketing authorisation.

The information with respect to a medicinal product must promote the rational use of the medicinal product, presenting it in an objective way, without exaggeration of its properties.

Promotional material must not be misleading or disguised:

- Exaggerations must be avoided with respect to the shape, size and cost of the promotional material.

- The promotional material must not include references to the National Organisation for Medicines (EOF), the European Medicines and Evaluation Agency (EMEA) and the committees operating under the responsibility thereof, or under the responsibility of the Ministry of Health, unless this is required by the competent authorities.
- Promotional material must be sent or distributed only to health professionals who need them or whom they concern, and pharmaceutical companies must regulate the frequency and volume of distribution.

9.3.11 INDIA[16]

Clause 4

Promotional information should be clear, legible, accurate, balanced, fair, objective and sufficiently complete to enable the recipient to form his or her own opinion of the therapeutic value of the pharmaceutical product concerned.

Promotional information should be based on an up-to-date evaluation of all relevant evidence and reflect that evidence clearly. It should not mislead by distortion, exaggeration, undue emphasis or omission, or in any other way. Every effort should be made to avoid ambiguity.

Absolute or all-embracing claims should be used with caution and only with adequate qualification and substantiation.

Descriptions such as 'safe' and 'no side effects' should generally be avoided and should always be adequately qualified.

9.3.12 IRELAND

Clauses 2, 3 and 7

Methods of promotion must never be such as to bring discredit upon, or reduce confidence in, the pharmaceutical industry. The promotion of a medicinal product must be consistent with the terms of the product authorisation. The following apply:

- Promotional material must not be disguised, e.g. where a pharmaceutical company pays for, secures or arranges the publication of promotional material in journals it should not resemble editorial matter.
- Promotional material must conform to good taste and be expressed so as to recognise the professional standing of the recipients.
- Postcards or exposed mailings, envelopes or wrappers must not carry matter that might be regarded as advertising to the lay public.
- The names or photographs of health professionals must not be used in a prominent manner or in a way that would contravene the ethical code of the profession.
- Promotional material must not imitate devices, copy slogans or layout used by other companies in a way that is likely to confuse or mislead.
- Brand names of products of other companies must not be used in comparison unless the prior consent of the companies concerned has been obtained.

9.3.13 ITALY[37]

Clause 2

The company is responsible for the information and promotional actions conducted on behalf of its products, even if this is arranged and/or performed by third persons (consultants, agents, agencies, etc.).

The information contents must always be documented. Exaggerated statements are not admissible, and nor may universal or hyperbolic assertions or indemonstrable comparisons with no objective basis be made.

9.3.14 JAPAN[38]

Clause 4

Member companies shall fully realise that brochures, advertisements in medical journals, internet web pages for the medical profession, audiovisual materials such as slides and video tape-recording, and other promotional materials are important media in dissemination of drug information, and they must produce and use those materials in compliance with the Pharmaceutical Affairs Law and relevant self-regulations. The statements contained in these materials must be correct, fair and objective, based on scientific data.

Statements regarding indications, dosage and administration, and any other statements, shall not deviate from the approved items. When scientific data are presented at international scientific meetings based on the attached guidelines, such statements can also refer to unapproved drugs (except for drugs not approved in any country).

9.3.15 MEXICO

No guidance found.

9.3.16 THE NETHERLANDS[39]

Clauses 3–5

Advertising must be in agreement with, and in the spirit of, the rules of conduct and comply with the following:

- Each written advertisement must, before distribution, be tested against the regulations of this code by the scientific department.
- No harm must be done to the reputation of the pharmaceutical industry or its products or to the reputation of practitioners.
- The advertising must not conflict with the officially approved SPC for the medicinal product, as prescribed in or by virtue of the Act.
- The advertising must be performed in such a way that the rational use of the medicinal product is encouraged from a pharmacotherapeutic perspective, so that the audience is not misled in any way.
- The advertising must be in compliance with the Act and meet the prevailing standards of good taste and conducts, showing respect for both the person at whom the advertising is aimed and colleagues in the sector.

9.3.17 NORWAY

No guidance found.

9.3.18 SPAIN[41]

Clauses 1, 3 and 4

A medicinal product cannot be promoted before the marketing authorisation allowing its sale or supply has been granted. This prohibition also covers medicines, authorised in another country, that have not obtained marketing authorisation in Spain. This regulation does not, however, imply a limitation to the right of the scientific community to be fully informed about medical and scientific progress, nor is it intended to restrict complete and adequate exchange of scientific information related to medicines or drug substances, including appropriate and objective dissemination of research findings in the scientific communication media and scientific congresses.

All parts of the advertising of a medicinal product must be consistent with the information contained in the applicable SPC and the approved indications. Any promotional activity or material should respect the special nature of the medicinal product and the professional standing of the target audience, and must not be likely to cause any offence or decrease the confidence in the pharmaceutical industry.

Promotional material should not imitate the products, slogans, presentation or general layout adopted by other companies in a way that is likely to mislead or confuse.

Postcards, other exposed mailings, envelopes or wrappers should not carry anything that could be regarded as advertising to the general public.

All material relating to medicines and their uses that is sponsored by a pharmaceutical company must clearly state that the company has sponsored it.

9.3.19 SWEDEN[42]

Articles 1 and 3

Drug information shall contain meaningful and balanced particulars dealing adequately with the favourable and unfavourable properties of the drugs.

This fundamental principle is further defined in the following rules of conduct and may serve as a guide in the interpretation of these rules. Information is permitted for medicinal products with marketing approval in Sweden. The information may not contain indications or dosages other than those approved by the Medical Products Agency, unless otherwise specified by this Agency. Drug information shall conform to professional standards of ethics and good taste. Offensive presentations are not permitted.

9.3.20 SWITZERLAND[43]

Clauses 131 and 132

Advertising to healthcare professionals for a specific medicinal product can be started only after it has received marketing authorisation from Swissmedic. The statements made when advertising to healthcare professionals must concur with the currently valid version of the approved professional information. Printed advertising (advertisements, pamphlets, brochures, etc.) to healthcare professionals must be easily legible in respect of font size and layout.

Advertising to healthcare professionals may not veil or obscure the actual intention. In professional media, advertisements are to be clearly distinguishable from the contributions for which the editors of the professional medium are responsible. The same applies to information in the edited part (PR texts, reports for the public and such like) that is triggered either directly or indirectly (e.g. via advertisements in the same medium).

9.3.21 TURKEY[44]

Clause 3

Promotion of a medicine must be in accordance with the terms of its marketing authorisation and consistent with the particulars in the SPC:

- Promotion must be informative, consistent with the scientific facts, reliable, fair, objective and clear.
- The promotion of a product should not be misleading by distortion, exaggeration, undue emphasis, omission or usage of unproven claims, or in any other way.
- Claims should not be stronger than scientific evidence warrants.
- Every effort should be made to avoid ambiguity.

9.3.22 THE UNITED KINGDOM[45]

Clause 3

- A medicine must not be promoted before the marketing authorisation that permits its sale or supply has been granted.

- The promotion of a medicine must be in accordance with the terms of its marketing authorisation and must not be inconsistent with the particulars listed in its SPC.
- Information, claims and comparisons must be accurate, balanced, fair, objective and unambiguous, and must be based on an up-to-date evaluation of all the evidence and reflect that evidence clearly. They must not mislead either directly or by implication, or by distortion, exaggeration or undue emphasis.
- Material must be sufficiently complete to enable the recipients to form their own opinion of the therapeutic value of the medicine.

9.3.23 THE UNITED STATES OF AMERICA

No guidance found.

9.4 Printed materials: contents and format

9.4.1 IFPMA[6]

Clauses 5 and 6

Required content All printed promotional materials other than reminder advertisements must be legible and include:

- the name of the product (normally the brand name)
- the active ingredients, using approved names where they exist
- the name and address of the pharmaceutical company or its agent responsible for marketing the product
- the date of production of the advertisement
- the abbreviated prescribing information.

Abbreviated prescribing information This should include:

- approved indication(s)
- dose
- method of use
- succinct statement of contraindications, precautions and side effects.

Reminder advertisements A 'reminder' advertisement is defined as a short advertisement containing no more than the name of the product and a simple statement of indications to designate the therapeutic category of the product. For 'reminder' advertisements, 'abbreviated prescribing information' may be omitted.

9.4.2 EFPIA[7]

Article 2

Subject to applicable national laws and regulations, all promotional material must include the following information clearly and legibly:

- essential information consistent with the SPC, specifying the date on which such essential information was generated or last revised
- the supply classification of the product
- when appropriate, the selling price or indicative price of the various presentations and the conditions for reimbursement by social security bodies.

Reminder advertisements Subject to applicable national laws and regulations, where an advertisement is intended only as a reminder, the above requirements need not be complied with, provided that the advertisement includes no more than the name of the medicinal product or its recommended international non-proprietary name (rINN), where this exists, or the trademark.

9.4.3 WHO[8]

Clauses 11 and 12

Some countries require advertisements to contain full PI, as defined by the approved scientific data sheet or similar document, for a given period from the date of first promotion or for the full product life. Advertisements that make a promotional claim should at least contain summary scientific information.

The following list illustrates the type of information that advertisements should usually contain:

- the name(s) of the active ingredient(s) using either the rINN or the approved generic name of the drug
- the brand name
- the content of active ingredient(s) per dosage form or regimen
- the name of other ingredients known to cause problems
- the approved therapeutic uses
- the dosage form or regimen
- side effects and major adverse drug reactions
- precautions, contraindications and warnings
- major interactions
- name and address of manufacturer or distributor
- reference to scientific literature as appropriate.

Reminder advertisements These should include at least:

- the brand name
- the rINN or approved generic name
- the name of each active ingredient
- the name and address of the manufacturer or distributor for the purpose of receiving further information.

9.4.4 AUSTRALIA[29]

Clause 2

Full disclosure PI The size of the type for this information must not be less than 1 mm as measured by the height of the font's letter 'e'.

With the exception of primary advertisements, full disclosure PI must accompany all promotional material for a period of 24 months from the date of marketing approval of a new chemical entity in Australia or longer, at the discretion of the company.

For new chemical entities listed on the Pharmaceutical Benefit Scheme (PBS), the full disclosure PI must accompany all promotional material, with the exception of primary advertisements, for at least 12 months from the initial PBS listing date.

Where a PI document has been approved by the Department of Health and Ageing, that document must be used in full without alteration unless approved by the Department. When used to accompany promotional material, it should appear under the heading 'Approved product information'.

Where a PI document has not been approved by the Department of Health and Ageing, the document must comply with the format described in the *Australian Guidelines for the Registration of*

Drugs.[52] When used to accompany promotional material, it should appear under the heading 'Full product information'.

Abridged disclosure PI The size of the type for this information must not be less than 1 mm as measured by the height of the font's lower case letter 'e'.

Abridged disclosure PI may be used after 24 months from the date of marketing approval of a new chemical entity in medical publications, except where there is a change of clinical significance. For new chemical entities listed on the PBS, the full PI must be used for at least 12 months from the initial PBS listing date.

Abridged disclosure PI must accurately reflect the full disclosure PI but may be a paraphrase or précis of the full disclosure PI.

Under the heading 'Abridged product information', the following should appear:

- approved indications for use
- contraindications
- clinically significant warnings
- clinically significant precautions for use
- clinically significant adverse effects and interactions
- available dosage forms
- dosage regimens and routes of administration
- dependence potential of clinical significance
- reference to special groups of patients (including Australian pregnancy categorisation if issued)
- boxed warnings.

Where the full disclosure PI does not include items under these headings, such headings are not required to be included in the document.

Minimum PI for primary advertisement A primary advertisement is the type of advertisement that is mandatory for advertising of either all new chemical entities or new indications for 24 months from the date of first advertising in medical publications, or longer, at the discretion of the company. Primary advertisements must also be used for at least 12 months after a change of clinical significance made to a product's PI. Primary advertisements may contain promotional claims provided that these adhere to the code, e.g. accurate, substantiated.

The size of the type for this information must not be less than 1.5 mm as measured by the height of the font's lower case letter 'e'.

The minimum PI required by a primary advertisement is as follows:

- approved indication(s) for use together with the dosage and method of use
- a succinct statement of the contraindications, precautions and side effects, including any boxed warnings that may appear in the full PI
- a clear and unambiguous statement for prescribers to review the PI before prescribing
- a statement to the effect that full disclosure PI is available on request from the company.

Changes of clinical significance or the addition of a boxed warning Where a change of clinical significance relating to product safety or the addition of a boxed warning is incorporated into the PI, it should be indicated in all representations of the PI for a period of 12 months from the date of change by an asterisk to a footnote in type size of not less than 2 mm: 'Please note change(s) in product information.'

The full text of the changed section should be included in any abridged PI during this period.

Where a company is not actively promoting the product, written advice of the change to PI should be forwarded to the appropriate healthcare professionals.

A secondary advertisement This is designed to reinforce information about a product, and may contain promotional claims. The use of a secondary advertisement in any issue of a publication that does not also contain a primary advertisement is not permitted:

- for 24 months from the first advertising of a new chemical entity
- for 12 months after a change of clinical significance made to the PI.

A secondary advertisement must contain:

- the brand name of the product
- the Australian approved name(s) of the active ingredient(s)
- the name of the supplier and the city, town or locality of the registered office
- a clear and unambiguous statement for prescribers to review
- the PI before prescribing
- a statement to the effect that further information is available on request from the supplier
- all PBS listings, including any restrictions.

A secondary advertisement must also contain one of the following:

- the full disclosure PI
- the abridged disclosure PI
- the minimum PI for primary advertisements
- the location of the PI within the same publication either by reference to the location of the PI or a PI index
- the location of the primary advertisement contained within the same publication by reference to the advertisers' index.

Reminder (short) advertisement A short advertisement is designed to remind prescribers of a product's existence but must not contain promotional claims. The sole use of a short advertisement in any one issue of a publication that does not also contain a primary advertisement is not permitted:

- for 24 months from first advertising a new chemical entity
- for 12 months after a change of clinical significance made to the PI.

A short advertisement must contain:

- the brand name of the product
- the Australian approved name(s) of the active ingredient(s)
- the name of the supplier and the city, town or locality of the registered office
- a statement to the effect that further information is available on request from the supplier
- all PBS listings, including any restrictions.

Short advertisements may contain:

- up to five words describing therapeutic class, but without the use of promotional phrases
- graphics
- a statement of available dosage forms
- a statement referring to the location of PI in a reference manual
- the website address of the company.

No other material is permitted.

9.4.5 BRAZIL[30]

Chapter 13

Any advertisement, publicity or promotion of prescription-only medicines is restricted to directed communication media, exclusively for the health professionals qualified to prescribe or dispense such products; these should include essential information compatible with the information registered at the National Agency of Sanitary Surveillance, such as the following:

- the tradename of the medicine
- the name of the active ingredient
- the generic name and the number of the registration at the National Agency of Sanitary Surveillance
- the indications
- the contraindications
- the cares and warnings (including the more frequent adverse reactions and drug interactions)
- the dosage
- the classification of the medicine in relation to prescription and distribution.

9.4.6 CANADA[31]

Clause 7

Indications for use of a pharmaceutical product must conform to the Health Canada-authorised product monograph or, if there is no monograph, the accepted prescribing information. If neither of the above exists, the Commissioner will make an evaluation after consultation with the appropriate Health Canada official(s) and clinical consultants.

Prescribing information must be presented legibly in a typeface that is not less than 6 or 7 point, and provide good contrast.

Prescribing information (when required) should form an integral part of the presentation or be attached to it.

Full disclosure prescribing information Full disclosure advertising/promotion systems (APSs) are designed to provide health professionals with sufficient background information on new pharmaceutical products to permit them to make a comprehensive assessment of risk/benefit, selection of patients and optimal therapeutic use. Advertisements for products that are new to the Canadian market must be accompanied by full disclosure prescribing information for a minimum of 2 years. Full disclosure prescribing information consists of a verbatim copy or equivalent of the prescribing information contained in the product monograph or Health Canada-accepted prescribing information, under the following headings:

- identification and classification of the product
- action and/or clinical pharmacology
- indications and clinical use
- contraindications
- warnings, precautions and adverse reactions
- symptoms and treatment of overdose
- dosage and administration
- special storage information
- availability
- a statement that the product monograph or full prescribing information is available from a stated Canadian address
- full name and address and website of manufacturer and/or Canadian distributor.

Abbreviated (condensed disclosure) prescribing information When a product has been available on the Canadian market for 2 years and if there have been no reports of previously unsuspected adverse effects of sufficient significance to warrant a warning letter from Health Canada or the manufacturer, the advertising can be accompanied by abbreviated (condensed disclosure) prescribing information.

This abbreviated form can be used because it is assumed that, after 2 years of clinical use, health professionals are familiar with the product, its indications and any significant problems associated with its therapeutic applications. Abbreviated prescribing information for second-entry products (generic alternative products) may be used from the date of introduction to the Canadian market, provided that the original product is eligible for this abbreviated information. Also, if more detailed information is required, it is readily available in the product monograph that is available from the sponsor and the *Compendium of Pharmaceutical and Specialties*.[53]

Abbreviated prescribing information must include the following:

- identification and classification of the product
- indications and clinical use
- contraindications
- warnings
- precautions
- significant adverse effects
- dosage and administration
- available dosage forms including the drug's federal schedule
- a statement that the product monograph or full prescribing information is available on request
- full name and address of the Canadian manufacturer or distributor.

Reminder advertising and promotion Reminder advertisements for established products keep the identity and therapeutic purposes of a pharmaceutical product before the health professions. Reminder APS prescribing information for pharmaceutical products may replace full disclosure advertisements only under the following conditions:

- A minimum period of at least 2 years has elapsed since the product was introduced to the Canadian market.
- When, over the past 2 years, there have been no reports of new adverse reactions of sufficient gravity to warrant a warning letter from Health Canada or the manufacturer.

Reminder advertising cannot contain graphics or text; it must NOT contain therapeutic or other claims of product merit, status or issues.

Reminder prescribing information MUST include the following:

- the brand and non-proprietary (generic) or chemical name(s) of the product, in juxtaposition
- the therapeutic or pharmacological classification of the product, or both
- a statement that the product monograph or full prescribing information is available on request from a stated Canadian address
- the full name and address of the manufacturer and/or Canadian distributor
- when required, a statement about special restrictions in usage and distribution
- any special labelling contraindications, warnings and precautions required by Health Canada, or specific precautions, warnings or contraindications that have been found to be important.

Reminder prescribing information at the discretion of the advertiser, may include the following:

- therapeutic indications that are supported in the most recent Health Canada-accepted product monograph or prescribing information

- a list of available dosage forms and strengths
- a quantitative list of active medicinal ingredients in each.

9.4.7 THE CZECH REPUBLIC[32]

Clauses 2 and 3

Journal advertising must comply with the following:

- The information required shall appear in each publication in a type size font of not less than 2 mm, and should appear on a background sufficiently contrasting for legibility.
- The prescribing information should be placed adjacent to the body of the advertisement. If this is not possible the advertisement must carry a statement in type size not less than 2 mm of where this can be found. This information must not be loose-leaf inserts.
- Care should be taken to ensure that, where an advertisement consists of a double sided or multiple page copy, the information contained on each individual page is not false or misleading when read in isolation.
- All promotional materials, including journal advertisements, must be accompanied by either full or abridged PI.
- Wherever required, PI must appear in a type size of small fonts not less than 2 mm (for format A4) on a background of sufficient contrast for legibility. For smaller format of promotional material, it is possible to decrease the size of fonts provided that they can be read easily and that the ethical committee will judge readability.
- Major headings should be easily identifiable. The date on which the last version of PI was approved by the State Institute for Drug Control (SÚKL) or for centrally registered products by the European Medicines Evaluation Agency (EMEA) must be included.
- PI must not be overprinted or interspersed with promotional phrases or graphics and must clearly identify any recent change of clinical significance.

Abbreviated (abridged) PI Abridged product information must accurately reflect the full PI and include the following:

- brand name of the product
- the rINN of the active ingredient
- approved indications for use
- contraindications
- clinically significant warnings
- clinically significant precautions for use
- clinically significant adverse events and interactions
- available dosage forms
- dosage regimens and routes of administration
- dependence potential of clinical significance
- reference to special groups of patients
- name and address of the registration holder
- registration number
- storage conditions.

Where the full PI does not include items under the aforementioned headings, such headings are not required to be included in the document.

Changes of clinical significance Where a change of clinical significance relating to product safety is incorporated into the PI, it should be indicated in all representations of the PI for a period of 12 months from the date of change by an asterisk to a footnote in type size of small fonts not less than 2 mm: 'Please note change in product information'.

The full text of the changed section should be included in any abridged PI during this period.

Reminder advertising and promotion A reminder can contain only the brand name of the product. It is designed to remind a prescriber of a product's existence, and must not contain any promotional claims. The sole use of a reminder within any one issue of a publication is not permitted before 12 months from first advertising of a new chemical entity

Reminder gimmicks must be reasonably related to the recipient's work as a healthcare professional and can be of maximum value CZK200 each.

Journal Advertising Journal Advertising must comply with the following:

The information required shall appear in each publication in a type size font of not less than 2 mm, and should appear on a background sufficiently contrasting for legibility.

The Prescribing Information should be placed adjacent to the body of the advertisement. If this is not possible the advertisement must carry a statement in type size not less than 2 mm to state where this can be found. This information must not be loose-leaf inserts.

Care should be taken to ensure that where an advertisement consists of a double sided or multiple page copy, the information contained on each individual page is not false or misleading when read in isolation.

9.4.8 FRANCE[33]

The head pharmacist is responsible for the content of the messages conveyed and of the scientific and economic quality of the paper and audiovisual aids used for medical representative visits and for compliance with the Charter. He or she signs and dates the documents under the company's name and his or her own name.

Obligatory wording When advertising documents refer to a medicinal product (commercial name, rINN, a slogan describing the product, etc.), the complete indication listed in the SPC for the medicinal product must be shown.

9.4.9 GERMANY[34]

Clause 10

Required content All promotional material relating to medicinal products must include the following information clearly and legibly:

- the name or the company name and domicile of the pharmaceutical manufacturer
- the name of the medicinal product
- the composition of the medicinal product
- the therapeutic indication
- the contraindications
- the side effects
- warnings and the extent required for the labelling of receptacles and outer packages
- the indication *verschreibungspflichtig* (prescription only)
- the date on which the information was generated or last revised.

For medicinal products that contain only one active ingredient, the name of the product should be followed by the name of the active ingredient. These names must be consistent with the package leaflet. The latter does not refer to reminder advertisements.

Reminder advertisement An advertisement is classed as a reminder if it exclusively refers to the name of the medicinal product or, in addition, to the name, company name, pharmaceutical manufacturer's trademark or active substance.

The medical sales representative must, when promoting individual medicinal products to healthcare professionals, supply a summary of the relevant product characteristics.

Forbidden content Advertisements may not contain any of the following:

- expertise, references or expert publications
- statements that the pharmaceutical is recommended, tested or used by physicians, dentists, veterinarians or other medical experts
- description of medical histories
- pictures of individuals in occupational clothing or who are performing the tasks of members of healthcare professions or occupations, or pharmaceutical business
- pictorial representation of changes in human anatomy or its parts caused by diseases, ailments or bodily injuries
- the effect of a pharmaceutical by means of comparative representation of the physical state or appearance before and after the application
- the response process to a pharmaceutical in the human body or its parts
- terms in a foreign language or professional terminology unless they have become fully integrated into common German usage
- a message that could provoke or exploit sentiments of anxiety or fear
- promotional speeches involving the offering/accepting of mailing addresses
- publications with an unclear advertising purpose
- publications that provide instructions on how to self-diagnose certain diseases, ailments, injuries or pathological problems in humans and treat them with the pharmaceuticals featured in the advertising measure
- third-party statements
- measures exclusively addressed to children aged under 14 years
- prize competitions, raffles or other procedures with random results
- distribution of free samples or vouchers
- information that the effect of a pharmaceutical is the same or superior to another pharmaceutical/treatment.

9.4.10 GREECE[35]

Articles 4, 5 and 18

Prescribing information on a medicinal product must be provided in a clear and easy-to-read manner in all promotional material, with the exception of abbreviated advertisements of up to one page. Prescribing information must constitute an integral part of the promotional material, must not be separate and should consist of the following:

- the brand name and the non-proprietary name of the medicinal product
- the qualitative and quantitative composition thereof in active ingredient(s)
- the name and domicile of the pharmaceutical company responsible for marketing the medicinal product
- the authorised indications
- the adverse reactions, warnings and counterindications relevant to the indications promoted
- any warnings approved or additionally imposed by the EOF or the authority that granted the marketing authorisation
- the classification of the medicinal product (i.e. for hospital use, under medical prescription only, etc.)
- the number and holder of the marketing authorisation
- information on the reimbursement status of the medicinal product (optional).

Information with respect to the dosage, the method of administration, the adverse reactions, warnings and counterindications, as well as any precaution, which must be included in promotional documents or entries, shall be presented in such a way as to enable the readers to assess the connection with the claims and indications of the product.

Abbreviated advertisements This type of advertisement is exempt from the obligation to include the prescribing information of the promoted medicinal product, provided that it fulfils the requirements of the present article.

Abbreviated advertisements may appear only in professional publications, namely publications that are sent or distributed exclusively to healthcare professionals and to nursing personnel. Scientific journals and publications, printed material of congresses, medical pharmaceutical books, etc. fall under this provision. A non-bound leaflet inserted in such a print is not considered an abbreviated advertisement (e.g. independent leaflets distributed through the medical press).

Abbreviated advertisements must include the following information:

- the name of the medicinal product, which may be the brand or non-proprietary name
- the name and address of the holder of the marketing authorisation
- the qualitative and quantitative composition in active ingredients
- in case additional information or claims are stated, the contraindications, warnings and adverse reactions must necessarily be stated
- any warning issued by the EOF, or the authority that issued the marketing authorisation, must be included in the advertisement
- a declaration that further information is available and shall be provided upon request by the holder of the marketing authorisation, or is included in the SPC, packages leaflet and monograph of the medicinal product.

Reminder advertisements Prescribing information for the medicinal product does not necessarily have to be included, if the item does not include more than the following information with respect to the medicinal product:

- the name of the medicinal product
- an indication that the name is a registered trademark
- the name of the person responsible for marketing.

9.4.11 INDIA[16]

Clauses 5 and 6

All printed promotional materials other than reminder advertisements must be legible and include the following:

- the name of the product (normally the brand name)
- the active ingredients, using approved names where they exist
- the name and address of the pharmaceutical company or its agent responsible for marketing the product
- date of production of the advertisement
- the abbreviated prescribing information.

Abbreviated prescribing information This should include the following:

- approved indication(s)
- dose
- method of use
- succinct statement of contraindications, precautions and side effects.

Reminder advertisements A 'reminder' advertisement is defined as a short advertisement containing no more than the name of the product and a simple statement of indications to designate the therapeutic category of the product. For 'reminder' advertisements, 'abbreviated prescribing information' may be omitted.

9.4.12 IRELAND[36]

Clause 7

All promotional material issued by a product authorisation holder, or with his or her authority, must be consistent with the requirements of this code.

Where the purpose of promotional material is to provide health professionals with sufficient information upon which to reach a decision for prescribing or use, the following minimum information must be given clearly and legibly:

- the number of the relevant product authorisation and the name and address of the holder of the authorisation
- a quantitative list of the active ingredients, using approved or other non-proprietary names, contained in each unit or dose
- recommended dosage, method of use and administration
- information as to whether or not the medicinal product is subject to medical prescription
- side effects, precautions and contraindications of the preparation in the recommended dosage
- a statement that additional information is available on request.

Reminder advertisement Where the purpose of the promotional material is to remind a health professional of the availability and the indication(s) of a medicinal product, the following information must be included:

- the name of the medicinal product
- a statement 'Full prescribing information is available on request', or words to that effect
- the number of the relevant product authorisation, and the name and address of the holder of the authorisation.

The indication(s) for the product may also be included. No statement of claim or other information about the product may be included.

9.4.13 ITALY[37]

Clause 2

The information material prepared by the company on its products and used to provide information to physicians must be based on official documents issued by the Ministry of Health when the drug is registered or successively approved by the Ministry on the basis of the pertinent laws in force.

9.4.14 JAPAN[38]

Clause 4

Statements about indications, dosage and administration, and any other statements shall not deviate from the approved items. When scientific data are presented at international scientific meetings based on the guidelines, such statements can also refer to non-approved drugs.

9.4.15 MEXICO

No guidance found.

9.4.16 THE NETHERLANDS[39]

Clause 8

Every written advertisement aimed at practitioners must comply with the instructions laid down in this code of conduct and must in every case state the following:

- the name of the medicinal product
- the name and address of the marketing authorisation holder
- the qualitative and quantitative composition of the active ingredients
- the pharmacotherapeutic group, if relevant
- the pharmaceutical form
- the major therapeutic indications
- the most important undesirable effects (showing frequency and severity)
- the most important warnings (precautionary measures for use)
- all contraindications.

Warnings and contraindications must be in a place and in a typeface that does justice to the importance of information. If, in the case of written advertising, the information referred to above is of such an extent that the text cannot in all reasonableness be accommodated within a standard-sized document, a cross-reference can be made to the place where this information can be found elsewhere in the relevant medium.

Reminder advertisement The criteria referred to above are not applicable if the written advertising aimed at practitioners is exclusively intended as a reminder of the name of the medicinal product and if it contains no data other than the following:

- the composition of the medicinal product
- the name of the pharmacotherapeutic group
- the name and address of the marketing authorisation holder
- practical information for the identification of the medicinal product to be supplied, without this involving any pharmacotherapeutic claims.

9.4.17 NORWAY

No guidance found.

9.4.18 SPAIN[41]

Clause 2

All printed promotional material should include the following information in a clear and legible form:

- essential information consistent with the data in the SPC, specifying the date on which it was prepared or last revised
- the prescription and dispensing conditions of the medicinal product
- the different presentations of the medicinal product and, when appropriate, the dosage and/or pharmaceutical form
- the selling price, the conditions for reimbursement by the national health system and, when appropriate and feasible, the estimated cost of the treatment.

Reminder advertisement Where the advertising is intended only as a reminder and the medicinal product has been authorised for at least 2 years, the above need not be complied with, provided that the advertising includes no more than the name of the product. In this case, the name of the medicinal product must be included and, if this is a brand name or an invented name and the product contains a single drug substance, it must be accompanied by the Spanish official name or, if unavailable, the rINN. The product logo and the name and logo of the pharmaceutical company may also be included, but no other information.

9.4.19 SWEDEN[42]

Article 17

Written information about a medicinal product that is contained in the Swedish compendium (FASS) must contain at least the following particulars, if the catalogue text or the SPC is not reproduced:

- the name of the medicinal product
- the formulation and, if appropriate, its strength
- the names of its active ingredients, stated by generic name, as well as quantities of such ingredients; the generic name shall be placed close by the name of the medicinal product where this first appears as a headline or an eye catcher
- a balanced statement of product characteristics; this description shall contain required particulars about pharmacological group or other accepted group affiliation, together with indication or area of indications
- the required warnings or limitations applicable to the use of the medicinal product.

9.4.20 SWITZERLAND[43]

Clause 134

Advertisements in professional media Advertisements must contain the following:

- The brand name of the medicinal product or a corresponding unmistakable identifying description, e.g. the description of the active ingredient together with the name of the manufacturing or distributing company.
- The active ingredients with the official abbreviated designation. If a medicinal product contains several active ingredients, then only the therapeutically more significant active ingredients must be cited, with the official abbreviated designation or a Swissmedic-approved designation; the other ingredients may be listed in an informative, summarised form.
- The prescription category authorised by Swissmedic.
- The name and the address of the company that is responsible for the medicinal product in Switzerland (holder of the Swissmedic marketing authorisation); this information must either be stated in the advertisement itself or be clearly seen in the professional medium where the advertisement appears.
- The indication that comprehensive information can be found in the professional information for the medicinal product and, if necessary, listing the medium in which the marketing authorisation holder makes it available to professionals who are entitled to prescribe, dispense or administer the medicinal products in humans, in accordance with the respective specifications of the legislation on therapeutic products.

Informative advertisements Advertisements that contain claims for the product must also include the following in addition to the items listed above:

- an approved indication
- dosage
- category of application and limitations to use
- adverse reactions and interactions.

Reminder advertisements These are advertisements that list solely the indications or the therapeutic category of the medicinal product; they contain no statements concerning the medicinal product's application.

Reminder advertisements must contain the following:

- the brand name of the medicinal product or a corresponding unmistakable identifying description, e.g. the description of the active ingredient
- the name of the manufacturing or distributing company
- the active ingredient(s) with the official abbreviated designation rINN.

Brand name advertising Should an advertisement be made exclusively for the brand name of a medicinal product, only the following are allowed:

- the official name (rINN) of the active ingredients
- the name of the company (holder of the Swissmedic marketing authorisation)
- the logo.

9.4.21 TURKEY[44]

Clauses 3, 4 and 5

Full advertisements A full advertisement is one that includes product claims and must include the prescribing information (also called succinct prescribing information or SPI) in a clear and legible manner. The prescribing information must form part of the promotion material, must not be separate from it and should include the following:

- the brand name of the medicine
- list of active ingredients, using approved rINNs where such exist, or other non-proprietary names; the rINNs or other names must be placed immediately adjacent to the most prominent display of the brand name, in a legible manner
- quantity of each active ingredient in a single unit dose
- at least one authorised indication for use consistent with the updated SPC
- a succinct statement of the information in the SPC relating to dosage and method of use
- the route of administration
- a succinct statement of major side effects and precautions
- major interactions
- contraindications, warning and precautions to be observed on administration of the product
- any information required or warning issued by the Ministry of Health, other authorised bodies or licensing authorities that must be included in advertisements
- name and address of the manufacturer, importer or distributor, as the case may be
- licence date and number
- a notice stating 'Please contact the company for detailed information'
- legal classification (prescription only or without prescription, narcotics or other controlled drugs, red and green prescription categories)
- public price of the sales packages (including VAT) and date of approval
- follow-up code (number) and printing date (or intended usage date) of the material
- the date of preparation and last update of the SPC or product leaflet.

The information specified above in relation to dosage, method of use, side effects, precautions and contraindications, and any warning that must be included in the advertisements, must be placed in such a position in the advertisement that its relationship to the claims and indications for the product can be readily seen by the reader.

In addition, on promotional materials the non-proprietary name of the medicine or a list of the active ingredients using approved names, where such exist, must appear immediately adjacent to the most prominent display of the brand name in a legible size.

In the case of a journal advertisement where the prescribing information does not appear on the same spread, a reference to where it can be found must appear on the outer edge of the page in a legible manner.

Promotional material other than advertisements appearing in professional publications must include the date on which the promotional material was drawn up or the last revision made.

Abbreviated advertisement or reminder advertisement This is defined as a short advertisement in a medical journal; the following should be included to comply with the regulation and code:

- the brand name of the medicine
- the rINN of the active substances
- the name and address of the manufacturer, importer or registration holder
- a note informing the prescriber that full information is available on request from the stated address.

Legibility The prescribing information is essential information that must be provided in promotional material and so it must be given in a clear and legible manner that assists readability. Legibility is not simply a question of type size. The following recommendations will help to achieve clarity:

- The type size should be such that a lower case 'c' is no less than 1 mm in height.
- Sufficient space should be allowed between lines to facilitate easy reading.
- A clear style of typesetting should be used.
- There should be adequate contrast between the colour of the text and the background.
- Dark print on a light background is preferable.
- Starting each section on a new line helps legibility.

When there are two or more commonly used rINNs, it is recommended to use the rINN in more common usage in continental Europe. It is considered a breach of the code when the open or closed chemical name or formula is given and the rINN omitted, whenever the rINN exists. Using a pale colour on a pale background (and vice versa), which results in difficulty of reading the rINN, is also considered a breach of the code.

Teaser advertisements Teaser campaigns can start before the grant of the marketing authorisation, so long as it does not contain the tradename or circumvent the spirit and letter of the code.

9.4.22 THE UNITED KINGDOM[45]

Clauses 4, 5, 9 and 18

The prescribing information must be provided in a clear and legible manner in all promotional material for a medicine, except for abbreviated advertisements and promotional aids that meet the requirements of the code.

The prescribing information must be positioned for ease of reference and must not be presented in a manner such that the reader has to turn the material round in order to read it, e.g. by providing it diagonally or around the page borders and it must form part of the promotional material and must not be separate from it.

The prescribing information consists of the following:

- the name of the medicine (which may be either a brand name or a non-proprietary name)
- a quantitative list of the active ingredients, using approved names where such exist, or other non-proprietary names; alternatively, the non-proprietary name of the product if it is the subject of an accepted monograph
- at least one authorised indication for use consistent with the SPC
- a succinct statement of the information in the SPC relating to the dosage and method of use relevant to the indications quoted in the advertisement and, where not otherwise obvious, the route of administration

- a succinct statement of common side effects likely to be encountered in clinical practice, serious side effects and precautions and contraindications relevant to the indications in the advertisement, giving, in an abbreviated form, the substance of the relevant information in the SPC, together with a statement that prescribers should consult the SPC in relation to other side effects
- any warning issued by the Medicines Commission, the Commission on Human Medicines, the Committee on Safety of Medicines (COSM) or the licensing authority that must be included in advertisements
- the cost (excluding VAT) of either a specified package of the medicine to which the advertisement relates, or a specified quantity or recommended daily dose, calculated by reference to any specified package of the product, except in the case of advertisements in journals printed in the UK that have more than 15 per cent of their circulation outside the UK, and audiovisual advertisements and prescribing information provided in association with them
- the legal classification of the product
- the number of the relevant marketing authorisation and the name and address of the holder of the authorisation or the name and address of the part of the business responsible for its sale or supply
- the date that the prescribing information was drawn up or last revised.

The information specified above in relation to dosage, method of use, side effects, precautions and contraindications, and any warning that is required to be included in advertisements, must be placed in such a position in the advertisement that the reader can appreciate its relationship to the claims and indications for the product.

In addition, the non-proprietary name of the medicine, or a list of the active ingredients using approved names where such exist, must appear immediately adjacent to the most prominent display of the brand name in bold type of a size such that a lower case ‘x’ is no less than 2 mm in height or in type of such a size that the non-proprietary name or list of active ingredients occupies a total area no less than that taken up by the brand name.

Abbreviated advertisement Advertisements are exempt from the requirement to include prescribing information provided that they comply with the following requirements:

- Abbreviated advertisements may appear only in professional publications, i.e. publications sent or delivered wholly or mainly to members of the health professions and/or appropriate administrative staff. A loose insert in such a publication cannot be an abbreviated advertisement.
- Abbreviated advertisements must be no larger than 420 cm^2 in size.
- Abbreviated advertisements must provide the following information in a clear and legible manner:
  - the name of the medicine (which may be either a brand or a non-proprietary name)
  - the non-proprietary name of the medicine or a list of the active ingredients using approved names where such exist
  - at least one indication for use consistent with the SPC
  - a statement that prescribers are recommended to consult the SPC before prescribing, particularly in relation to side effects, precautions and contraindications
  - the legal classification of the product
  - any warning issued by the Medicines Commission, the Commission on Human Medicines, the COSM or the licensing authority that must be included in advertisements
  - the name and address of the holder of the marketing authorisation or the name and address of the part of the business responsible for its sale or supply
  - a statement that further information is available on request to the holder of the marketing authorisation or that it may be found in the SPC.

- In addition, the non-proprietary name of the medicine, or a list of the active ingredients using approved names where such exist, must appear immediately adjacent to the most prominent display of the brand name in bold type of a size such that a lower case 'x' is no less than 2 mm in height or in type of such a size that the non-proprietary name or list of active ingredients occupies a total area no less than that taken up by the brand name.
- In addition, abbreviated advertisements must include prominent information about adverse event-reporting mechanisms.
- Abbreviated advertisements may, in addition, contain a concise statement consistent with the SPC, giving the reason why the medicine is recommended for the indication(s) given.

Reminder advertisements The prescribing information for a medicine does not have to be included on a promotional aid (reminder item) if it includes no more than the following about a medicine:

- the brand or non-proprietary name of the medicine
- an indication that the name of the medicine is a trademark
- the name of the company responsible for marketing the product.

A promotional aid (reminder item/advertisement) may bear the names of more than one medicine.
Teaser advertisements Teaser advertising is where promotional material is intended to elicit an interest in something that will be happening soon, e.g. a new product or indication, without actually providing any information about it. This type of advertising and promotion is not acceptable in the UK.

9.4.23 THE UNITED STATES OF AMERICA

No guidance found.

9.5 Provision of reprints

9.5.1 IFPMA

No guidance found.

9.5.2 EFPIA

No guidance found.

9.5.3 WHO

No guidance found.

9.5.4 AUSTRALIA[29]

Clause 3

The general interpretation and conclusions of any reprints of journal articles, proceedings of symposia or summaries of literature used in promotion must be consistent with the PI for both the sponsor's products and any competitor's products with which a comparison is being made.

Healthcare professionals may request literature on subjects not covered by the PI such as non-approved indications. Although it is not acceptable routinely to disseminate such literature where unsolicited, it is acceptable to provide such information on individual request, provided that the literature or accompanying communication clearly identifies that it refers to a product or indication not approved in Australia. If the product is approved in Australia, the Australian approved PI must accompany it.

Reprints themselves do not need to be accompanied by PI, but it must be included with any accompanying material (e.g. letter) or presentation made that makes promotional claims.

9.5.5 BRAZIL

No guidance found.

9.5.6 CANADA[31]

Clause 5

Reprints of scientific and medical papers may be distributed from trade booths, provided that they are reprinted verbatim and comply with the marketing authorisation.

9.5.7 THE CZECH REPUBLIC

No guidance found.

9.5.8 FRANCE

Medical sales representatives may distribute only reprints that comply with the product licence or the Transparency Opinion. These reprints must have been reviewed, approved and dated by the Pharmacien Responsible and notified to AFSSAPS. In addition to the reprint the sales representative must also provide a copy of the Summary of Product Characteristics and Transparency opinion.

9.5.9 GERMANY

There are no specific national rules on the distribution of reprints.

9.5.10 GREECE[35]

Articles 11 and 18

Reprints from medical and scientific bibliography or personal communications must accurately reflect the meaning of the author. Quotations relating to medicinal products, which are taken from public communications, i.e. radio, TV or medical congresses or symposia, must not be used without the official permission of the speaker.

Care must be taken to reflect the current views of the authors.

It is permitted to offer scientific publications to legal entities directly connected with the provision of healthcare and medical training.

9.5.11 INDIA

No guidance found.

9.5.12 IRELAND[36]

Clauses 3 and 11

All reprints of articles included in mailings must include prescribing information or abbreviated prescribing information as appropriate, and may be supplied to individual health professionals.

Promotional materials can include reasonably brief abstracts of, or quotations from, articles; in such material references to authors' names in a bibliography of published works must be included. Authors' names should not be used in a prominent manner in promotional material.

Quotations from medical literature, or from personal communications received from health professionals, must accurately reflect the meaning of the author and the significance of the study.

Before a product is licensed, scientific papers may be provided at international congresses in accordance with the IPHA code of marketing practice as a means of exchange of medical and scientific information during the development of a preparation.

9.5.13 ITALY

Reprints can only be distributed on an unsolicited basis if they are consistent with the product licence.

9.5.14 JAPAN

No guidance found.

9.5.15 MEXICO

No guidance found.

9.5.16 THE NETHERLANDS

No guidance found.

9.5.17 NORWAY

No guidance found.

9.5.18 SPAIN[41]

Scope of Code vii

Originals, reprints, literal translations of scientific articles and abstracts published in scientific sources of recognised prestige are acceptable, provided that they do not contain printed, stamped or electronically linked trademarks or tradenames of medicines, advertising slogans or other advertising material, whether or not related to this information.

This type of scientific information may be accompanied by publicity of the company, but, regardless of the mass medium used (journals, bulletins, books, etc. or audiovisual materials stored on optical, magnetic, electronic or other media), it must not have any connection with that scientific information, so that its handling, reading, display, listening, etc. will be separate.

Clause 6

Quotations from medical and scientific literature or from personal communications should accurately reflect the opinion of the author.

Quotations relating to medicines taken from public broadcasts, e.g. on radio and TV, and from private events, such as medical conferences or symposia, should not be used without the formal authorisation of the speaker.

9.5.19 SWEDEN

No guidance found.

9.5.20 SWITZERLAND

No guidance found.

9.5.21 TURKEY[44]

Clause 14

Distribution of scientific medical books and medical periodicals is not restricted under the code.

9.5.22 THE UNITED KINGDOM[45]

Clause 11

Unsolicited reprints of articles in journals must not be provided unless the articles have been refereed.

Provision of unsolicited articles about a medicine constitutes promotion and therefore all the requirements of the code must be observed. This means that the reprint must be in accordance with the terms of the marketing authorisation of the product. It should also be certified for use according to the normal processes for promotional material.

When providing a reprint, it should be accompanied by prescribing information, but this need not be an integral part of it.

9.5.23 THE UNITED STATES OF AMERICA[52]

The Washington Legal Foundation[52] (WLF), a non-profit foundation involved in shaping public policy, brought a series of legal challenges to FDA regulations. These have resulted in legal decisions that have defined circumstances under which off-label information may be distributed legally and within FDA regulations.

Unabridged reprints or copies of peer-reviewed scientific publications and unabridged reference publications that contain off-label information about a clinical investigation involving a product, written by a third party, may be distributed in certain circumstances. All reprint materials must be accurate, objective, scientifically rigorous, and balanced with respect to risks and benefits. Reprint materials do not include abstracts, letters to the editor, materials regarding phase 1 trials in healthy people, flagged reference publications containing little or no substantive discussion of the relevant clinical investigation, or publications regarding observations in four or fewer people that do not reflect any systematic attempt to collect data.

Reprints should bear the WLF sticker and this sticker must be permanently affixed to the front of the reprint and state, 'This information concerns a use that has not been approved by the Food and Drug Administration.' If the reprint contains information regarding both approved and unapproved uses, the statement shall be modified to identify the unapproved new use or uses.

Reprints must be accompanied by the product labelling, a bibliography of additional articles (reports of clinical investigations, both supporting and not supporting the new use, that have been previously published in a scientific reference publication or scientific journal) unless the reprint already contains a bibliography, and any additional information required by the FDA.

CHAPTER

10

Internet and Electronic Communication Media

10.1 Internet and other audiovisual material

10.1.1 IFPMA[6]

Clause 6

Electronic materials, including audiovisuals The same requirements that apply to printed materials also apply to electronic promotional materials and websites. Websites must comply with the following:

- the identity of the pharmaceutical company and the intended audience should be readily apparent
- the content should be appropriate for the intended audience
- the presentation (content, links, etc.) should be appropriate and apparent to the intended audience
- country-specific information should comply with local laws and regulations.

10.1.2 EFPIA[7]

Annex B

The following guidelines may need adaptation to meet individual country requirements.

Transparency of website origin, content and purpose Each website shall clearly identify the following:

- the identity and physical and electronic addresses of the sponsor(s) of the website
- the source(s) of all information included on the website, the date of publication of the source(s), and the identity and credentials (including the date credentials where received) of all individual/institutional providers of information included on the website
- the procedure followed in selecting the content included on the website
- the target audience of the website (e.g. healthcare professionals, patients and the general public, or a combination thereof)
- the purpose or objective of the website.

Table 10.1 Summary of requirements relating to internet sites

	Promotional content must be password protected?	Target audience must be readily identified?	Must contain sponsor/company identification?	Must be a warning when user is leaving site via links, etc.?	Specific warning that content applies to country of origin?	Other
Australia	Must be restricted to HCPs – secure system required to prevent access by general public	Yes	Address and identity of the company	Yes, specific in the case of the general public		Only educational content to be accessed by the general public
Brazil	Accessible exclusively to HCPs					
Canada	Appropriate security, e.g. passwords	Yes	Yes, on home page and/or each sponsored page	Yes	Yes, on each page containing PI	Printed copy of the content must be available for initial approval
The Czech Republic	Must be restricted to HCPs					
France	Websites originated by French companies must be restricted to HCPs	The target audience and the type of information must be published	A website must show a company's identity, and must include a postal address		Published information that is intended for those in foreign countries must be clearly described as such	Disease awareness campaigns permissible to the general public; they must not reference a specific product or therapy class Advertising of medicinal products aimed at health professionals is allowed. The advertisement must be submitted to AFSSAPS within 8 days of its publication
Germany	No particular provision – general rules of law and FSA guidance apply					
Greece	Yes, should be restricted to HCPs and appropriate administrative staff	Yes, specific wording required				Electronic promotional material must comply with provisions that apply to printed promotional materials
India	Not necessarily, but content must comply with rules that apply to promotion and advertising generally	The identity of the intended audience should be readily apparent	The identity of the pharmaceutical company should be readily apparent			
Ireland	No specific guidance					
Italy	No specific guidance; the access to websites containing information about POMs must be restricted to HCPs					
Japan	Not necessarily; password protected although content should be restricted to HCPs	Yes, access should be linked to user, confirming that they are in intended audience	Yes			All content is appropriate and links are both appropriate and apparent to intended audience

Mexico	'Normally' restricted to HCPs, although no specific guidance					
The Netherlands	Must be restricted to HCPs		Name and address of person responsible	See specific guidance		Use of company name, indications and brands in an internet address is permitted Information must be kept up to date
Norway	No specific guidance; any information on POMs should not be available to the general public and provided only after confirmation from the user that they are HCPs					
Spain	Specific measures need to be taken to ensure that content is accessible to HCPs only	Yes, specific warnings are required, stating that the content is for HCPs only				All promotional materials must have a primarily technical, scientific or professional content
Sweden	Yes, but not necessary to password protect	Yes, must be clearly labelled				Same rules as advertising in any other Swedish media
Switzerland	Not necessarily, but content must comply with rules that apply to promotion and advertising generally	Yes	Yes			Access must be provided to the last Swissmedic-approved version of the corresponding professional information for the product(s) featured
Turkey	Must be limited to HCPs	Yes, specific messages required for different target groups	Addresses, contact numbers of the website owner and site designer should be shown on the main page	Yes; in addition specific warnings about content of links that the site owner does not control		Websites should have a main page. Promotion should not feature on the main page, but rather address and contact numbers of website owner The last date of actualisation has to be given

(continued)

TABLE 10.1 Continued

	Promotional content must be password protected?	Target audience must be readily identified?	Must contain sponsor/company identification?	Must be a warning when user is leaving site via links, etc.?	Specific warning that content applies to country of origin?	Other
The UK	Generally be limited to HCPs and appropriate administrative staff via password protection	If no access restriction the target audiences must be clearly segregated	Sponsorship must be clearly declared	Yes		The public should not be encouraged to access content not intended for them Requirements are the same as for printed material A hard copy of the content must be certified
The USA	No	Promotion on the internet is being examined as part of an FDA working group and DDMAC is developing an agency-wide policy to address how advertising and promotion of FDA-regulated products will be regulated on the internet				

AFSSAPS, French Agency for the Safety of Health Products; DDMAC, Division of Drug Marketing, Advertising and Communication Agency (the USA); FDA, US Food and Drug Administration Agency; FSA, German code of conduct; HCPs, healthcare professionals; PI, product information; POMs, prescription only medicines.

Content

- Information included in the website shall be regularly updated and shall clearly display, for each page and/or item, as applicable, the most recent date when such information was updated.
- Examples of the information that may be included in a single website or in multiple websites are:
  - general information on the company
  - health education information
  - information intended for healthcare professionals (as defined in the EFPIA code), including any promotion
  - non-promotional information intended for patients and the general public about specific medicinal products marketed by the company.

General information on the company Websites may contain information that would be of interest to investors, the news media and the general public, including financial data, descriptions of research and development programmes, discussion of regulatory developments affecting the company and its products, information for prospective employees, etc. These guidelines or provisions of medicines advertising law do not regulate the content of this information.

Health education information Websites may contain non-promotional health education information about the characteristics of diseases, methods of prevention, and screening and treatments, as well as other information intended to promote public health. They may refer to medicinal products, provided that the discussion is balanced and accurate. Relevant information may be given about alternative treatments, including, where appropriate, surgery, diet, behavioural change and other interventions that do not require use of medicinal products. Websites containing health education information must always advise individuals to consult a healthcare professional for further information.

Information for healthcare professionals Any information on websites directed to healthcare professionals that constitutes promotion (as defined in the EFPIA code) must comply with applicable code(s) (as defined in the EFPIA code) and any other industry codes of practice governing the content and format of advertisement and promotion of medicinal products. Such information must be clearly identified as information for healthcare professionals, but need not be encrypted or otherwise restricted.

Non-promotional information for patients and the general public Subject to any applicable national laws and regulations, websites may include non-promotional information for patients and the general public on products distributed by the company (including information on their indications, side effects, interactions with other medicines, proper use, reports of clinical research, etc.), provided that such information is balanced, accurate and consistent with the approved summary of product characteristics (SPC). For each product that is discussed, the website must contain full, unedited copies of the current SPC and patient leaflet. These documents should be posted in conjunction with other information about the products or be connected with that discussion by a prominent link advising the reader to consult them. In addition, the website may provide a link to the full, unedited copy of any public assessment report issued by the Committee for Medicinal Products for Human Use or a relevant national competent authority. Brand names should be accompanied by recommended international non-proprietary names (rINNs).

The website may include links to other websites containing reliable information on medicinal products, including websites maintained by government authorities, medical research bodies, patient organisations, etc. The website must always advise individuals to consult a healthcare professional for further information.

Email enquiries A website may invite electronic mail communications from healthcare professionals and patients or the general public seeking further information about the company's products or other matters (e.g. feedback with regard to the website). The company may reply to such communications in the same manner as it would reply to enquiries received by post, telephone or other media. In communications with patients or members of the general public, discussion of personal medical matters must be avoided. If personal medical information is revealed, it must be held in confidence. Where appropriate, replies shall recommend that a healthcare professional be consulted for further information.

Links from other websites Links may be established to a company-sponsored website from websites sponsored by other individuals, but companies should not establish links from websites designed for the general public to company-sponsored websites that are designed for healthcare professionals. In the same manner, links may be established to separate websites, including websites sponsored by the company or other individuals. Links should ordinarily be made to the home page of a website or otherwise managed so that the reader is aware of the identity of the website.

Website addresses in packaging Subject to any applicable national laws and regulations, uniform resource locators (URLs) of company-sponsored websites that comply with these guidelines may be included in packaging of medicinal products.

Scientific review Companies should ensure that scientific and medical information prepared by them for inclusion in their websites is reviewed for accuracy and compliance with the applicable code(s). The scientific service established may perform this function or it may be entrusted to other appropriately qualified individuals.

Privacy The website must conform to legislation and applicable codes of conduct governing the privacy, security and confidentiality of personal information.

10.1.3 WHO[8]

No guidance found.

10.1.4 AUSTRALIA[29]

Clause 3

Internet in general Information provided by a pharmaceutical company on the internet must contain the following:

- It must include the address and identity of the company.
- The intended audience should be readily apparent on the site.

- It should be made clear when the reader is leaving the site and being directed to a site that the company has not developed.
- A link to the text of the code of conduct on the Medicines Australia website must not be used to imply endorsement of the website

Information available to the general public Information that can be accessed by members of the general public via the internet must be educational and not promotional. It is permissible to provide a brief non-promotional summary of the company's products that are available in Australia. This information should:

- be in accordance with the product's current approved product information (PI)
- be current, accurate, balanced and contain information about the product's precautions, adverse reactions, warnings, contraindications and interactions
- contain information about current research or clinical data that would assist members of the general public to understand how this product works, its uses and compliance advice
- be a full copy of the product's consumer medicine information (CMI); it must not be amended, abridged or displayed in a promotional manner.

Reference or linkages to reputable information sources providing valuable educational material about a disease area are allowed. However, a clear screen displaying the following statements must appear before the information can be accessed:

- The information that a reader is about to be referred to may not comply with the Australian regulatory environment and refer to the CMI.
- The intent of providing this material is informational and not as advice.
- Any information provided by this source should be discussed with the reader's healthcare professional and does not replace his or her advice.

Information available to healthcare professionals Promotional material must be accessible to healthcare professionals only via a secure system that is designed to prevent access by members of the general public. Companies must take all reasonable steps to ensure that these information sources are appropriate and will enhance the appropriate prescribing, dispensing and usage of medicines in Australia. Any promotional material provided to healthcare professionals via the internet must comply with the requirements for other promotional items.

10.1.5 BRAZIL[30]

Chapter 5

Internet Advertising and promotion of prescription-only medicines (POMs) via the internet are allowed only via sites that are accessible exclusively to professionals duly qualified to prescribe or to administer medicines.

The identity of the supplier and his or her 'geographical address' must be included in the advertising message of advertisements for the promotion of over-the-counter medicines.

10.1.6 CANADA[31]

Clause 6

Internet The same rules and regulations that apply to print-based product claims and advertising apply to electronic on-line activities controlled by pharmaceutical companies.

These electronic media must be submitted to the Pharmaceutical Advertising Advisory Board (PAAB) before presentation to health professionals.

The following guidelines apply to websites and other online activities such as banner ads, email marketing campaigns, patient drug therapy compliance programmes, search engine optimisation techniques, including all activities where the intended or probable audience is Canadian health professionals. The following rules apply:

- Prescribing information should form an integral part of the presentation or be attached to it, when the item is distributed to the health professional.
- The name of the pharmaceutical company sponsor should be stated clearly on the home page of every website or on a sponsored web page.
- Sponsors should not provide the text of a meta-data descriptor that contains direct or implied product claims to a search engine. Keywords and other meta-data tags that refer to competitor products are prohibited.
- Banner or pop-up ads that contain either direct or implied product claims must include risk – benefit fair balance and have a hyperlink to the prescribing information.
- Third-party links to websites where entry is in close proximity to content that contravenes PAAB guidelines are prohibited. A message should appear telling the viewer when they are leaving the sponsor's website.
- Promotion of a website that contains promotional information by non-web-based mechanisms, e.g. sales representatives, direct mail, journal ads, would require prior PAAB clearance review of the website content.
- Appropriate security measures, e.g. password protection, should be used to restrict the target audience as applicable by federal law. A statement such as 'this product information is intended only for residents of Canada' should appear on each web page containing PI.
- The investor information section of a corporate website should be clearly identified, e.g. 'Information intended for investors'. The content should be non-promotional in nature and be consistent with Health Canada guidelines on advertising. Promotional content would require PAAB pre-clearance review.
- Concepts relating to sponsored chat rooms, postings, bulletin boards and other forms of interactive online communication programs must be submitted for PAAB pre-clearance review.
- Sponsors are expected to ensure compliance with federal and provincial laws with regard to collection and utilisation of personal information.
- Websites must conform to current industry standards for maintaining security, accuracy and privacy of the information both on the site and that it has collected. For physician, patient or consumer requests for information through a sponsored programme, the sponsor should provide an appropriate mechanism (e.g. registration for password protection) to determine the regulatory category of the person requesting the information online.
- For pre-clearance review of online materials, the sponsor should submit a printed copy of the entire material and provide the proposed material online where possible or when the PAAB reviewer believes that it is necessary to complete a review.
- On previously approved existing websites, sponsors should submit, to the PAAB for pre-clearance review, all changes to content that fall under the PAAB Code of Advertising Acceptance before adding that information to the site.

10.1.7 THE CZECH REPUBLIC[32]

Clause 3

Internet Czech law prohibits the promotion of prescription products to the general public and therefore access to promotional areas of company intranet sites must be restricted to healthcare professionals.

Electronic promotional material Electronic promotional material designed by companies to promote products directly to healthcare professionals includes:

- software programs used by medical representatives during interchanges with healthcare professionals
- external computer-generated programs that promote products, e.g. prescribing and dispensing software.

All computer-based promotional material must comply with all relevant provisions of this code in the same way as printed materials (see Chapter 6). PI must be readily accessible via the computer-based material or offered to an audience in a group situation on completion of the presentation. Where the PI is included in interactive data system, instructions for accessing it must be clearly displayed.

Audiovisual promotional material This must be accompanied by a document that contains the following information:

- the brand name of the medicinal product
- the INN of the active ingredient(s)
- the name of the registration holder and its mailing address in Czech Republic
- full or abridged Product Information
- other data required by legal provisions.

Where an audiovisual item is demonstrated, the Product Information document must be given to the individual reviewing the promotional material, or offered to the audience in a group situation on completion of the presentation. The INN should appear adjacent to the most prominent presentation of the trade name.

10.1.8 FRANCE[33]

French law prohibits the advertising of POMs to the general public but does permit (pursuant to Article L5122–1 of the French Public Health Code) disease awareness campaigns. Disease awareness campaigns must not refer directly or indirectly to a specific product or therapeutic class.

Although French law is, in principle, applicable to information available to the French public, it has not been possible for the AFSSAPS or LEEM to regulate websites that originate in foreign countries. However, in the case of websites that French pharmaceutical companies originate access to areas that promote POMs must be restricted to healthcare professionals.

There is a Charter in France for internet communications, which gives the following recommendations.

General recommendations A website must show a company's identity and include a postal address. It must also state the target audience and the type of information published.

Information is regularly updated and the date of the last update must be clearly stated.

Published information that is intended for those in foreign countries must be clearly described as such.

A pharmaceutical company's website must expressly indicate those pages that are promotional, e.g. by clearly stating 'advertisement' or 'promotional communication' on every page. A product name or logo can be sufficient to highlight the promotional nature if it is clearly presented as advertising.

The site should be designed in such a way that promotional sections are separate from information and services sections.

Websites and corporate information The corporate information section of a website must be independent of promotional sections and identified as such at least on the homepage/site layout page/site plan.

Pharmaceutical companies can publish corporate information on the internet, in the same form as when it was published through other media, as outlined in article R.5124–67 of the Code of Public Health. This is available to the general public.

Corporate information must be scientific, technical or financial in nature (e.g. a company's annual report) and must not promote a medicinal product. A company's medicinal products, direction, and research and development activities can be referred to only on the condition that it is for information purposes only and not promotional.

Hypertext links can be created among a group's various corporate sites.

Websites and advertising of medicinal products The provisions of the Code of Public Health govern the advertising of medicinal products.

Advertising aimed at the general public can be for just medicinal products that do not require a medical prescription and are not reimbursed by health insurance schemes, and the marketing authorisation (MAA) should therefore have no restrictions in terms of advertising aimed at the general public. Advertising is monitored by the AFSSAPS. Advertising of all other medicinal products aimed at the general public is not allowed, apart from the exceptions outlined in the texts.

Advertising of medicinal products aimed at health professionals is allowed. The advertisement must be submitted to the AFSSAPS within 8 days of its publication.

10.1.9 GERMANY[14]

Internet There is no particular provision in German law with regard to the advertising of medicines on the internet and no particular guidance in the German code of conduct (FSA). Therefore the general rules of law and FSA guidance apply as for other forms of promotional advertising (see Chapter 6) i.e. websites containing promotional information on prescription only medicines should be limited to health professionals.

10.1.10 GREECE[35]

Clause 23

Internet Websites must comply with the following:

- Promotional material available on the internet must be restricted to healthcare professionals and suitable administrative personnel, who will obtain access by entering a password.
- Promotional material for medicinal products addressed to healthcare professionals on the internet must in principle all have a technical, scientific or professional content.
- Electronic promotional material must comply with all relevant provisions of this code that apply to printed promotional materials.
- Promotional material must include a characteristic and legible warning which states that the information contained on the web page is exclusively addressed to healthcare professionals who are authorised to prescribe or supply medicinal products and, therefore, specific training is necessary for the correct interpretation.

10.1.11 INDIA[16]

Clause 6

Electronic materials, including audiovisuals The same requirements that apply to printed materials also apply to electronic promotional materials and websites.

Websites must comply with the following:

- The identity of the pharmaceutical company and of the intended audience should be readily apparent.
- The content should be appropriate for the intended audience.

- The presentation (content, links, etc.) should be appropriate and apparent to the intended audience.
- India-specific information should comply with local laws and the Drugs and Magic remedies Act.

10.1.12 IRELAND[36]

Clause 7

Internet There is no specific guidance on the use of the internet in the Irish code of conduct, but advertising on the internet is subject to the same rules as other advertising. Advertising on the internet for POMs must therefore be restricted to healthcare professionals.

Electronic promotional material All promotional material (including electronic media) issued by a product authorisation holder, or with his or her authority, must be consistent with the requirements of the code. Audiovisual material must be accompanied by all appropriate printed material.

10.1.13 ITALY[37]

Internet There is no specific legal or self-regulatory guidance on advertising of medicines on the internet, so the guidance for other types of advertising applies.

The access to websites containing information about POMs must be restricted to physicians and pharmacists.

10.1.14 JAPAN[38]

Clause 4

Internet Member companies shall fully realise that brochures, advertisements in medical journals, internet web pages for the medical profession, and audiovisual materials such as slides, video and other promotional materials are important media in the dissemination of drug information. These items should be produced in compliance with the Pharmaceutical Affairs Law and relevant self-regulations. The statements contained therein shall be correct, fair and objective, based on scientific data.

The advertisement of prescription-only medicines to the general public is prohibited and access to websites providing information about these products should be restricted to healthcare professionals, but it is not necessary to password protect these sites. The following requirements should be met:

- The identity of the pharmaceutical company and the intended audience should be readily apparent.
- Access to the website can be gained only upon confirmation of the intended audience.
- The content is appropriate for the intended audience.
- Links are both appropriate and apparent to the intended audience.

10.1.15 MEXICO[20]

Internet There is no specific guidance on the use of the internet in Mexico but advertising on it is subject to the same rules as other advertising. COFEPRIS therefore requires pharmaceutical company advertising on the internet for prescription-only medicines to be restricted to healthcare professionals. Although no rules have been laid down for these levels of security, it is normally administered via the company granting user name and password protection.

10.1.16 THE NETHERLANDS[39]

Guidelines for advertising and information on POMs on the internet

Internet Advertising for POMs to the general public is forbidden.

The *Code geneemiddelenreclame* (CGR) has very specific and detailed guidance on the use of the internet for advertising of medicines, which states the following:

- The use of company names, indications and brands in an internet address is permitted.
- The name and address of the individuals responsible for the site must be mentioned.

- Medical and scientific information on the site must be kept up to date.
- If a website contains information about a specific medicine, it must contain an abbreviated package insert or direct link to this information.
- Linking from a site aimed at the general public to another site is allowed, unless the link is invitational and to a site intended for healthcare professionals.
- If a cross-reference is made to a third party site, this must be clearly indicated.
- Banners on sites aimed at the general public may not advertise POMs. However, sites may state an email address where patients can request information.

10.1.17 NORWAY[22]

Internet There are no particular rules about advertising on the internet and therefore the general rules apply. According to the Norwegian Manufacturers Association, access to information about POMs should not be available to the general public and should be conditional upon users indicating that they are healthcare professionals.

10.1.18 SPAIN[41]

Clause 8

Internet Promotional materials for medicines directed at healthcare professionals to be disseminated through the internet must have a primarily technical, scientific or professional content. In addition the following should apply:

- Measures must be taken to ensure that this advertising is accessible only to these professional groups.
- Promotional material must include a prominent and clearly legible warning indicating that the information contained on the web page is intended only for health professionals qualified to prescribe or dispense medicines.
- Specialised training is therefore required for its adequate interpretation.

10.1.19 SWEDEN[24]

Internet The advertising of POMs on the internet is subject to the same rules as advertising in any other Swedish medium (see Chapter 6).

The pharmaceutical company should divide websites into those intended for healthcare professionals, the public or the press and they must be clearly labelled as to their target audience, but it is not necessary to password protect them.

10.1.20 SWITZERLAND[43]

Clause 15

Internet Information to healthcare professionals about medicines provided over the internet by companies, their agents or with their approval must comply with the rules that apply to promotion and advertising.

Furthermore, the following must be clearly evident from the internet presentation:

- Which company operates or sponsors the website, either directly or indirectly.
- Which information on the website is intended for healthcare professionals and which for the lay public.
- If a company provides information about a medicine on its website, the healthcare professional must also have access, at this site, to the last-approved version by Swissmedic of the corresponding professional information for this medicinal product.

- In addition, when advertising or providing information to healthcare professionals over the internet, the companies observe the relevant legislation on therapeutic products and the recommendations by the IFPMA and EFPIA.

10.1.21 TURKEY[44]

Clause 17

Internet Internet sites are within the scope of the code and pharmaceutical companies are responsible for the website created by them or in their name under their authority:

- Information gathered from visitors should be kept confidential.
- Information given at the site has to be prepared by individuals who specialise in the subject.
- The sources and name of the person preparing the information have to be clarified; otherwise appropriate explanation should be given. Websites should have a main page.
- Promotion of medicinal products should not feature on the main page.
- The addresses, contact numbers of the website owner, site designer and the like should be clearly shown on the main page.
- The owner of the website assigns an employee responsibility for the site and his or her name is shown on the main page.
- The last date of actualisation has to be given.
- Information and links about the community have to be featured on the main page.
- It should bear the sign 'the information given at this site cannot replace a consultation with a physician or pharmacist'.
- For information about the community and explanation on diseases, accessible and clear references should be given. The content of the information given has to be appropriate for the target audience.

Access to promotional material in relation to POMs, must be limited to health professionals and related staff. The web pages prepared for physicians/pharmacists have to be separated from those for the general public and must contain the following information:

- It should state 'this part is prepared for physicians/pharmacists' and 'information given at these pages and promotional activities are subject to the code of practice'.
- Information that does not comply with the monograph and short PI approved by the Ministry of Health (even if it is approved in other countries) cannot be used on the internet for product promotion.
- It should be made clear when a user is leaving any of the company's sites or those sponsored by the company, or is being directed to an external site.
- There should be a warning about links for which the site owner is not responsible for the content, and also that they may contain information not in line with the laws and that information may be different to the texts approved by the MoH.
- It is the responsibility of the company preparing the site to update the available information in line with scientific developments and product-related information.

10.1.22 THE UNITED KINGDOM[45]

Clause 21

Internet Access to promotional material directed to a British audience on the internet in relation to POMs should generally be limited to health professionals and appropriate administrative staff. If, however, access restriction is not applied, a pharmaceutical company or company-sponsored website must provide information for the public as well as promotion to health professionals, with the sections for each target audience clearly separated and the intended audience identified. This is to avoid the public needing to access material for health professionals except by choice. The *MHRA Blue Guide*[54] states that the public should not be encouraged to access material that is not intended for them:

- Requirements are the same as for printed materials.
- Prescribing information is required on all promotional material.
- The non-proprietary name must be clearly displayed adjacent to the most prominent (usually first) display of the brand name.
- The black triangle must be clearly displayed adjacent to the most prominent (usually first) display of the brand name.
- Access must be password protected.
- Sponsorship should be clearly declared.
- It should be clear if a user is leaving the company website and/or moving to a non-company site.
- A hard copy of the information on a website must be certified.
- Information or promotional material about POMs that is placed on the internet outside the UK will be regarded as coming within the scope of the code if it was placed there by a UK company or an affiliate of a UK company, or at the instigation or with the authority of such a company, and it makes specific reference to the availability or use of the medicine in the UK.
- Medicines may be advertised in a relevant, independently produced, electronic journal intended for health professionals or appropriate administrative staff, which can be accessed by members of the public.
- It should be made clear when a user is leaving any of the company's sites or sites sponsored by the company, or is being directed to an external site that does not belong to the company.

The *MHRA Blue Guide* states that each page of an advertisement for a POM should be clearly labelled as intended for health professionals.

Public assessment reports (European or UK), SPCs, package leaflets and reference material for POMs may be included on the internet and be accessible by members of the public, provided that they are not presented in such a way as to be promotional in nature.

Information on clinical trials as agreed in the Joint Position on the Disclosure of Clinical Trial Information via Clinical Trial Registries and Databases 2005 may be available at a UK or non-UK website.

10.1.23 THE UNITED STATES OF AMERICA[28]

Internet Promotion on the internet is being examined as part of an FDA working group and the Division of Drug Marketing, Advertising and Communications (DDMAC) is developing an agency-wide policy to address how advertising and promotion of FDA-regulated products will be regulated on the internet.

No specific level of security is required for websites that promote the use of POMs.

10.2 Emails and faxes

10.2.1 IFPMA

No guidance found.

10.2.2 EFPIA[7]

No guidance found.

10.2.3 WHO

No guidance found.

10.2.4 AUSTRALIA

No guidance found.

10.2.5 BRAZIL

No guidance found.

10.2.6 CANADA

No guidance found.

10.2.7 THE CZECH REPUBLIC

Clause 3

Unsolicited telegrams, telexes and electronic transmissions, or replicas thereof, must not be used for promotional purposes.

10.2.8 FRANCE[33]

Charte internet

Advertisements for medicinal products sent to email distribution lists (emails, spam) require an advertising registration or licence application.

Promotional emails As for other internet-based communication, promotional emails require registration.

For the repeated sending of emails such as newsletters, the possibility of unsubscribing at any time must be made available to health professionals.

10.2.9 GERMANY[34]

Section 13

Advertising shall not unreasonably molest healthcare professionals. Unreasonable molestation is where the advertiser can recognise that the recipient does not desire it:

- The use of faxes, automated calling systems or emails for promotion is prohibited except with the prior permission of the recipient. When using email, permission may be assumed if the company have received the email address from the recipient. The recipient must be clearly informed in any email that he or she may object to the use of an email at any time.
- The permission to be given by the addressee of the advertising action must not be obtained by using any inducement or subterfuge, in particular by misleading the addressee as to the identity of the medical sales representative or the company represented by him or her.
- Mailing lists may be used for promotion only if the data included therein are kept up to date. Requests by healthcare professionals to be removed from promotional mailing lists must be complied with.

10.2.10 GREECE[35]

Article 9

Telephone communications, telephone messages, email and telefax must not be used for promotional purpose without the recipient's prior consent.

10.2.11 INDIA

No guidance found.

10.2.12 IRELAND

Clause 10

The use of faxes, text messages, email, automated calling systems and other electronic data communications must not be used for promotional purposes, except when requested or with prior permission of the recipient.

10.2.13 ITALY

No guidance found.

10.2.14 JAPAN[38]

Clause 7

Oral advertising via the telephone is not permitted except by prior arrangement with the practitioner concerned.

10.2.15 MEXICO

No guidance found.

10.2.16 THE NETHERLANDS

No guidance found.

10.2.17 NORWAY

No guidance found.

10.2.18 SPAIN

No guidance found.

10.2.19 SWEDEN

No guidance found.

10.2.20 SWITZERLAND

No guidance found.

10.2.21 TURKEY[44]

Clause 9

Telephone, text messages, email, telemessages, facsimile, automated calling systems and other electronic data communications must not be used for promotional purposes, except when requested or with prior permission of the recipient.

10.2.22 THE UNITED KINGDOM[45]

Clause 9

The telephone, text messages, email, telemessages, facsimile, automated calling systems and other electronic data communications must not be used for promotional purposes, except with the prior permission of the recipient.

10.2.23 THE UNITED STATES OF AMERICA

No guidance found.

CHAPTER 11

Research

11.1 Clinical research

Clinical research, if conducted according to good clinical practice (GCP) guidelines, is not normally considered promotional; however, research that is conducted by pharmaceutical companies will usually have some impact on the commercialisation of the company's product and therefore care needs to be taken as to how this is organised.

It is important to ensure that all research is conducted with a primarily scientific or educational purpose or it may be deemed as disguised promotion. Therefore, it is important that study documentation should not be promotional in appearance or feature brand names of products.

There are several ways to debase the research process for marketing purposes[50] and this must be avoided and is reflected in the clauses of many of the codes of conduct referred to in this chapter.

Post-marketing surveillance

Many adverse effects of drugs do not emerge until after they are on the market, so it makes scientific sense to gather data on patients taking new drugs. These trials are often published in major journals because they give important data on adverse effects.[50] Therefore these types of studies are of value, but only if properly conducted. Many of the codes now refer to specific rules for conducting this type of study. In the past, they have been used for marketing purposes as a way of getting doctors to prescribe a drug, with doctors often being paid substantial sums 'for expenses'.

Seeding and switching trials[50]

Pharmaceutical companies have, in the past, conducted trials simply to get doctors to prescribe their drug. These 'seeding trials' were often scientifically meaningless and have no clear research question and no controls. They were conducted on a large scale, and 'investigators' (often ordinary doctors, not researchers) were paid to enter patients into the trial. A variant is a 'switching trial' in which a doctor is paid to switch patients from their usual treatment to the new treatment. These sorts of trials will rarely make it into major journals, but many may be published somewhere and then be used to promote the drug.

Equivalence trials

An equivalence trial is one that shows that one drug is as good as another; these are termed 'equivalence' studies or, if insufficiently powered, they may show only 'non-inferiority' They are particularly difficult to interpret, because the trial is not large enough to be able to show that one treatment is better than another, but not small enough to be meaningless. Many trials funded by pharmaceutical companies are in these categories.[50] It is less a matter of suppressing unfavourable results and more a matter of making sure that a trial is not funded that will work against the sponsor.

Doses

This is a method that pharmaceutical companies have used to ensure that results are favourable for their products during a comparative study with a competitor. The study design uses a dose of the competitor drug that is lower or higher than optimal, in this way endeavouring to show that the competitor is less effective or has more side effects than the company's product.

11.1.1 IFPMA

No guidance found.

11.1.2 EFPIA

No guidance found.

11.1.3 WHO

No guidance found.

11.1.4 AUSTRALIA[29]

Clause 8

The following provisions apply to research whether it is carried out directly by the company or by a contractor acting under its direction. Companies must ensure that the requirements of Australia's privacy legislation are complied with during any research activity, and that any research activities are undertaken by suitably qualified and experienced individuals or organisations:

- Post-marketing surveillance studies should have scientific or medical merit and objectivity and not be designed for, or conducted as, a promotional exercise.
- Post-marketing surveillance studies must have a formal protocol and a requirement for data collection, and generate a report.
- When a company is intending to carry out a post-marketing surveillance study it must advise the Adverse Drug Reactions Advisory Committee (ADRAC) of its intention.
- Only patients being treated for approved indications of the product are to be included in the post-marketing surveillance study.
- Decisions by the medical profession to prescribe the product should be based solely on their clinical judgement.
- No starter packs or free trade packs should be distributed as part of the post-marketing surveillance study.
- Any payment to the medical profession must be commensurate with the work involved and not based on the number of prescriptions written.
- Pharmaceutical companies must report suspected adverse drug reactions noted during post-marketing surveillance studies.
- A prompt report on the outcome of the study should be provided to participating doctors and the ADRAC.

General Clinical trials of products approved for registration are not covered by the above categories and are considered to be subject to the Therapeutic Goods Administration's *Guidelines for Good Clinical Research Practice (GCRP) in Australia.*[55]

11.1.5 BRAZIL

No guidance found.

11.1.6 CANADA[31]

Clause 9

Post-registration clinical studies are defined as any study that is conducted after Health Canada's Notice of Compliance (NOC) has been issued for a medicine.

The main goal of a post-registration clinical study will be to obtain and evaluate data on safety and/or efficacy, cost-effectiveness, quality of life or other socioeconomic factors that have to do with clinical use of the medicine.

- Post-registration clinical studies must provide a scientific framework for investigation of the medicine in broader or special populations.
- All post-registration clinical studies must have a clearly defined goal that is amenable to scientific review and testing.
- The member must ensure that post-registration clinical studies are designed/approved and administered by qualified people in the medical/scientific department, using the same kinds of methodology (i.e. the planning, protocol development, monitoring and data interpretation) that apply to pre-marketing trials. Other member representatives' roles in the process must be limited to the distribution and collection of materials pertinent to the study, on behalf of the medical/scientific department.
- Post-registration clinical studies must be carried out in accordance with the Canadian Food and Drugs Act and Regulations, other applicable federal and provincial legislation, and guidelines issued by Health Canada.
- Post-registration clinical studies must be carried out using a written protocol that will provide answers to specific research questions. The protocol must be designed to ensure scientifically meaningful results, and should contain details about study objective, study population, methodology, information to be obtained and data collection method.
- Researchers must collect data according to the protocol and keep the research results on file with the member as required by applicable law and/or regulations.
- After the data are collected, but before the study is published, the researchers and medical/scientific department of the member must jointly review the scientific evaluations of data.
- Researchers' pay must reflect costs incurred in conducting the study, such as professional fees, salaries of study staff and laboratory tests. Payment may be in the form of a monetary grant, travel to attend scientific and medical meetings, or equipment, provided that the last is needed for and relevant to the study.
- Payment to researchers must not be based on continuing administration of the medicine under study to patients after the researcher has completed the study protocol.

11.1.7 THE CZECH REPUBLIC[32]

Clause 9

The following provisions apply to market research and post-marketing surveillance, whether the research is carried out directly by the manufacturer or by another company acting under its direction.

This section does not apply to evaluations being carried out as clinical trials (consistent with GCP) according to the Act on Pharmaceuticals.

Non-interventional studies In this type of study the medicinal product is prescribed in the usual manner in accordance with the terms of the marketing authorisation. The assignment of the patient to a particular therapeutic strategy is not decided in advance by a trial protocol but falls within current practice, and the prescription of the medicine is clearly separated from the decision to include the patient in the study. No additional diagnostic or monitoring procedures shall be applied to the patients and epidemiological methods shall be used for the analysis of collected data.

They must fulfil the following criteria:

- They must have scientific or medical merit and not be designed for, or conducted as, a promotional exercise.
- They must concern regulatory approved products used in approved indications and can include, but not only, non-interventional trials, observational trials, post-marketing surveillance and post-authorisation safety studies.
- The objective of the study must be to obtain real clinical evaluation of the use of the product studied. The information collected must include clinical data, safety data and/or quality-of life data to describe clinical experience sufficiently.
- The MAFS executive director has to be notified before the start, and the protocol of the study and study report forms must be submitted.
- The executive director ensures the confidentiality of the submitted documentation.
- If a complaint is made by another member company, the executive director makes available all study documentation submitted to the ethical committee.
- The ethical committee will randomly check up to 10 per cent of the submitted non-interventional studies to see if they fulfil criteria described in the code of conduct.

11.1.8 FRANCE[33]

The presentation of an ongoing or future clinical study in an advertisement, based on one or more medicinal products, and especially presentation of the objectives, the protocol, demographic characteristics of patients or interim results, is not acceptable because this does not provide complete information to prescribers and could, in certain cases, constitute anticipation of the results that are incomplete and not yet validated.

Clinical trial agreements with a French trial centre must be submitted to CNOM for prior review. Companies are required to advise a health professional if the opinion of CNOM is negative. Proceeding with the trial after a negative opinion may have tax implications and this should be reviewed carefully before proceeding.

11.1.9 GERMANY[34]

Scientific information on pharmaceuticals as part of the preparation/implementation of clinical trials in particular is not considered to be advertising.

Payments to health institutions for their collaboration in research must be paid into a separate funding account and permission to participate in this research must be obtained from the institution prior to the research commencing.

11.1.10 GREECE[35]

Clause 10

Clinical assessments, post-marketing surveillance, experience programmes and post-authorisation studies must not constitute a disguised promotion. Such assessments, programmes and studies must be performed mainly for a scientific or educational purpose. In all clinical trials, the following principles must be applied:

- All participants in a clinical trial must respect ethical and professional principles and guidelines such as the Helsinki Declaration and the International Conference on Harmonisation (ICH) guidelines for GCP.
- Each trial must have a relevant scientific and therapeutic purpose. It must not be performed in view of increasing sales or prescribing.
- The purpose of the trial must always be the improvement of therapeutic, diagnostic methods and/or medical knowledge to the best interest of patients.
- The purpose of the trial must be declared in advance. The trial protocols must be compiled in such a way as to ensure success of the aim of the trial and that valid conclusions are drawn.
- Clinical trials are carried out only on approval by the competent authorities – the National Ethics Committee and the National Organisation for Medicines (EOF).
- Patients participating in the trial must know who is sponsoring the trial.
- The physician must not receive any remuneration or compensation for the mere inclusion of patients in clinical trials.
- The physician may receive remuneration for his or her work in the trial. Remuneration must be given in connection with the work provided and must be declared to the competent authorities. Remuneration must not be connected with the expected outcome of the trial.
- Data on safety, efficacy and other important clinical results with respect to marketed products must be truthfully published on the internet, irrespective of the outcome of the trial within the year after the marketing authorisation has been granted.
- In publications, lectures and other presentations, the identity of the sponsor must be known.
- The physician may receive remuneration for lectures relating to the clinical trial and the results.
- When presenting clinical trials, the physician must make known his or her connections with all the companies of the therapeutic area covered by his lecture.

11.1.11 INDIA

No guidance found.

11.1.12 IRELAND[36]

Clause 16

Post-marketing surveillance studies, pharmacoeconomic studies, non-interventional trials, clinical audit programmes and the like, which have been commissioned, undertaken or provided by companies, must never be promotional in nature and must be conducted primarily with a scientific or educational purpose. This clause does not preclude the use of the data generated from such studies to support claims in promotion.

11.1.13 ITALY

Clinical trials must be carried out according to specific regulations laid down in the circular of the Ministry of Health September 2002. Pharmaceutical companies can provide investigators involved in these trials with instruments and software support as specified by Farmaindustria. These instruments can only be on loan for the duration of the study.

11.1.14 JAPAN[38]

Clause 5

Member companies shall properly recognise the objectives of post-marketing surveillance (PMS), i.e. the establishment of the appropriate usage of marketed pharmaceuticals, and shall conduct such PMS activities on a scientific basis, in strict compliance with relevant laws and regulations, as well as relevant self-regulations. These activities shall not be misused as a means of promotion.

11.1.15 MEXICO

No guidance found.

11.1.16 NORWAY

No guidance found.

11.1.17 THE NETHERLANDS

No guidance found.

11.1.18 SPAIN[41]

Clause 14

Post-authorisation studies should be conducted in compliance with the requirements of the applicable legislation and with a primarily scientific or educational purpose. They should not be used as a means of promotion or inducement to prescribe.

Design and follow-up of post-authorisation studies shall be the responsibility of the companies' medical or clinical research departments. Medical representatives shall not be involved in the studies other than in logistic aspects.

11.1.19 SWEDEN

No guidance found.

11.1.20 SWITZERLAND

No guidance found.

11.1.21 TURKEY[44]

Clause 7

Post-authorisation studies can be conducted only after proper vetting by relevant authorities. Such studies or programmes should not be carried out as disguised promotion. Adherence to the letter of the existing regulations will not be accepted as sufficient proof for a study to be considered to adhere to the spirit of the code.

Post-marketing studies should not be carried out and used in order to influence physicians, and should not be disguised as research

11.1.22 THE UNITED KINGDOM[45]

Clause 9

Post-marketing surveillance studies, clinical assessments and the like must be conducted with a primarily scientific or educational purpose. Clinical research is not subject to the code unless any activities or materials become promotional.

Study documentation should not be promotional in appearance or feature brand names of products.

11.1.23 THE UNITED STATES OF AMERICA

No guidance found.

11.2 Market research

Market research, although mentioned in a number of the codes, is not normally considered promotional if conducted correctly. Care must be taken to ensure that it and the materials used in the research are non-promotional, otherwise it may be considered disguised promotion. The results of the market research can be used promotionally in some countries, with Turkey being an exception. Therefore, if considering using market research promotionally, individual country rules regarding this should be checked.

To be considered bona fide market research the following general points will normally apply:

- The research must be clearly identified as such and the fact that it is sponsored by a pharmaceutical company must be clearly stated, (in some countries the company who is sponsoring the research must be named).
- There should be a research question.
- Market research materials should not be branded.
- The participants in the market research should be selected for their relevance to the research objective.
- The payment for participation must be commensurate with the time taken and also be appropriate to the normal commercial rate for the participant

11.2.1 IFPMA
No guidance found.

11.2.2 EFPIA
No guidance found.

11.2.3 WHO
No guidance found.

11.2.4 AUSTRALIA[29]
Clause 8
The sole purpose of these activities must be to collect data and not to be a means of promoting to and/or rewarding healthcare professionals. It should comply with the following:

- Market research studies must be clearly identified as such when the initial approach is made.
- Any payment must be kept to a minimum and should not exceed a level commensurate with the work involved.
- It should not be possible to confuse market research with a competition; it should be a genuine initiative to collect relevant and useful information to enhance the quality use of medicines.

11.2.5 BRAZIL
No guidance found.

11.2.6 CANADA[31]
Clause 12
Market research links the consumer, customer and public to the marketer through information that points out and defines marketing opportunities and problems, that generates, refines and evaluates marketing programmes, that monitors marketing performance and that improves understanding of marketing as a process.

Market research details the information needed to address these issues, designs the method for collecting information, manages and implements the data collection process, analyses the results, and communicates the findings and their implications. This section applies to market research carried out within the framework of various forums including studies, individual and group interviews, and focus groups.

The following general principles should apply:

- The purpose of an individual or group interview must be made clear to the participant(s).
- Market research must not be a disguise for selling or developing sales contacts.
- Market research must not deliberately sway the opinion(s) of the participant(s).
- Honoraria offered to healthcare professionals who gather or provide market research information should be based on rates similar to (and not higher than) their usual rate of pay.
- Even when a consent form is not signed, the confidentiality of participant(s) must be preserved. The identity of the participant(s) must not be revealed for purposes of promoting products to them in the future.

11.2.7 THE CZECH REPUBLIC[32]

Clause 9

- Market research studies must be clearly identified as such when the initial approach is made. Any payment must be kept to a minimum and should not exceed a level commensurate with the work involved.
- Promotion must not be represented as market research or research of any type. Market research is not to be carried out by sales representatives or any other position involved in sales activities, unless there is no payment to the physician who is taking part in the research.

The requirements for conducting post-marketing surveillance studies also apply to market research studies.

11.2.8 FRANCE[33]

Opinion polls or surveys should just report the opinions of those surveyed on their attitudes and behaviour.

A poll can be conducted of an opinion leader when it is assumed that the renown, experience or recognised scientific history will have an impact on the expression of their point of view.

Polls can use a 'panel of experts' or an expert committee upon the request of a company, in order to express a consensual opinion, based on scientific arguments in a given therapeutic area.

Polls can involve a panel of health professionals, selected randomly, whose opinions reflect their consensual opinions, based on scientific arguments in a given therapeutic area.

Polls can use a panel of consumers with a view to conducting specific or periodic studies.

The advertising message for a medicinal product, primarily based on the results of opinion polls, is in principle not allowed, except if the results of these polls match the marketing authorisation, Transparency Commission opinions and the proper use of the medicinal product.

11.2.9 GERMANY

No guidance found.

11.2.10 GREECE

No guidance found.

11.2.11 INDIA

No guidance found.

11.2.12 IRELAND[36]

Clause 16

Methods used for market research must never be such as to bring discredit upon or reduce confidence in the pharmaceutical industry. The following provisions apply whether the research is carried out by the company or by an organisation acting on its behalf:

- Access must not be gained by subterfuge.
- Incentives must be kept to a minimum and be commensurate with the work that is involved.
- Questions intended to solicit disparaging references to competing preparations or companies must be avoided.
- Market research must not be used as a form of disguised promotion

11.2.13 ITALY

No guidance found.

11.2.14 JAPAN

No guidance found.

11.2.15 MEXICO

No guidance found.

11.2.16 THE NETHERLANDS

No guidance found.

11.2.17 NORWAY

No guidance found.

11.2.18 SPAIN

No guidance found.

11.2.19 SWEDEN

No guidance found.

11.2.20 SWITZERLAND

No guidance found.

11.2.21 TURKEY[44]

Clause 7

Market research activities, post-marketing surveillance and experience programmes, observational and post-authorisation studies, clinical assessments and the like must not be disguised promotion. Such assessments, programmes and studies should not be carried out for any other purpose than collecting information on the company's own or competitive products, with a primarily scientific or educational purpose. It must comply with the following:

- Market research material need not reveal the company's name, but must nevertheless state that a pharmaceutical company sponsors it.

- Market research material, from internal or external sources, should be examined to ensure that it does not contravene the code.
- External information from a reputable source does not guarantee its suitability under the code.
- Market research results should not be used in promotion.

11.2.22 THE UNITED KINGDOM[45]

Clauses 9 and 10

Material relating to medicines and their uses, whether or not promotional in nature, that is sponsored by a pharmaceutical company must clearly indicate that it has been sponsored by that company.

- The only exception to this is market research material, which need not reveal the name of the company involved but must state that a pharmaceutical company is the sponsor. The declaration of sponsorship must be sufficiently prominent to ensure that readers of sponsored material are aware of it at the outset.
- Where market research is carried out by an agency on behalf of a pharmaceutical company, the agency must reveal the name of its client to the Prescription Medicines Code Practice Authority when the authority requests it to do so. When commissioning market research, a company must take steps to ensure that its identity would be so made known to the authority should a request for that information be made.
- Market research activities, post-marketing surveillance studies, clinical assessments and the like must not be disguised promotion. The use to which the statistics or information is put may be promotional. The two phases must be kept distinct.
- Market research material should be examined to ensure that it does not contravene the code.
- Where market research is carried out by an agency on behalf of a pharmaceutical company, the agency must reveal the name of its client to the Prescription Medicines Code Practice Authority when the authority requests it to do so.

11.2.23 THE UNITED STATES OF AMERICA

No guidance found.

APPENDIX 1

Contact Information

Country	Geographical address	Website
International	International Federation of Pharmaceutical Manufacturers and Associations (IFPMA) 30 rue de St Jean PO Box 758 1211 Geneva 13 Switzerland Tel: 00 41 22 338 3200 Fax: 00 41 22 338 3299	www.ifpma.org/News/news_market.aspx
	European Federation of Pharmaceutical Industries and Associations (EFPIA) Rue du Trone 108 B-1050 Brussels Belgium	www.efpia.org/6_publ/codecon/Promomedicines2004.pdf
	World Health Organization (WHO) Avenue Appia 20 1211 Geneva 27 Switzerland Tel: 00 41 22 791 2111 Fax: 00 41 22 791 3111	www.who.int
Australia	Medicines Australia 16 Napier Close Deakin ACT 2600 Australia Tel: 00 61 6 282 6888 Fax: 00 61 6 282 6299	www.medicinesaustralia.com.au/pages/page5.asp
	Therapeutic Goods Administration PO Box 100 Woden, ACT 2606 Australia Tel: 00 61 6 6232 8757 Fax: 00 61 6 6232 8659	www.tga.gov.au/advert
	Australian Medical Association 42 Macquarie Street Barton, ACT 2600 Australia or PO Box 6090 Kingston, ACT 2604 Australia Tel: 00 61 2 6270 5400 Fax: 00 61 2 6270 5499	www.ama.com.au/web.nsf/doc/WEEN-5GJ7MH
Brazil	Anvisa No contact information available	Unknown

Country	Geographical address	Website
Canada	Health Canada Tunney's Pasture Address Locator 0701C Ottawa Ontario K1A 0K9 Canada Tel: 00 1 613 948 7973 Fax: 00 1 613 948 7996	www.hc-sc.gc.ca/dhp-mps/advert-publicit/index_e.html
	Canada Pharma 55 Metcalfe Street Suite 1220 Ottawa Ontario K1P 6L5 Canada Tel: 00 1 613 236 0455 Fax: 00 1 613 236–6756	www.canadapharma.org/Industry_Publications/Code/CodeDocuments_e.html
Canada	Pharmaceutical Advertising Advisory Board (PAAB) 375 Kingston Rd Suite 200 Pickering Ontario L1V 1A3 Canada Tel: 00 1 905 509 2275 Fax: 00 1 905 509 2486	www.paab.ca/index_en.html
Czech Republic	MAFS No contact information available	No website
France	Charte de la Visité Médicale	www.leem.org/industrie/pres9.htm
	Doctors Advisory Body	www.conseil-national.medecin.fr
	Agence Française de Sécurité Sanitaire des Produits de Santé (AFSSAPS) Saint Denis 143 147 boulevard Anatole France 93285 Saint-Denis Cedex France Tel: 00 33 01 5587 3000	http://afssaps.sante.fr/ang/indang.htm
Germany	FSA FS Arzneimittelindustrie eV Friedrichstr. 50 10117 Berlin Germany Tel: 00 49 30 2065 9144 Fax: 00 49 30 2065 9200	www.fs-arzneimittelindustrie.de/FSA.nsf/0/96B7C4558CCF60AB80256EA80047F0AE/$file/Kodex-englisch_02.12.05.pdf
	VFA	www.vfa.de/en/vfa_en/kdx_en.html
Greece	Hellenic Association of Pharmaceutical Companies	http://sfee.gr/article/english/252/148/index.htm
India	Organisation of Pharmaceutical Producers of India Peninsula Chambers Ground Floor Ganpatrao Kadam Marg Lower Parel Mumbai 400 013 India Tel: 00 91 22 2491 8123, 00 91 22 2491 2486, 00 91 22 5662 7007 Fax: 00 91 22 2491 5168	www.indiaoppi.com/guidelines.htm
Ireland	Irish Pharmaceutical Healthcare Association Franklin House 140 Pembroke Road Dublin 4 Ireland Tel: 00 3 53 660 3350 Fax: 00 3 53 668 6672	www.ipha.ie

Country	Geographical address	Website
Italy	Farmindustria Largo del Nazareno 3/8 Rome 187 Italy Tel: 00 39 0667 5801 Fax: 00 39 0667 86494	www.efpia.org/6_publ/codecon/Italiancodeofpractice.pdf
Japan	Japan Pharmaceutical Manufacturers Association Torii Nihonbashi Building 3–4–1 Nihonbashi-Honcho Chuo-Ku Tokyo 103–0023 Japan Tel: 00 81 03 3241 0326 Fax: 00 81 03 3242 1767	
The Netherlands	Code geneemiddelenreclame (CGR) No contact information on website	www.cgr.nl/index.cfm?pageid=4637
Norway	Legemiddelindustriforeningen Grev Wedels plass 9 Postboks 734 Sentrum N-0105 Oslo Norway Tel: 00 47 2316 1500 Fax: 00 47 2316 1501	www.lmi.no/digimaker/documents/Rules_governing_ drug_information_._uten_fotnoter_LX5fX32488er.pdf
Spain	Farmaindustria Serrano 116 Madrid 28006 Spain Tel: 00 34 91 515 9350 Fax: 00 34 91 563 7380	www.farmaindustria.es/index_secundaria_codigo.htm
Sweden	Läkemedelsindustriföreningen (LIF) Box 17608 118 92 Stockholm Sweden Tel: 00 46 08 462 3700 Fax: 00 46 08 462 0292	www.lif.se/Branschinformation/Overenskommelser/agreements.asp www.lif.se/eng/ethical_rules.asp
Switzerland	SGCI Chemie Pharma Schweiz Postfach 8035 Zürich Switzerland	www.sgci.ch/plugin/template/sgci/*/11388
Turkey	AIFD Barbaros Bulvarı No. 121 TEV Orhan Birman İş Merkezi Balmumcu Istanbul Turkey Tel: 00 90 212 267 1600 (pbx) Fax: 00 90 212 273 1179	www.aifd.org.tr/_publish/documents/ilkelerkitabiing.pdf
The UK	Association of the British Pharmaceutical Industry (ABPI) 12 Whitehall London SW1A 2DY UK Tel: 00 44 20 7930 3477 Fax: 00 44 20 7747 1414	www.abpi.org.uk/publications/pdfs/pmpca_code2006.pdf
	Medicines and Healthcare Regulatory Agency (MHRA) Tel: 00 44 20 7084 2000	www.mhra.gov.uk/home/groups/pla/documents/ websiteresources/con007552.pdf www.mhra.gov.uk/home/groups/comms-ic/documents/ publication/con007555.pdf

Country	Geographical address	Website
The USA	Pharmaceutical Research Manufacturers of America (PhRMA) 950 F Street, NW Washington DC 20004 USA Tel: 00 1 202 835 3400 Fax: 00 1 202 835 3414	www.phrma.org/ code_on_interactions_with_healthcare_professionals/ www.phrma.org/files/DTCGuidingprinciples.pdf
	Food and Drug Administration (FDA) 5600 Fishers Lane Rockville MA 20857 USA Tel: 00 1 888 463 6332	www.fda.gov/cder/ddmac/ www.fda.gov/cder/ddmac/

APPENDIX

2

References

[1] Abbasi K, Smith R. No more free lunches. Patients will benefit from doctors and drug companies disentangling. *BMJ* 2003;**326**:1155–1156.

[2] The House of Commons Health Committee. *The Influence of the Pharmaceutical Industry*, 4th report 2004–5, Vol. 1 (www.publications.parliament.uk/pa/cm200405/cmselect/cmhealth/42/42.pdf).

[3] Boseley S. Drug Firms a danger to health. *The Guardian* 26 June 2006.

[4] Woods P Sales and marketing practices for prescription medicines: New rules in a new environment. *Regulatory Rapporteur* 2005;**2**(11).

[5] PriceWaterhouseCooper's Health Research Institute. *Recapturing the Vision: Integrity driven performance in the pharmaceutical industry*, 2005 (www.pwc.com/extweb/pwcpublications.nsf/docid/E8A194168C19DE678525726100550B91).

[6] International Federation of Pharmaceutical Manufacturers and Associations. *Code of Marketing Practices*, April 2006 (www.ifpma.org/pdf/IFPMA-TheCode-FinalVersion-30May2006–EN.pdf).

[7] European Federation of Pharmaceutical Industries and Associations. *Code of Practice for the Promotion of Medicines*, November 2004 (www.efpia.org/Objects/2/Files/Promomedicines2004.pdf).

[8] World Health Organization. *Criteria for Medicinal Drug Promotion*. Geneva: WHO, 1985 (www.who.int/medicinewww.fda.gov/cder/ddmac/docs/collect/edmweb/pdf/whozip08e/whozip08e.pdf).

[9] International Comparative Legal Guide to Pharmaceutical Advertising: Australia, 2006 (www.ICLG.co.uk).

[10] International Comparative Legal Guide to Pharmaceutical Advertising: Brazil, 2006 (www.ICLG.co.uk).

[11] International Comparative Legal Guide to Pharmaceutical Advertising: Canada, 2006 (www.ICLG.co.uk).

[12] International Comparative Legal Guide to Pharmaceutical Advertising: Czech Republic, 2006 (www.ICLG.co.uk).

[13] International Comparative Legal Guide to Pharmaceutical Advertising: France, 2006 (www.ICLG.co.uk).

[14] International Comparative Legal Guide to Pharmaceutical Advertising: Germany, 2006 (www.ICLG.co.uk).

[15] International Comparative Legal Guide to Pharmaceutical Advertising: Greece, 2006 (www.ICLG.co.uk).

[16] Organisation of Pharmaceutical Producers of India January 2007

[17] International Comparative Legal Guide to Pharmaceutical Advertising: Ireland, 2006 www.ICLG.co.uk

[18] International Comparative Legal Guide to Pharmaceutical Advertising: Italy, 2006 (www.ICLG.co.uk).

[19] International Comparative Legal Guide to Pharmaceutical Advertising: Japan, 2006 (www.ICLG.co.uk).

[20] International Comparative Legal Guide to Pharmaceutical Advertising: Mexico, 2006 (www.ICLG.co.uk).

[21] International Comparative Legal Guide to Pharmaceutical Advertising: Netherlands, 2006 (www.ICLG.co.uk).

[22] International Comparative Legal Guide to Pharmaceutical Advertising: Norway, 2006 (www.ICLG.co.uk).

[23] International Comparative Legal Guide to Pharmaceutical Advertising: Spain, 2006 (www.ICLG.co.uk).

[24] International Comparative Legal Guide to Pharmaceutical Advertising: Sweden, 2006 (www.ICLG.co.uk).

[25] International Comparative Legal Guide to Pharmaceutical Advertising: Switzerland, 2006 www.ICLG.co.uk

[26] International Comparative Legal Guide to Pharmaceutical Advertising: Turkey, 2006 (www.ICLG.co.uk).

[27] International Comparative Legal Guide to Pharmaceutical Advertising: England, 2006 (www.ICLG.co.uk).

[28] *International Comparative Legal Guide to Pharmaceutical Advertising*. USA, 2006 (www.ICLG.co.uk).

[29] Medicines Australia. *Code of Conduct*, 14th edn. January 2003 (www.ifpma.org/EthicalPromotion/content/pdfs/AU_EN_Code.pdf).

[30] Agencia Nacional de Vigilancia Sanitaria (National Health Surveillance Agency Brazil). Resolution RDC No. 102, November 2000.

[31] Canadian Pharmaceutical Advertising Advisory Board. *Code of Advertising Acceptance*, January 2006 (www.paab.ca/index_en.html).

[32] Czech Republic. *MAFS Code of Conduct*, January 2005 (www.ifpma.org/EthicalPromotion/content/pdfs/CZ_EN_Code.pdf).

[33] Agence Française de Sécurité Sanitaire des Produits de Santé (AFSSAPS) (http://afssaps.sante.fr/htm/5/recopub/indrepub.htm).

[34] German Freiwillige Selbstkontrolle für die Arzheimittelindustrie (FSA). *Code of Conduct of the Members of the Association*, February 2004 (www.fs-arzneimittelindustrie.de/FSA.nsf/0/96B7C4558CCF60AB80256EA80047F0AE/$file/Kodex-englisch_02.12.05.pdf).

[35] Hellenic Association of Pharmaceutical Companies. Code *of Practice on the Promotion of Prescription Only Medicinal Products*, January 2006 (http://sfee.gr/article/english/252/148/index.htm).

[36] Irish Pharmaceutical Healthcare Association. *Code of Marketing Practice for the Pharmaceutical Industry*, 6th edn, December 2005 (www.ipha.ie/htm/info/download/Publications/IPHA%20Code%206th%20Edition%20–%20Final%20Sept%2006.pdf).

[37] *Italian Farmindustria s Code of Professional Conduct*, January 2004 (www.efpia.org/6_publ/codecon/Italiancodeofpractice.pdf).

[38] Japan Pharmaceutical Manufacturers Association. *Promotion Code for Prescription Drugs*, April 2004 (www.jpma.or.jp/english/isuues/index.html).

[39] Netherlands CGR Foundation. *Code of Conduct for Pharmaceutical Advertising* (www.cgr.nl/index.cfm?pageid=4637).

[40] Norwegian Legemiddelindustriforeningen. *Committee for Drug Information Rules governing Drug Information*, June 2005 (www.ifpma.org/EthicalPromotion/content/pdfs/NO_EN_Code.pdf).

[41] *Farmaindustria Spanish Code of Practice for the Promotion of Medicines*, January 2004 (www.farmaindustria.es/Index_secundaria_ingles.htm).

[42] Swedish Association of the Pharmaceutical Industry. *Code of Marketing Practice*, June 2002 (www.lif.se/pdf/Rules_drug_information.pdf).

[43] Swiss Society of Chemical Industries. Code *of Conduct of the Pharmaceutical Industry in Switzerland* (Pharma Code), December 2003 (www.sgci.ch/plugin/template/sgci/*/27686).

[44] Turkish Association of Research Based Pharmaceutical Companies. *Code of Ethical Promotion Practices for Medicinal Products*, November 2005 (www.aifd.org.tr/_publish/documents/ilkelerkitabiing.pdf).

[45] The Association of British Pharmaceutical Industry. *Code of Practice*, 2006 (www.abpi.org.uk/publications/pdfs/pmpca_code2006.pdf).

[46] Pharmaceutical Research and Manufacturers of America. *Code on Interactions with Healthcare Professionals*, July 2002 (www.phrma.org/code_on_interactions_with_healthcare_professionals).

[47] Les enterprises du médicament, France Medical Visit Charter, December 2004 (www.leem.org/htm/accueil/accueil.asp).

[48] USA Federal Anti-Kickback Statute: 42 U.S.C. § 1320a-7b (www.gpoaccess.govv/uscode).

[49] The Healthcare Conventions and Exhibitions Associations (HCEA) (www.hcea.org).

[50] Washington Legal Foundation (www.wlf.org).

[51] Smith R (ed.) Medical journals and pharmaceutical companies: uneasy bedfellows. *BMJ* 2003;**326**:1202–1205.

[52] *Australian Guidelines for the Registration of Drugs*, Vol. 1 (www.tga.health.gov.au/docs/html/tganews/news27/dseb.htm).

[53] Canadian Pharmaceutical Association. *Compendium of Pharmaceutical and Specialties*, 2007 (www.pharmacists.ca/content/about_cpha/who_we_are/publications_products/inside_publications.cfm#cps).

[54] Medicines and Healthcare Regulatory Agency. *MHRA Blue Guide* (www.mhra.gov.uk/home/groups/pl-a/documents/websiteresources/con007552.pdf).

[55] *Guidelines for Good Clinical Research Practice in Australia* (www.tga.gov.au/docs/pdf/euguide/ich/ich13595.pdf).

APPENDIX 3

Abbreviations

AAD	American Academy of Dermatology
ABPI	Association of the British Pharmaceutical Industry
ACCC	Australian Competition and Consumer Commission
ADRAC	Adverse Drug Reactions Advisory Committee
AFSSAPS	French Agency for the Safety of Health Products (Agence Française de Sécurité Sanitaire des Produits de Santé)
AIFA	Italian Medicines Agency
Anvisa	Brazilian Sanitation Agency
APS	advertising/promotion scheme
ASAI	Advertising Standards Authority for Ireland
ASC	Advertising Standards Canada
BAH	German Federal Association of Pharmaceutical Manufacturers
BHIVA	British HIV Association
BPI	German Association of the Pharmaceutical Industry
BtMG	German Narcotics Act
CEP	clinical evaluation package
CEPS	Economic Committee of Health Products (France)
CGR	Code geneemiddelenreclame
COFEPRIS	Federal Commission for Protection Against Sanitary Risks (Mexico)
Conar	Brazilian Advertising Self Regulation Council
CNOM	Consiel national de l'Ordre des Médecins
CNOP	Consiel national de l'Ordre des Pharmacists
COSM	Committee on Safety of Medicines (the UK)
CRP	Complaints Resolution Panel (Australia)
CSI	consumer medicine information
DAH	German Aids Society
DDMAC	Division of Drug Marketing, Advertising and Communication Agency (the USA)
EASL	European Association for Study of the Liver
EFPIA	European Federation of Pharmaceutical Industries and Associations
EMEA	European Medicines and Evaluation Agency
EOF	National Organisation for Medicines (Greece)
FDA	Food and Drug Administration Agency (the USA)
FDCA	Food, Drug and Cosmetic Act (the USA)

FPHC	French Public Health Code
FSA	German code of conduct
FTC	Federal Trade Commission (the USA)
GCP	good clinical practice
HA	health authority
HC	Health Canada
HCEA	Healthcare Conventions and Exhibitions Associations (the USA)
HWG	Heilmittelwerbegesetz (Advertising in the Field of Healthcare) (Germany)
IAMA	Industry Association Medicines Australia
IFPMA	International Federation of Pharmaceutical Manufacturers and Associations
IMB	Irish Medicines Board
IMSS	Mexican Institute of Social Security
IPHA	Irish Pharmaceuticals Health Authority
ISSSTE	Institute of Social Security and Services for Government Workers (Mexico)
JPMA	Japan Pharmaceutical Manufacturers Association
LEEM	Les enterprises du médicament (French Pharmaceutical Companies Association)
LIF	Swedish Association of the Pharmaceutical Industry
LMI	Norwegian Association of Pharmaceutical Manufacturers
MAA	Marketing authorisation application
MAFS	International Association of Pharmaceutical Companies (the Czech Republic)
MHLW	Ministry of Health Labour and Welfare (Japan)
MHRA	Medicines and Healthcare Regulatory Agency (the UK)
MHWS	Ministry of Health Labour and Sports (the Netherlands)
NCPI	National Chamber of the Pharmaceutical Industry (Mexico)
NMA	Norwegian Medicines Agency
OPPI	Organisation of Pharmaceutical Producers of India
PAAB	Pharmaceutical Advertising Advisory Board (Canada)
PBS	Pharmaceutical Benefit Scheme (Australia)
PhRMA	Pharmaceutical Research Manufacturers of America (the USA)
PI	product information
PMCPA	Prescription Medicines Code of Practice Authority (the UK)
POM	prescription-only medicine
rINN	recommended international non-proprietary name
SFEE	Hellenic Association of Pharmaceutical Companies
SMPA	Swedish Medical Products Agency
SPC	summary of product characteristics
SSCI	Swiss Society of Chemical Industries
SÚKL	State Institute for Drug Control (the Czech Republic)
TGA	Therapeutic Goods Administration (Australia)
TP Act	Trade Practices Act
UWG	Unfair Competition Act (Germany)
VFA	German Association of Research-based Pharmaceutical Companies
WAIDS	World Congress of AIDS

Index